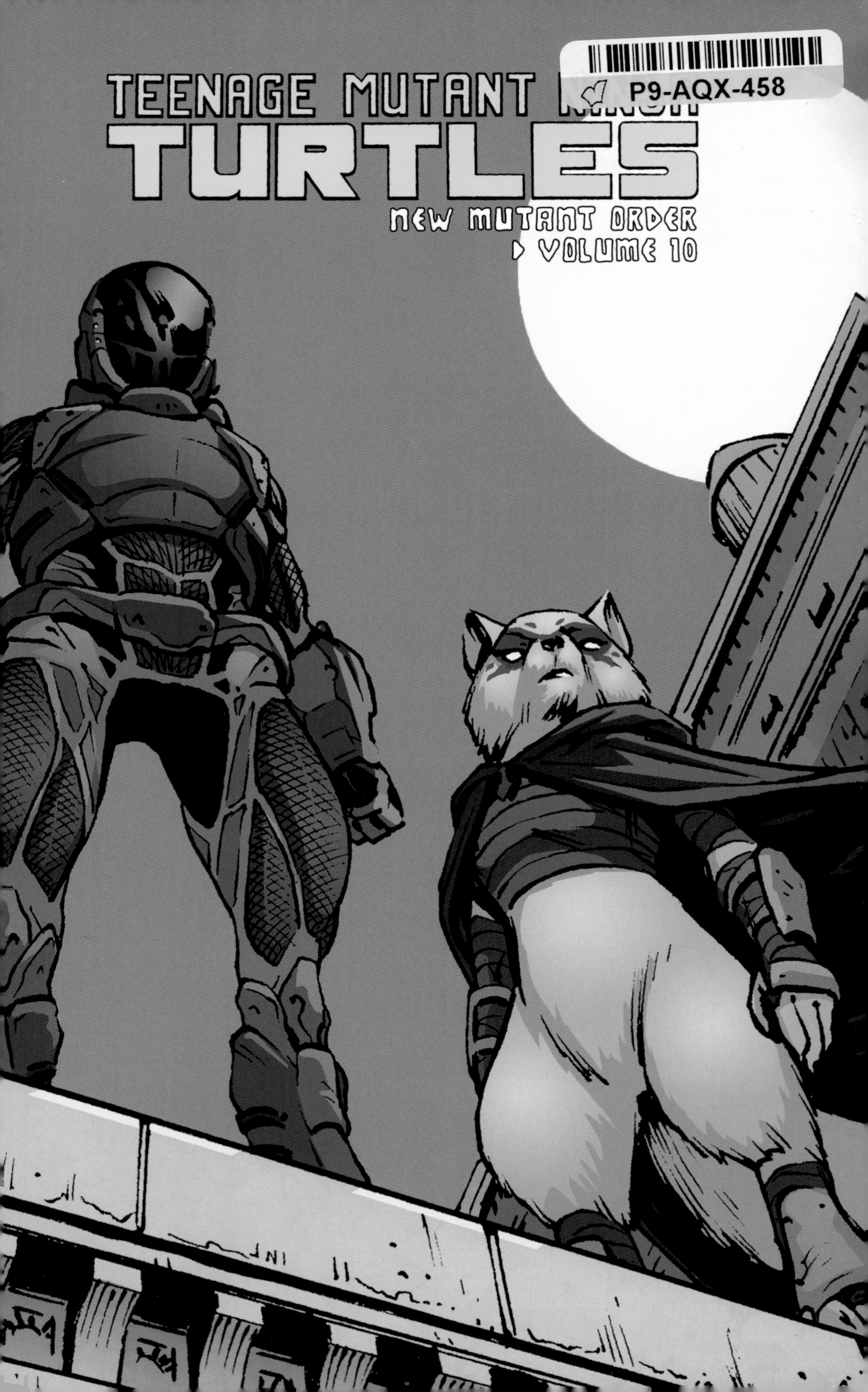
TEENAGE MUTANT
TURTLES
NEW MUTANT ORDER
VOLUME 10

Special thanks to Joan Hilty, Linda Lee, and Kat van Dam for their invaluable assistance.

ISBN: 978-1-63140-233-3

For international rights, contact licensing@idwpublishing.com

19 18 17 16   3 4 5 6

Ted Adams, CEO & Publisher
Greg Goldstein, President & COO
Robbie Robbins, EVP/Sr. Graphic Artist
Chris Ryall, Chief Creative Officer/Editor-in-Chief
Matthew Ruzicka, CPA, Chief Financial Officer
Dirk Wood, VP of Marketing
Lorelei Bunjes, VP of Digital Services
Jeff Webber, VP of Licensing, Digital and Subsidiary Rights
Jerry Bennington, VP of New Product Development

IDW
www.IDWPUBLISHING.com

Facebook: facebook.com/idwpublishing
Twitter: @idwpublishing
YouTube: youtube.com/idwpublishing
Tumblr: tumblr.idwpublishing.com
Instagram: instagram.com/idwpublishing

Originally published as TEENAGE MUTANT NINJA TURTLES issues #37–40.

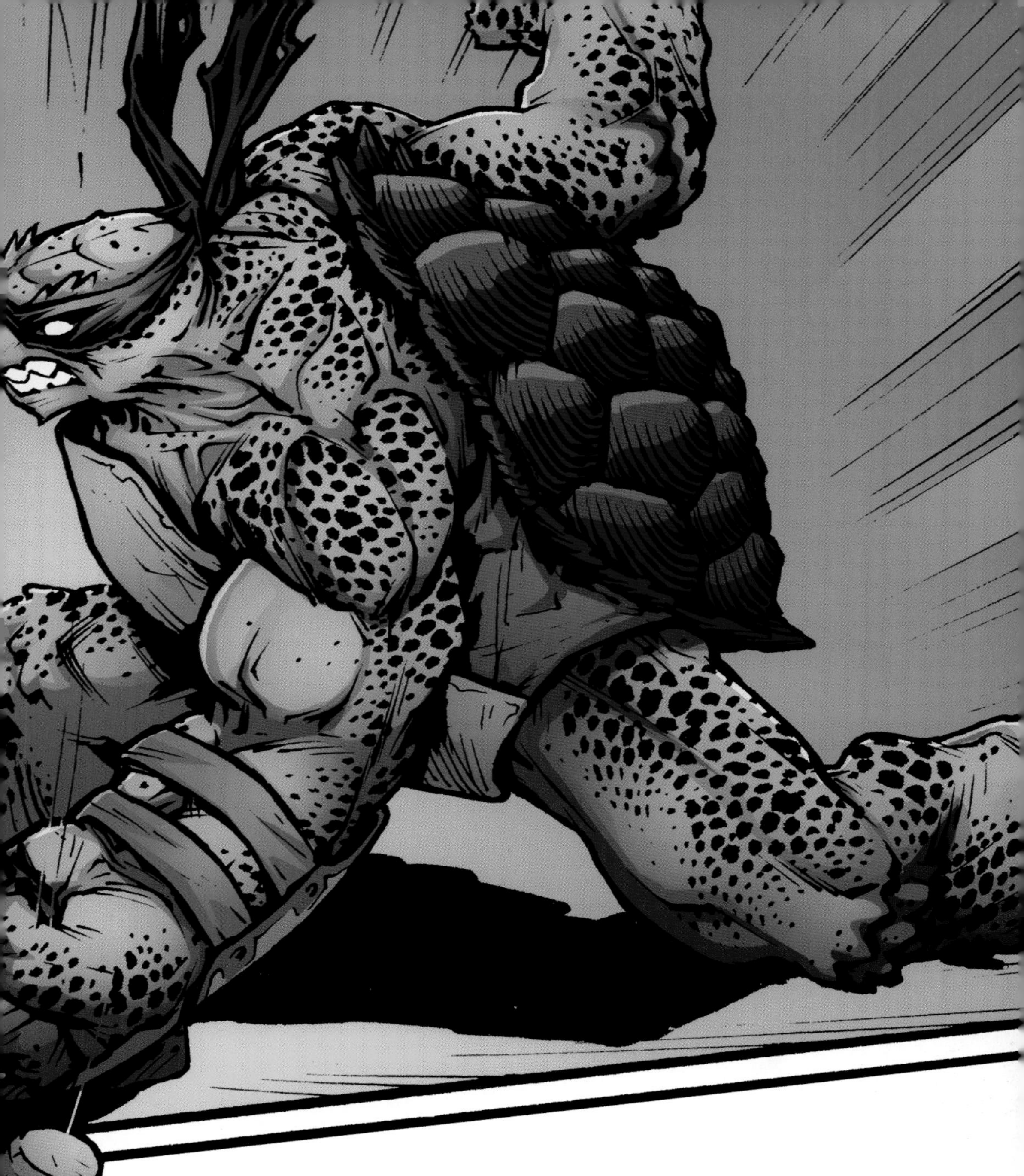

Story by Kevin Eastman, Bobby Curnow, and Tom Waltz · Script by Tom Waltz

Art by Cory Smith (Ch. 1) and Mateus Santolouco (Ch. 2-4)

Colors by Ronda Pattison · Letters by Shawn Lee

Series Edits by Bobby Curnow

Cover by Mike Henderson

Collection Edits by Justin Eisinger & Alonzo Simon

Production by Gilberto Lazcano

Based on characters created by Peter Laird and Kevin Eastman

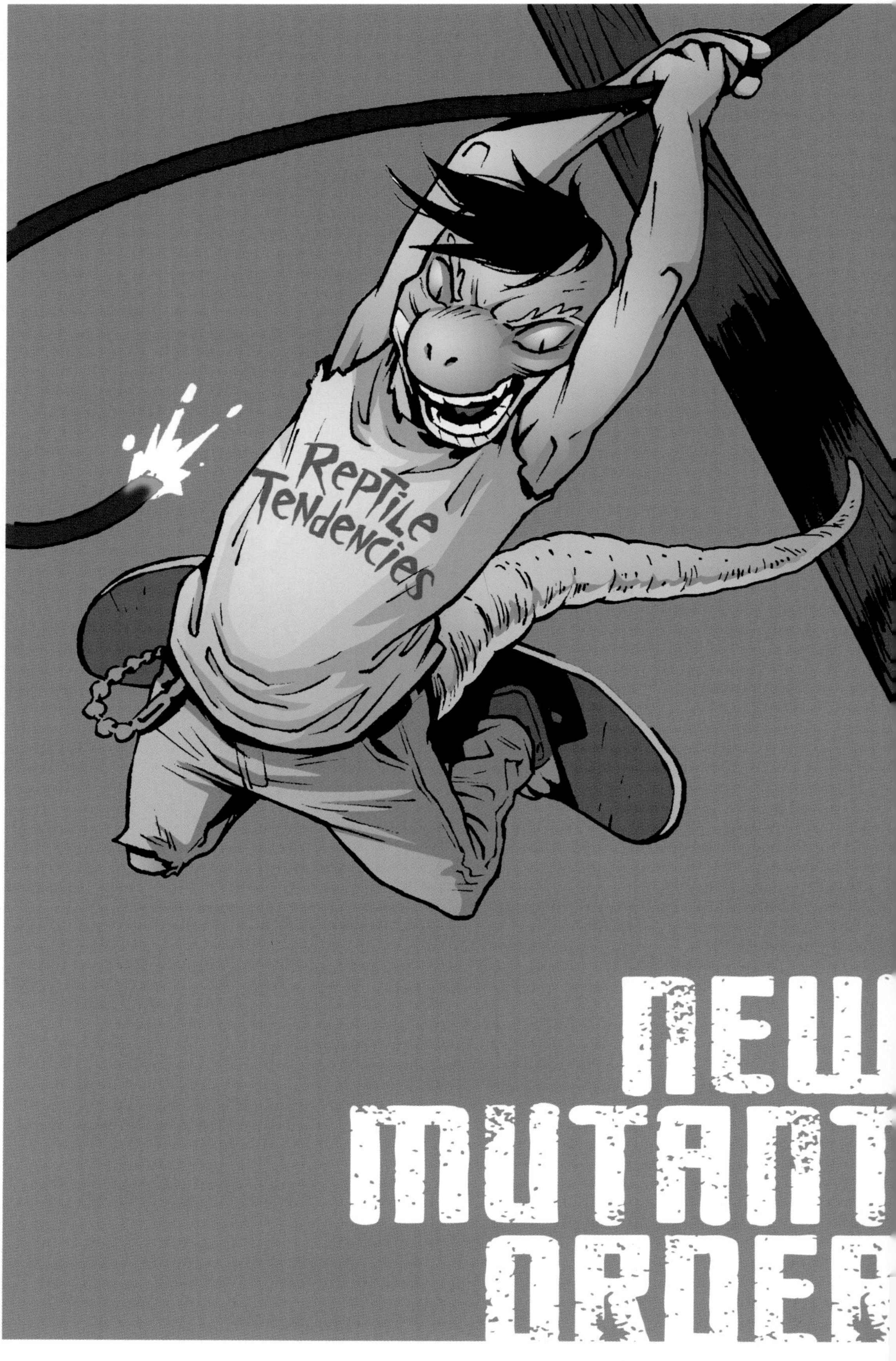
Reptile Tendencies
NEW
MUTANT
ORDER

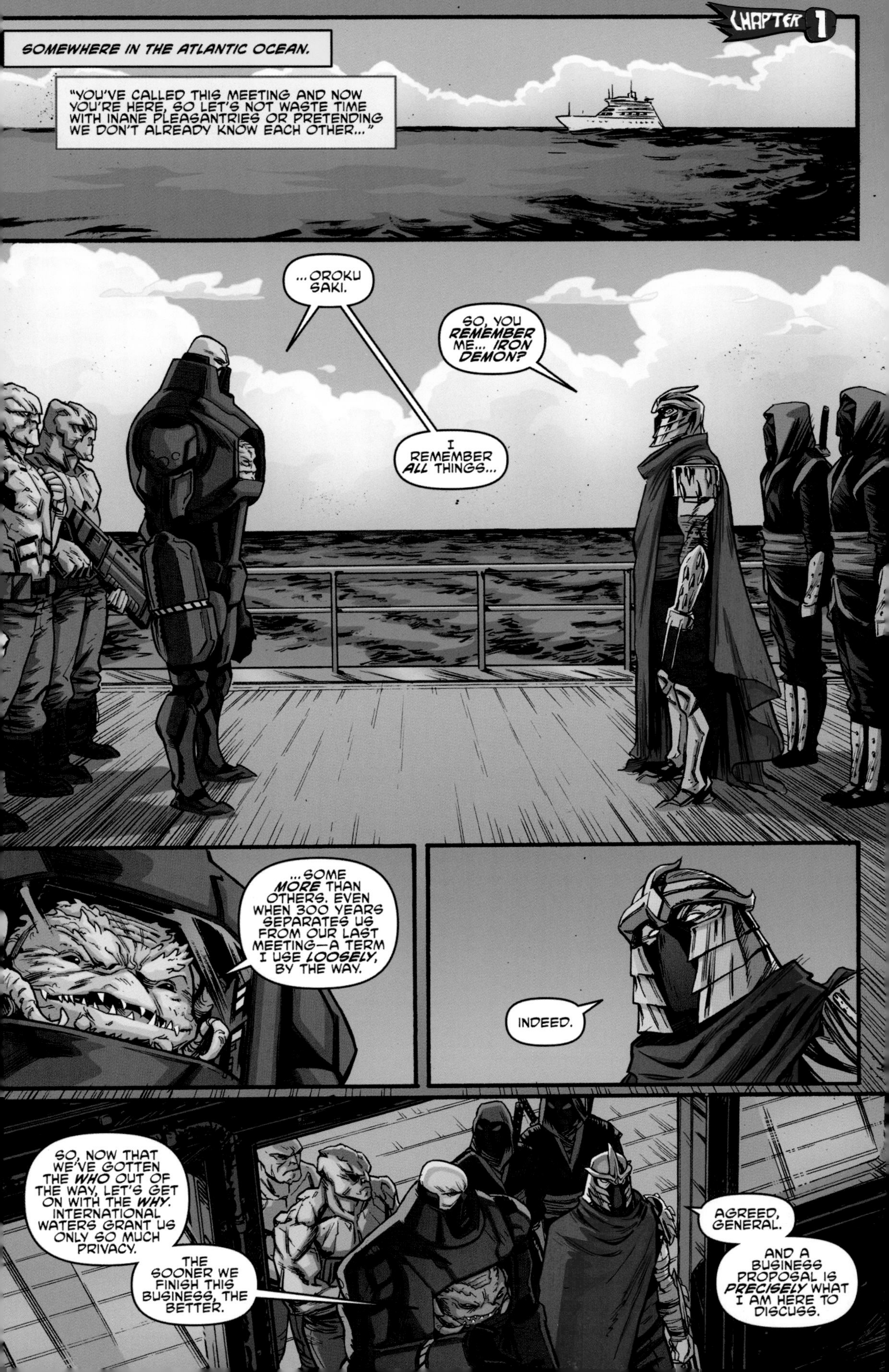
CHAPTER 1
SOMEWHERE IN THE ATLANTIC OCEAN.
"YOU'VE CALLED THIS MEETING AND NOW YOU'RE HERE, SO LET'S NOT WASTE TIME WITH INANE PLEASANTRIES OR PRETENDING WE DON'T ALREADY KNOW EACH OTHER..."
...OROKU SAKI.
SO, YOU *REMEMBER* ME... *IRON DEMON?*
I REMEMBER *ALL* THINGS...
...SOME *MORE* THAN OTHERS. EVEN WHEN 300 YEARS SEPARATES US FROM OUR LAST MEETING—A TERM I USE *LOOSELY*, BY THE WAY.
INDEED.
SO, NOW THAT WE'VE GOTTEN THE *WHO* OUT OF THE WAY, LET'S GET ON WITH THE *WHY*. INTERNATIONAL WATERS GRANT US ONLY SO MUCH PRIVACY.
THE SOONER WE FINISH THIS BUSINESS, THE BETTER.
AGREED, GENERAL.
AND A BUSINESS PROPOSAL IS *PRECISELY* WHAT I AM HERE TO DISCUSS.

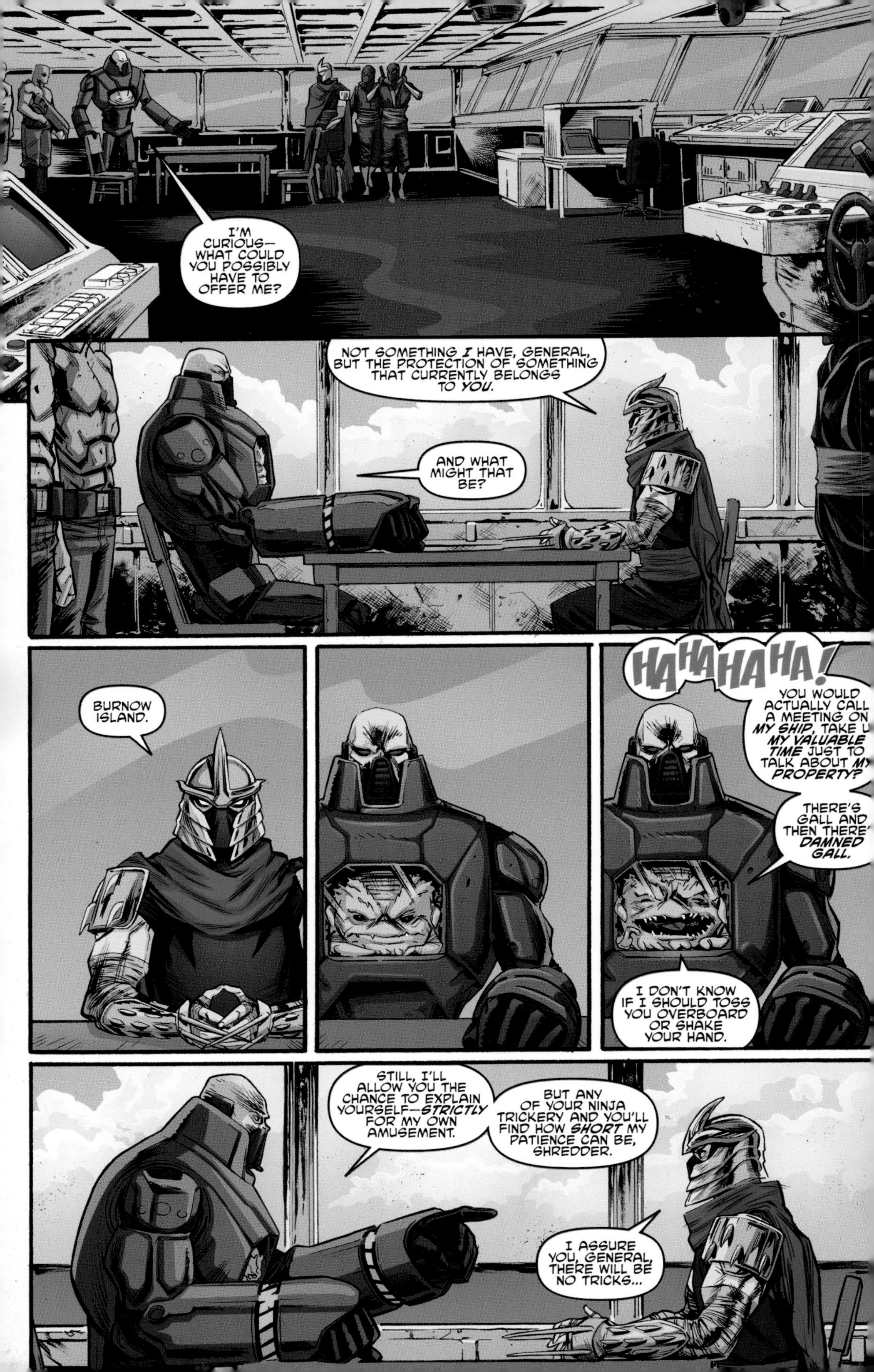
I'M CURIOUS— WHAT COULD YOU POSSIBLY HAVE TO OFFER ME?
NOT SOMETHING I HAVE, GENERAL, BUT THE PROTECTION OF SOMETHING THAT CURRENTLY BELONGS TO YOU.
AND WHAT MIGHT THAT BE?
BURNOW ISLAND.
HAHAHAHA!
YOU WOULD ACTUALLY CALL A MEETING ON MY SHIP, TAKE U MY VALUABLE TIME JUST TO TALK ABOUT MY PROPERTY?
THERE'S GALL AND THEN THERE' DAMNED GALL.
I DON'T KNOW IF I SHOULD TOSS YOU OVERBOARD OR SHAKE YOUR HAND.
STILL, I'LL ALLOW YOU THE CHANCE TO EXPLAIN YOURSELF—STRICTLY FOR MY OWN AMUSEMENT.
BUT ANY OF YOUR NINJA TRICKERY AND YOU'LL FIND HOW SHORT MY PATIENCE CAN BE, SHREDDER.
I ASSURE YOU, GENERAL, THERE WILL BE NO TRICKS...

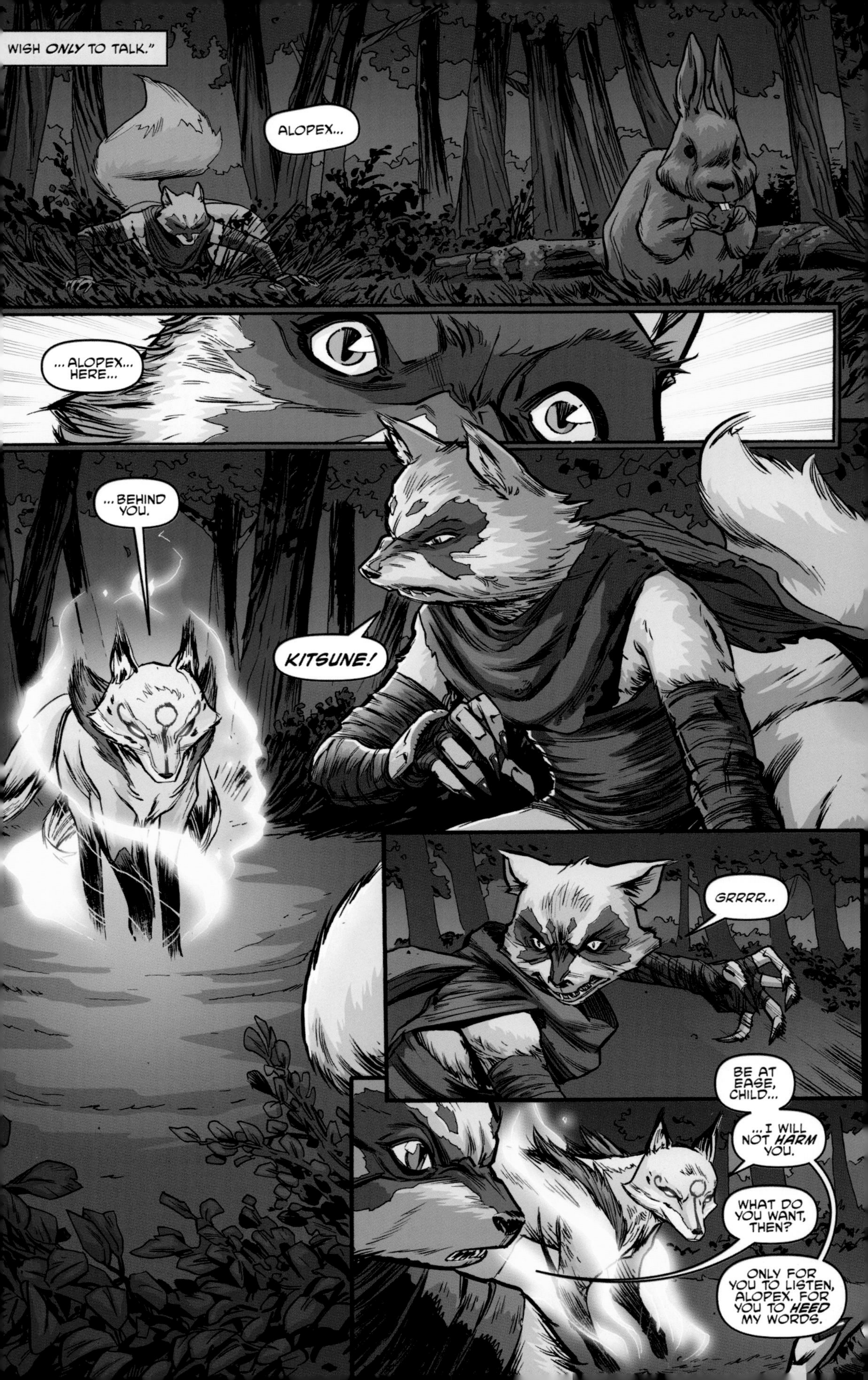
WISH ONLY TO TALK."
ALOPEX...
...ALOPEX... HERE...
...BEHIND YOU.
KITSUNE!
GRRRR...
BE AT EASE, CHILD...
...I WILL NOT HARM YOU.
WHAT DO YOU WANT, THEN?
ONLY FOR YOU TO LISTEN, ALOPEX. FOR YOU TO HEED MY WORDS.

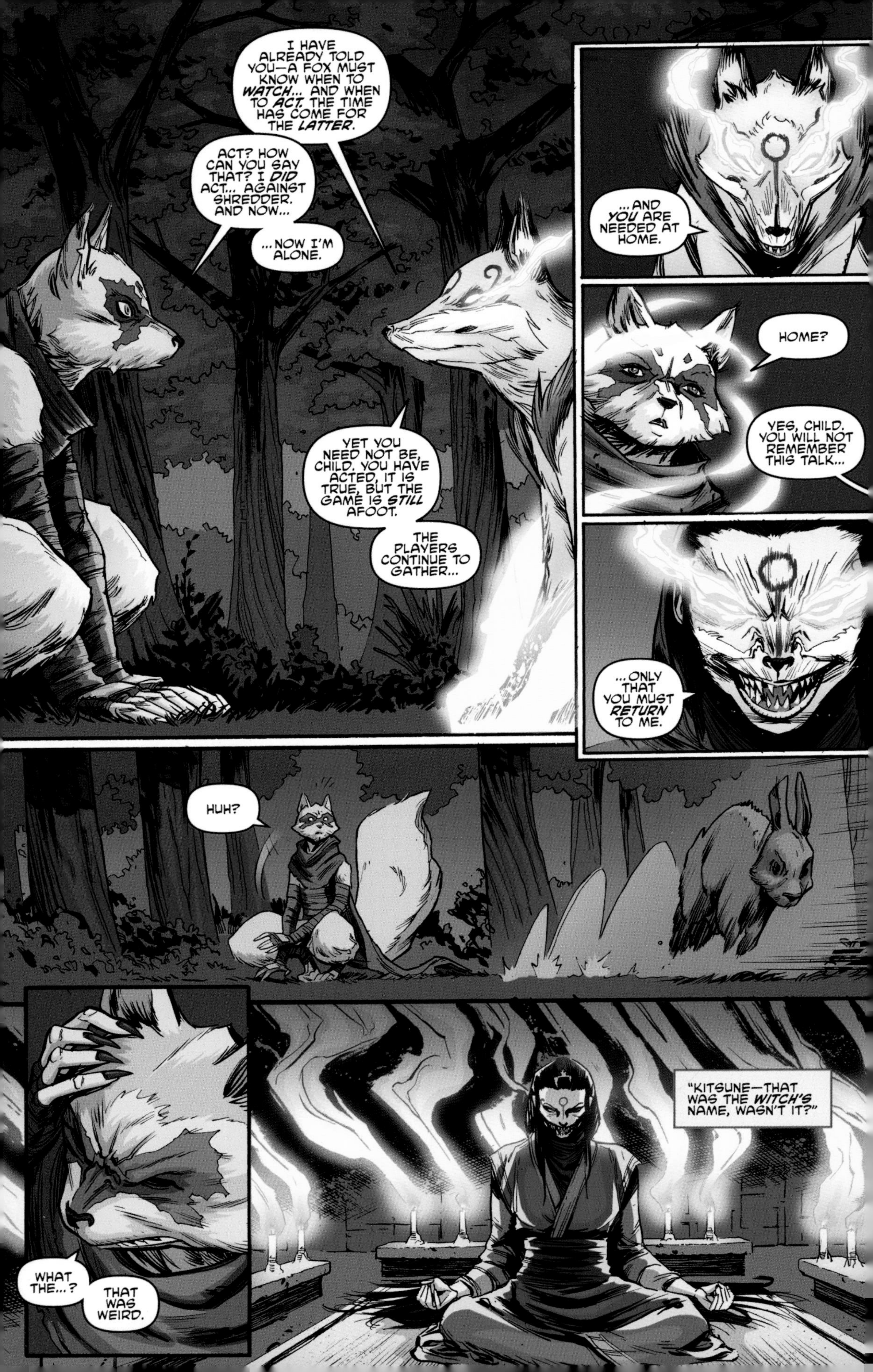
I HAVE ALREADY TOLD YOU—A FOX MUST KNOW WHEN TO WATCH... AND WHEN TO ACT. THE TIME HAS COME FOR THE LATTER.
ACT? HOW CAN YOU SAY THAT? I DID ACT... AGAINST SHREDDER. AND NOW...
...NOW I'M ALONE.
YET YOU NEED NOT BE, CHILD. YOU HAVE ACTED, IT IS TRUE, BUT THE GAME IS STILL AFOOT.
THE PLAYERS CONTINUE TO GATHER...
...AND YOU ARE NEEDED AT HOME.
HOME?
YES, CHILD. YOU WILL NOT REMEMBER THIS TALK...
...ONLY THAT YOU MUST RETURN TO ME.
HUH?
WHAT THE...?
THAT WAS WEIRD.
"KITSUNE—THAT WAS THE WITCH'S NAME, WASN'T IT?"

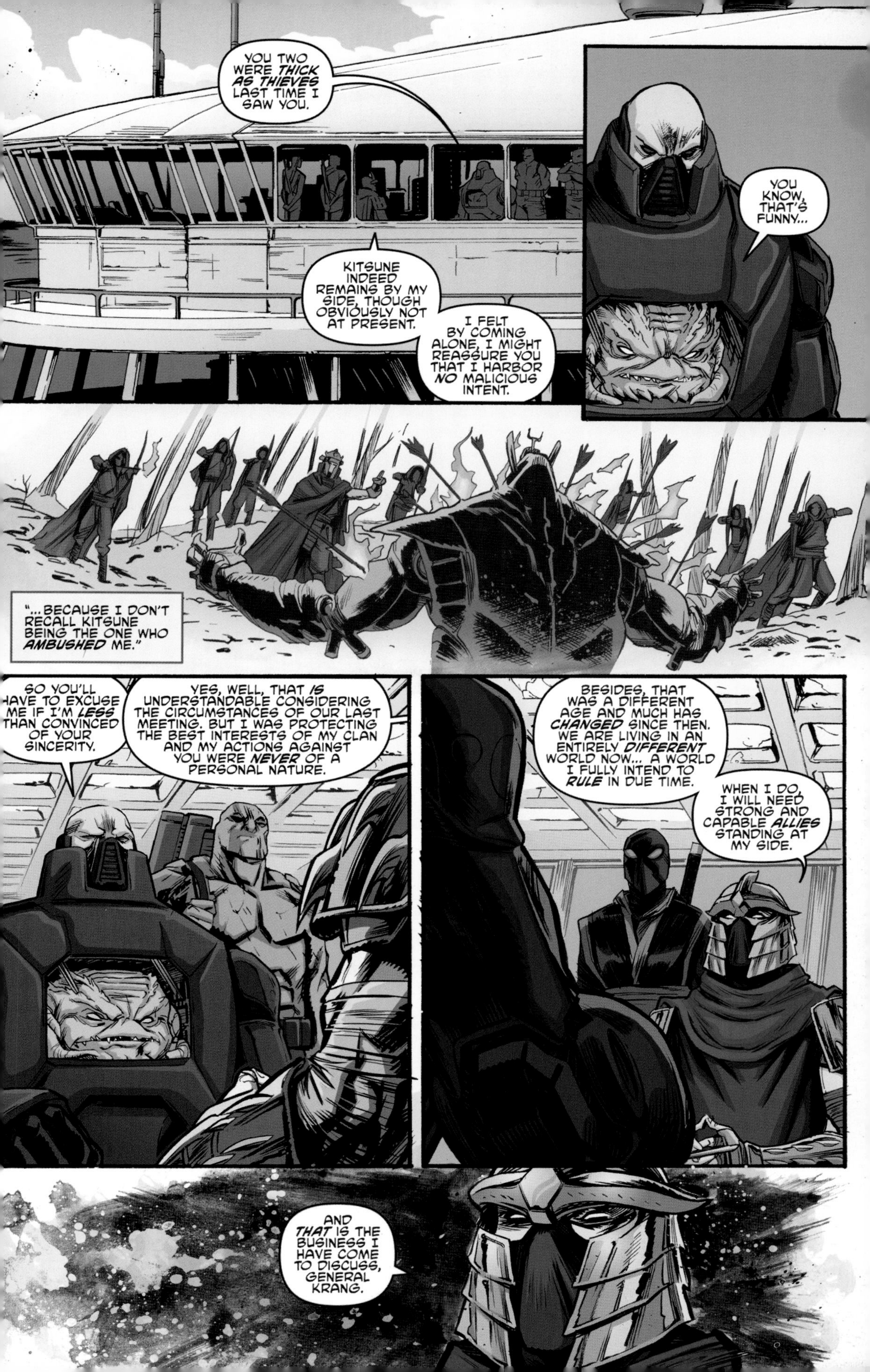

YOU TWO WERE *THICK AS THIEVES* LAST TIME I SAW YOU.
KITSUNE INDEED REMAINS BY MY SIDE, THOUGH OBVIOUSLY NOT AT PRESENT.
I FELT BY COMING ALONE, I MIGHT REASSURE YOU THAT I HARBOR *NO* MALICIOUS INTENT.
YOU KNOW, THAT'S FUNNY...
"...BECAUSE I DON'T RECALL KITSUNE BEING THE ONE WHO *AMBUSHED* ME."
SO YOU'LL HAVE TO EXCUSE ME IF I'M *LESS* THAN CONVINCED OF YOUR SINCERITY.
YES, WELL, THAT *IS* UNDERSTANDABLE CONSIDERING THE CIRCUMSTANCES OF OUR LAST MEETING. BUT I WAS PROTECTING THE BEST INTERESTS OF MY CLAN AND MY ACTIONS AGAINST YOU WERE *NEVER* OF A PERSONAL NATURE.
BESIDES, THAT WAS A DIFFERENT AGE AND MUCH HAS *CHANGED* SINCE THEN. WE ARE LIVING IN AN ENTIRELY *DIFFERENT* WORLD NOW... A WORLD I FULLY INTEND TO *RULE* IN DUE TIME.
WHEN I DO, I WILL NEED STRONG AND CAPABLE *ALLIES* STANDING AT MY SIDE.
AND *THAT* IS THE BUSINESS I HAVE COME TO DISCUSS, GENERAL KRANG.

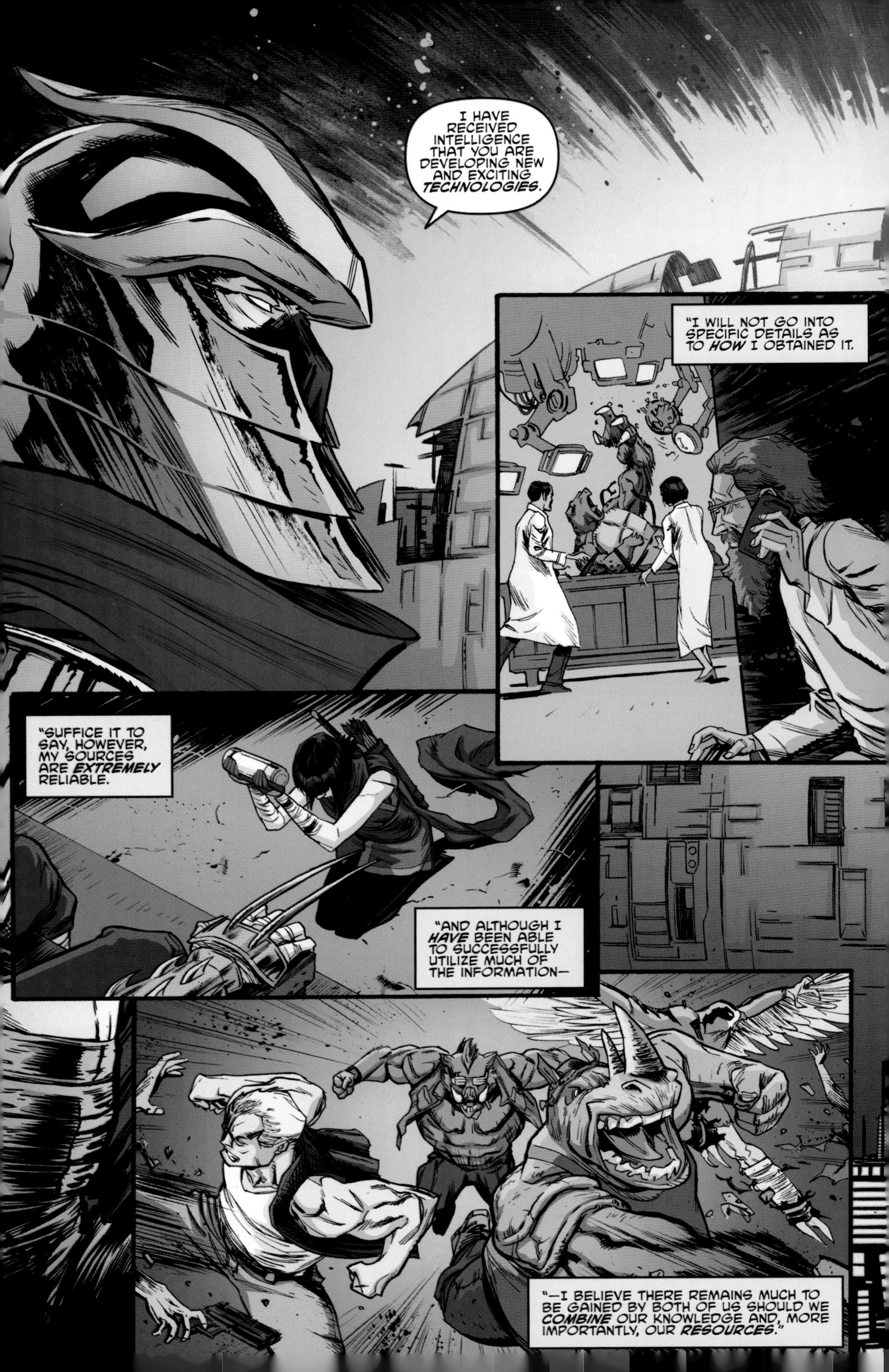
I HAVE RECEIVED INTELLIGENCE THAT YOU ARE DEVELOPING NEW AND EXCITING *TECHNOLOGIES*.
"I WILL NOT GO INTO SPECIFIC DETAILS AS TO *HOW* I OBTAINED IT.
"SUFFICE IT TO SAY, HOWEVER, MY SOURCES ARE *EXTREMELY* RELIABLE.
"AND ALTHOUGH I *HAVE* BEEN ABLE TO SUCCESSFULLY UTILIZE MUCH OF THE INFORMATION—
"—I BELIEVE THERE REMAINS MUCH TO BE GAINED BY BOTH OF US SHOULD WE *COMBINE* OUR KNOWLEDGE AND, MORE IMPORTANTLY, OUR *RESOURCES*."

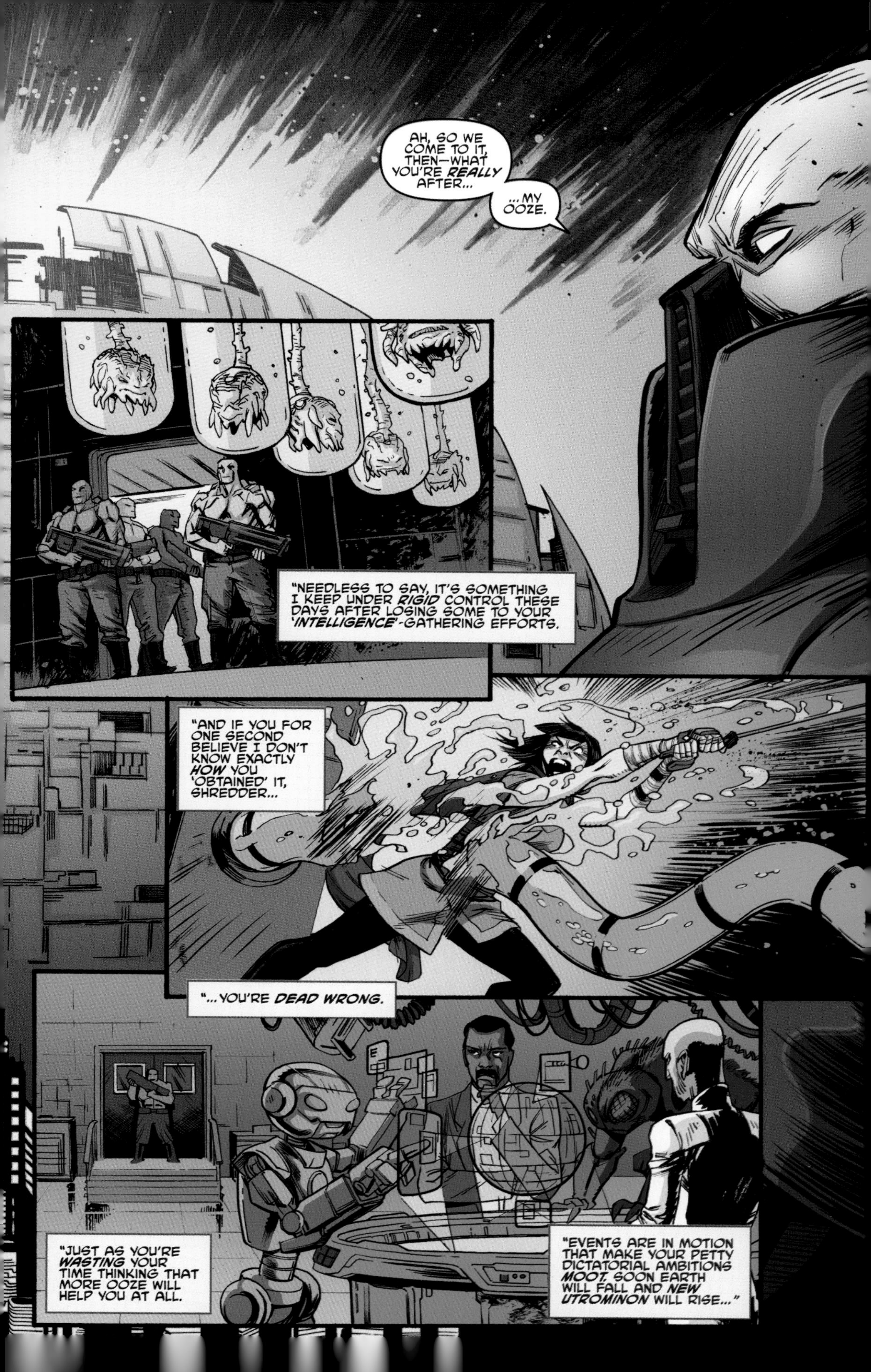
AH, SO WE COME TO IT, THEN—WHAT YOU'RE REALLY AFTER...
...MY OOZE.
"NEEDLESS TO SAY, IT'S SOMETHING I KEEP UNDER RIGID CONTROL THESE DAYS AFTER LOSING SOME TO YOUR 'INTELLIGENCE'-GATHERING EFFORTS.
"AND IF YOU FOR ONE SECOND BELIEVE I DON'T KNOW EXACTLY HOW YOU 'OBTAINED' IT, SHREDDER...
"...YOU'RE DEAD WRONG.
"JUST AS YOU'RE WASTING YOUR TIME THINKING THAT MORE OOZE WILL HELP YOU AT ALL.
"EVENTS ARE IN MOTION THAT MAKE YOUR PETTY DICTATORIAL AMBITIONS MOOT. SOON EARTH WILL FALL AND NEW UTROMINON WILL RISE..."

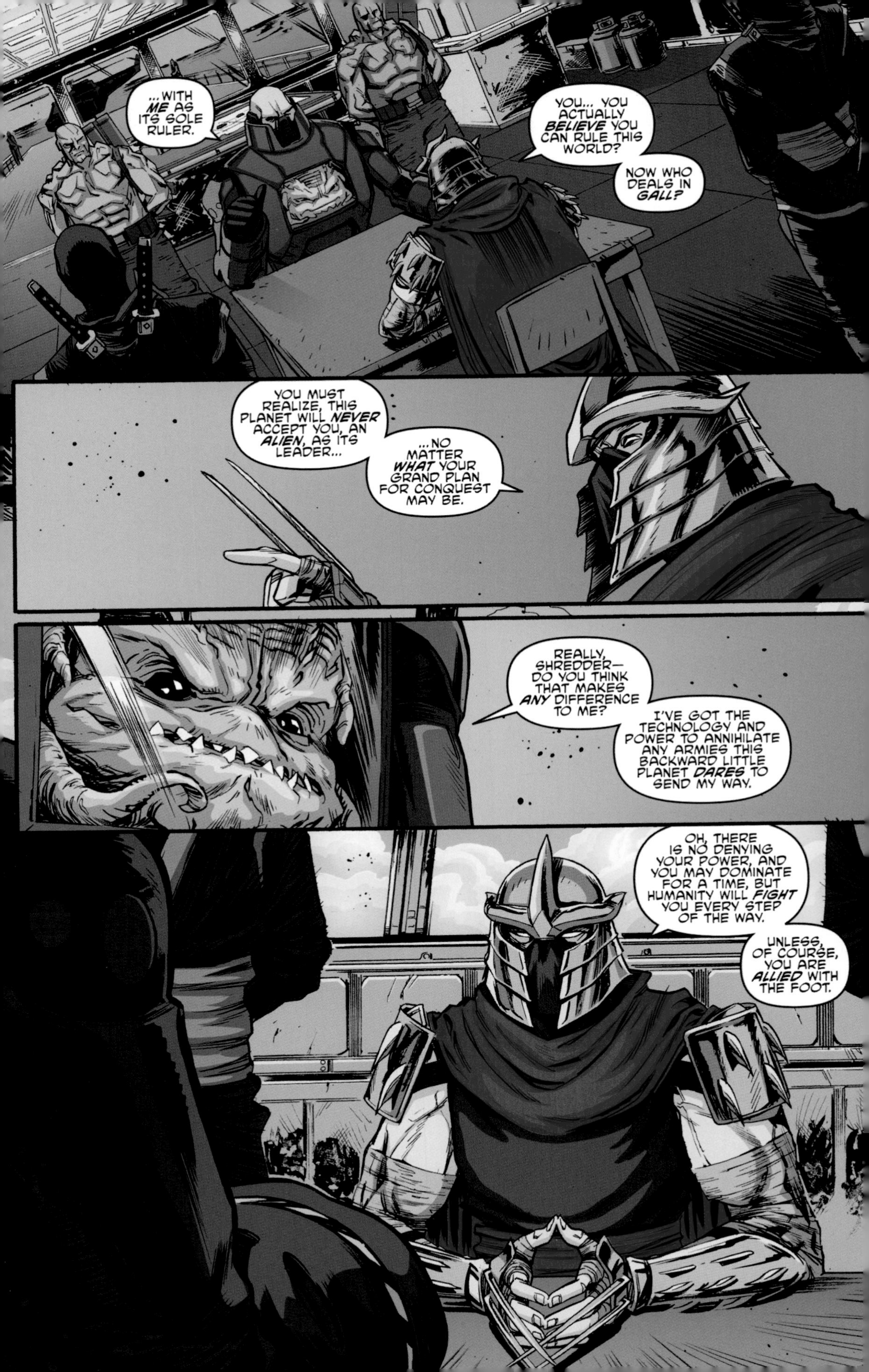
...WITH *ME* AS ITS SOLE RULER.
YOU... YOU ACTUALLY *BELIEVE* YOU CAN RULE THIS WORLD?
NOW WHO DEALS IN *GALL?*
YOU MUST REALIZE, THIS PLANET WILL *NEVER* ACCEPT YOU, AN *ALIEN*, AS ITS LEADER...
...NO MATTER *WHAT* YOUR GRAND PLAN FOR CONQUEST MAY BE.
REALLY, SHREDDER— DO YOU THINK THAT MAKES *ANY* DIFFERENCE TO ME?
I'VE GOT THE TECHNOLOGY AND POWER TO ANNIHILATE ANY ARMIES THIS BACKWARD LITTLE PLANET *DARES* TO SEND MY WAY.
OH, THERE IS NO DENYING YOUR POWER, AND YOU MAY DOMINATE FOR A TIME, BUT HUMANITY WILL *FIGHT* YOU EVERY STEP OF THE WAY.
UNLESS, OF COURSE, YOU ARE *ALLIED* WITH THE FOOT.

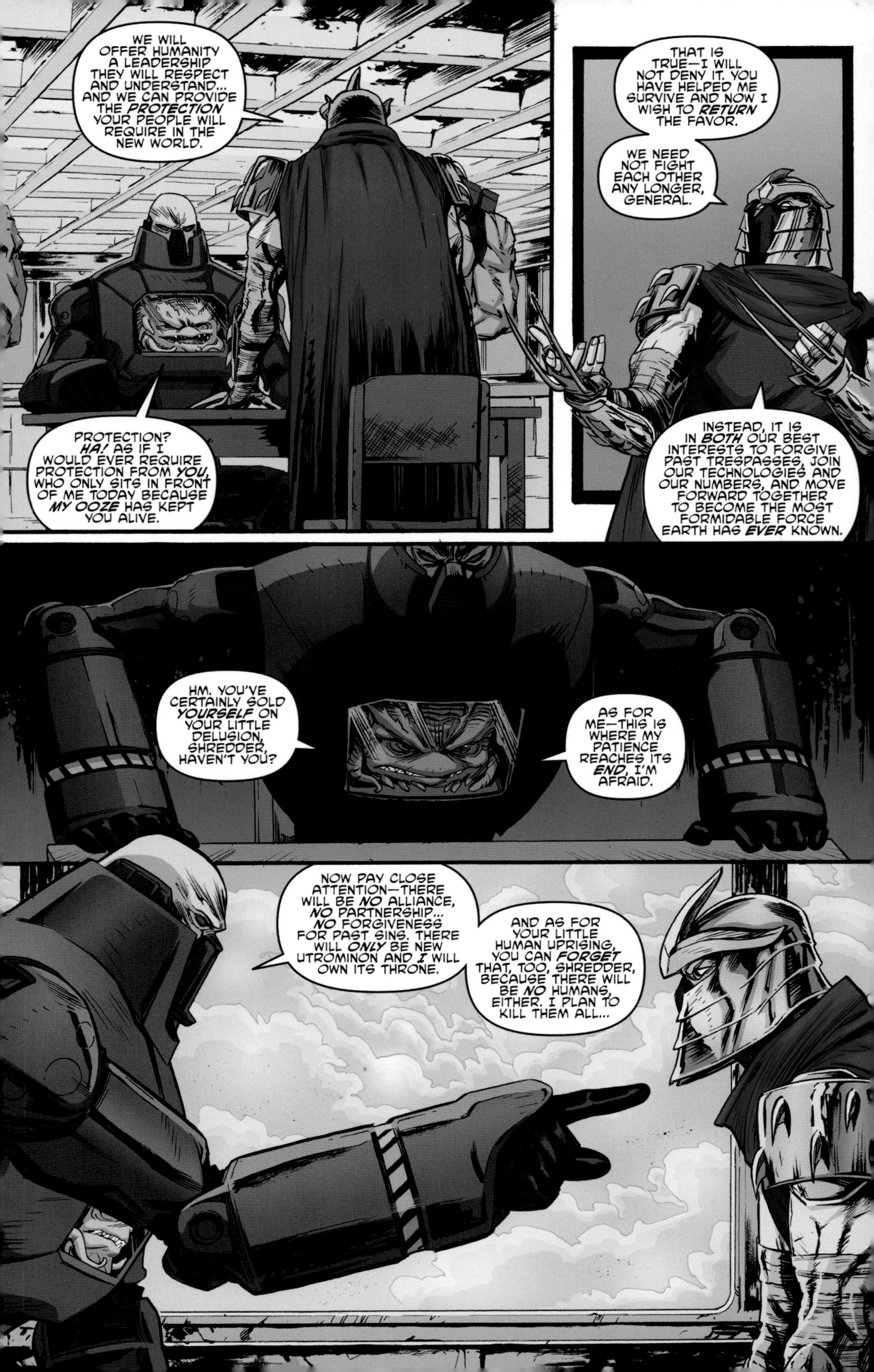
WE WILL OFFER HUMANITY A LEADERSHIP THEY WILL RESPECT AND UNDERSTAND... AND WE CAN PROVIDE THE PROTECTION YOUR PEOPLE WILL REQUIRE IN THE NEW WORLD.
PROTECTION? HA! AS IF I WOULD EVER REQUIRE PROTECTION FROM YOU, WHO ONLY SITS IN FRONT OF ME TODAY BECAUSE MY OOZE HAS KEPT YOU ALIVE.
THAT IS TRUE—I WILL NOT DENY IT. YOU HAVE HELPED ME SURVIVE AND NOW I WISH TO RETURN THE FAVOR.
WE NEED NOT FIGHT EACH OTHER ANY LONGER, GENERAL.
INSTEAD, IT IS IN BOTH OUR BEST INTERESTS TO FORGIVE PAST TRESPASSES, JOIN OUR TECHNOLOGIES AND OUR NUMBERS, AND MOVE FORWARD TOGETHER TO BECOME THE MOST FORMIDABLE FORCE EARTH HAS EVER KNOWN.
HM. YOU'VE CERTAINLY SOLD YOURSELF ON YOUR LITTLE DELUSION, SHREDDER, HAVEN'T YOU?
AS FOR ME—THIS IS WHERE MY PATIENCE REACHES ITS END, I'M AFRAID.
NOW PAY CLOSE ATTENTION—THERE WILL BE NO ALLIANCE, NO PARTNERSHIP... NO FORGIVENESS FOR PAST SINS. THERE WILL ONLY BE NEW UTROMINON AND I WILL OWN ITS THRONE.
AND AS FOR YOUR LITTLE HUMAN UPRISING, YOU CAN FORGET THAT, TOO, SHREDDER, BECAUSE THERE WILL BE NO HUMANS, EITHER. I PLAN TO KILL THEM ALL...

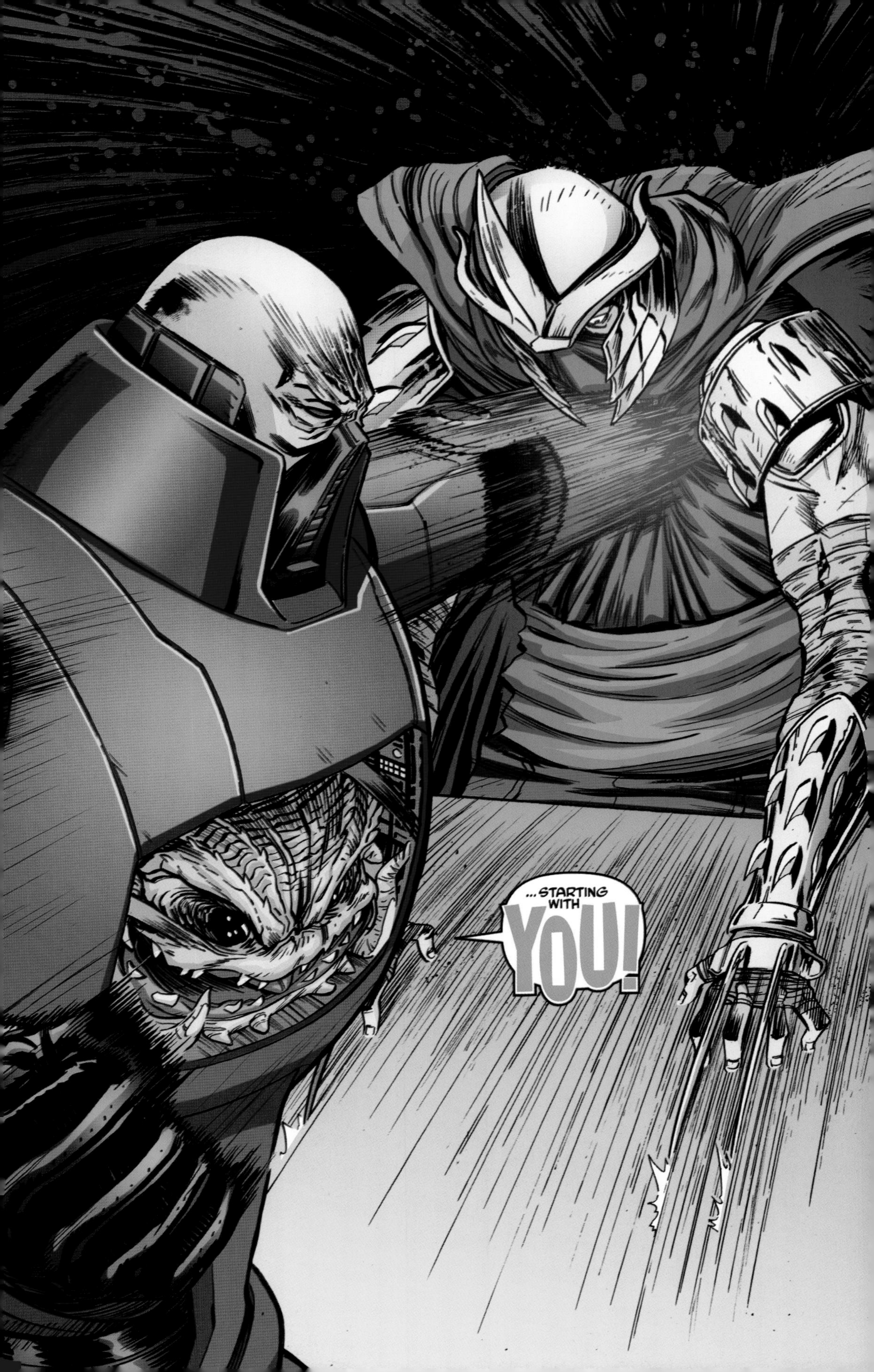
...STARTING WITH YOU!

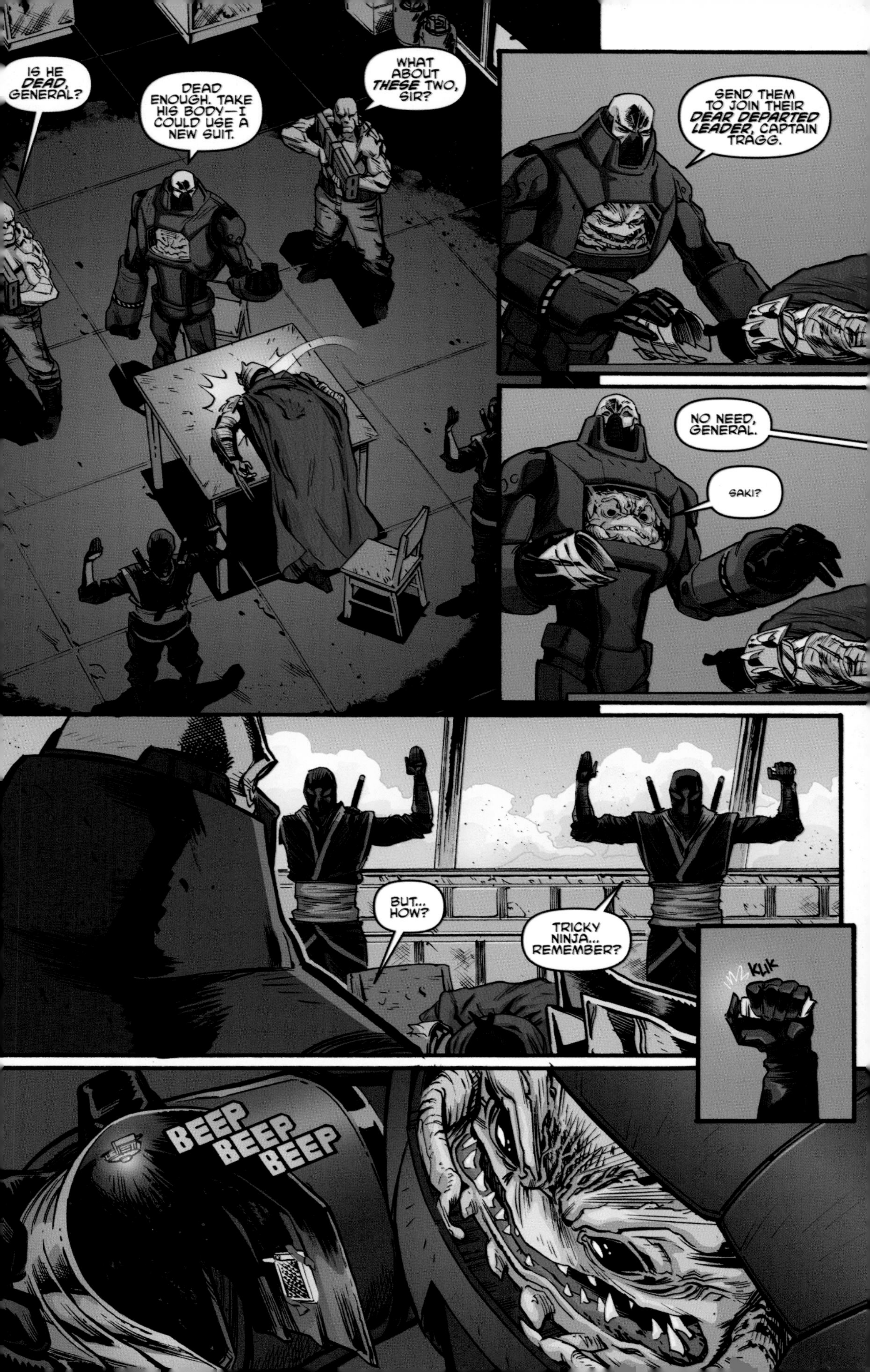
IS HE DEAD, GENERAL?
DEAD ENOUGH. TAKE HIS BODY—I COULD USE A NEW SUIT.
WHAT ABOUT THESE TWO, SIR?
SEND THEM TO JOIN THEIR DEAR DEPARTED LEADER, CAPTAIN TRAGG.
NO NEED, GENERAL.
SAKI?
BUT... HOW?
TRICKY NINJA... REMEMBER?
KLIK
BEEP BEEP BEEP

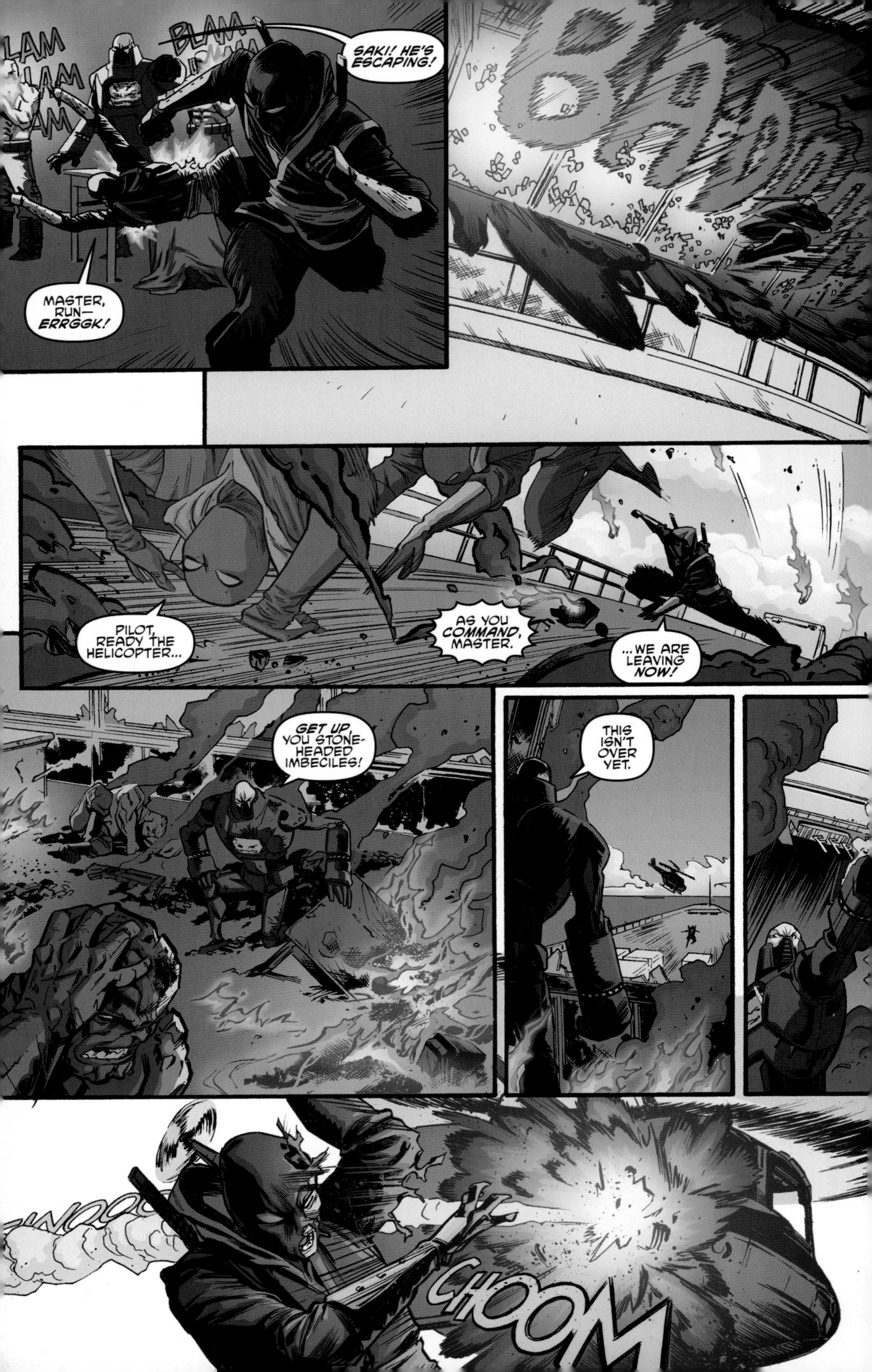
BLAM
BLAM
BLAM
BLAM
SAKI! HE'S ESCAPING!
MASTER, RUN— ERRGGK!
PILOT, READY THE HELICOPTER...
AS YOU COMMAND, MASTER.
...WE ARE LEAVING NOW!
GET UP YOU STONE-HEADED IMBECILES!
THIS ISN'T OVER YET.
CHOOM

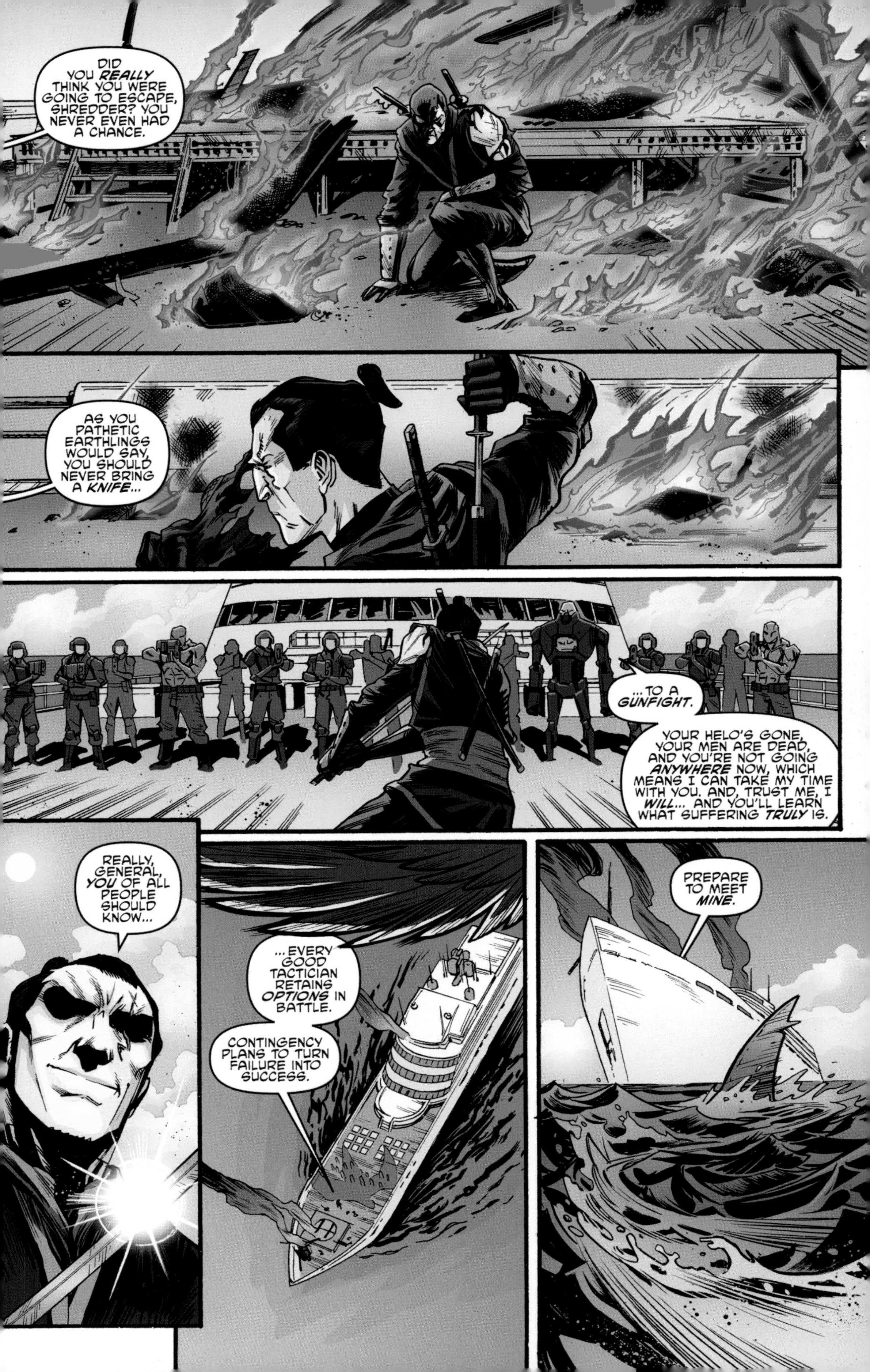
DID YOU REALLY THINK YOU WERE GOING TO ESCAPE, SHREDDER? YOU NEVER EVEN HAD A CHANCE.
AS YOU PATHETIC EARTHLINGS WOULD SAY, YOU SHOULD NEVER BRING A KNIFE...
...TO A GUNFIGHT.
YOUR HELO'S GONE, YOUR MEN ARE DEAD, AND YOU'RE NOT GOING ANYWHERE NOW, WHICH MEANS I CAN TAKE MY TIME WITH YOU. AND, TRUST ME, I WILL... AND YOU'LL LEARN WHAT SUFFERING TRULY IS.
REALLY, GENERAL, YOU OF ALL PEOPLE SHOULD KNOW...
...EVERY GOOD TACTICIAN RETAINS OPTIONS IN BATTLE.
CONTINGENCY PLANS TO TURN FAILURE INTO SUCCESS.
PREPARE TO MEET MINE.

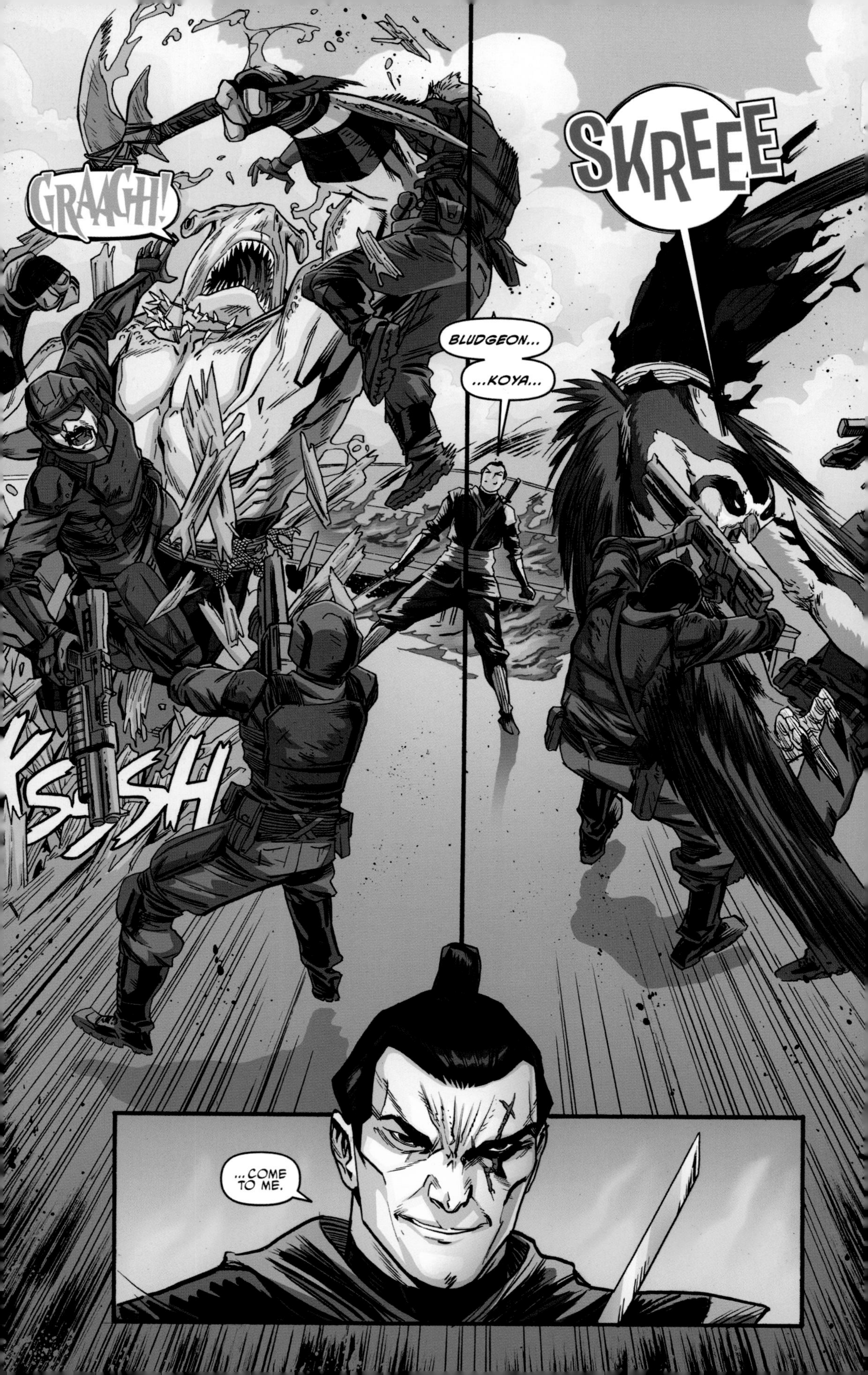
GRAAGH!
SKREEE
BLUDGEON...
...KOYA...
KSSSH
...COME TO ME.

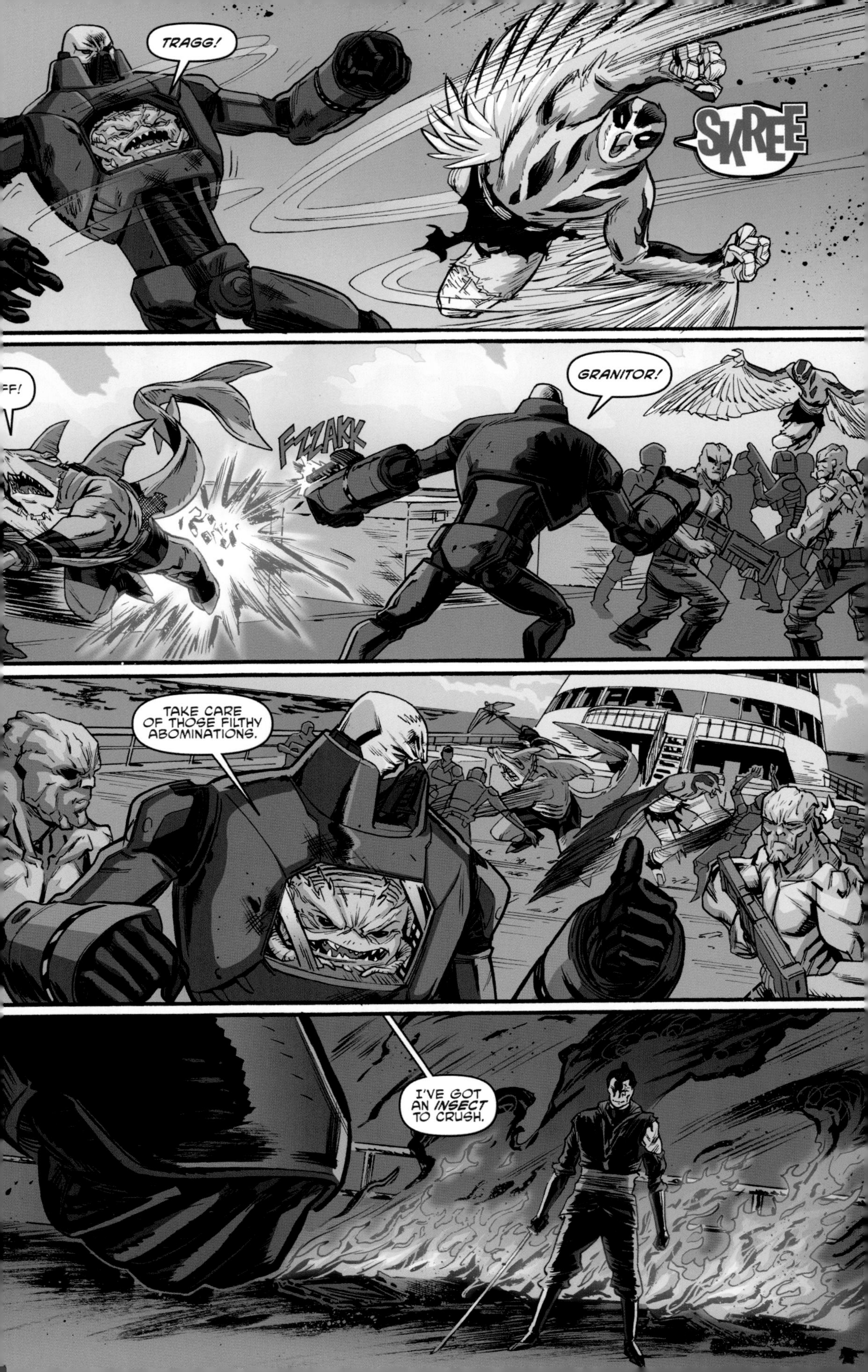
TRAGG!
SKREE
FF!
FZZAKK
GRANITOR!
TAKE CARE OF THOSE FILTHY ABOMINATIONS.
I'VE GOT AN *INSECT* TO CRUSH.

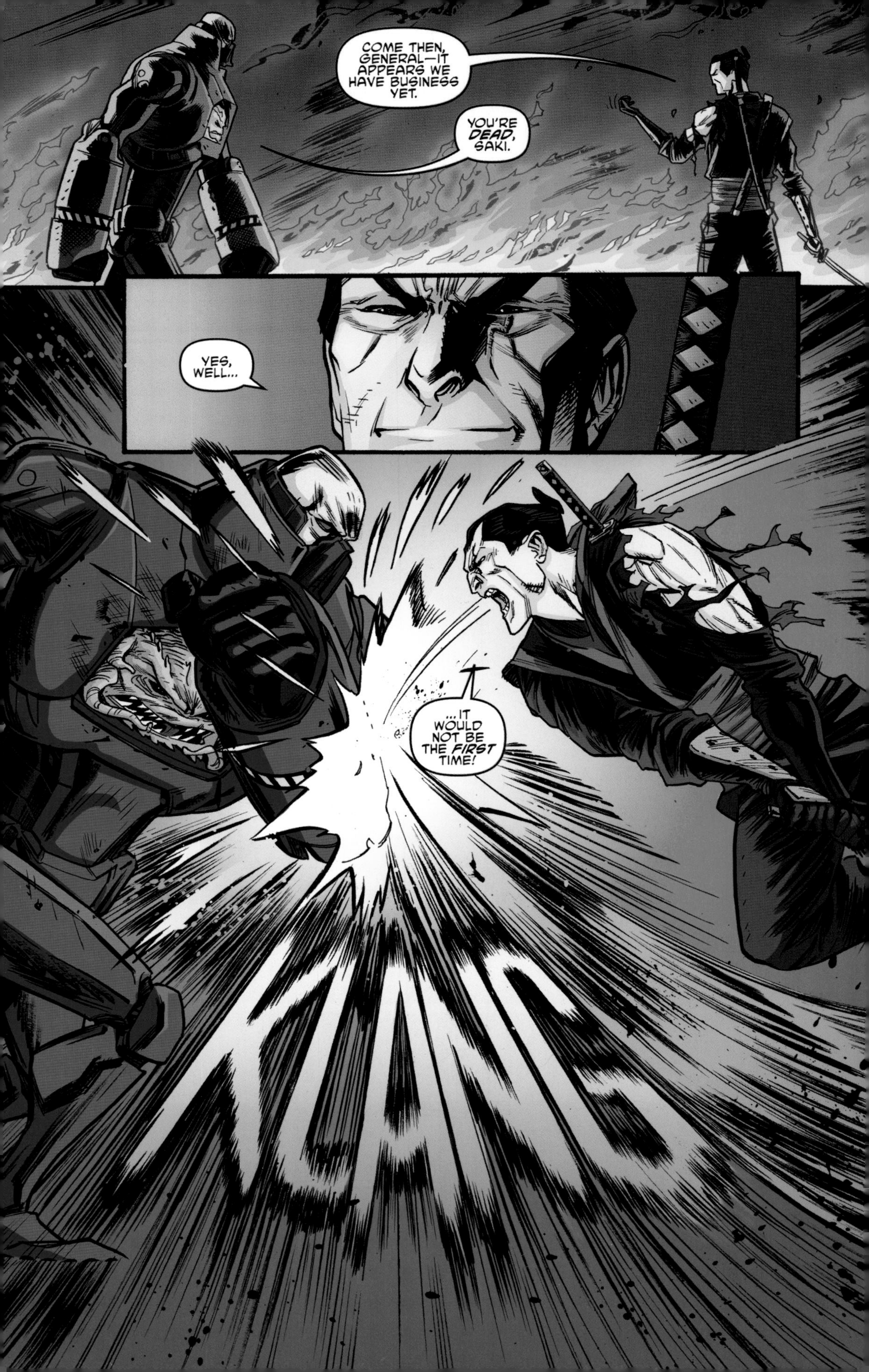
COME THEN, GENERAL—IT APPEARS WE HAVE BUSINESS YET.
YOU'RE *DEAD*, SAKI.
YES, WELL...
...IT WOULD NOT BE THE *FIRST* TIME!

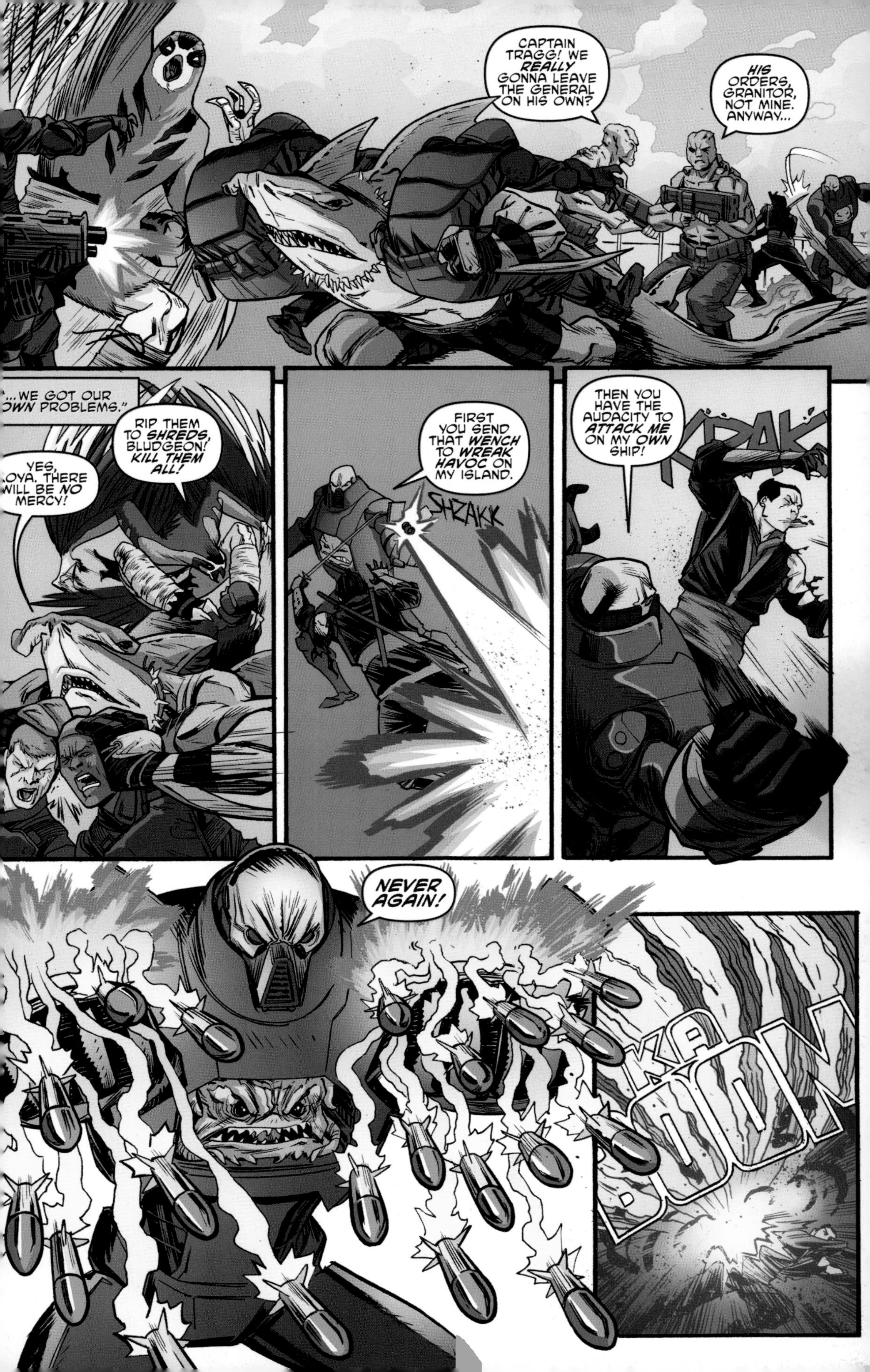

CAPTAIN TRAGG! WE *REALLY* GONNA LEAVE THE GENERAL ON HIS OWN?
HIS ORDERS, GRANITOR, NOT MINE. ANYWAY...
"...WE GOT OUR *OWN* PROBLEMS."
RIP THEM TO *SHREDS*, BLUDGEON! *KILL THEM ALL!*
YES, KOYA. THERE WILL BE *NO* MERCY!
FIRST YOU SEND THAT *WENCH* TO *WREAK HAVOC* ON MY ISLAND.
SHRAKK
THEN YOU HAVE THE AUDACITY TO *ATTACK ME* ON MY *OWN* SHIP!
KRAK
NEVER AGAIN!
KA-DOOM

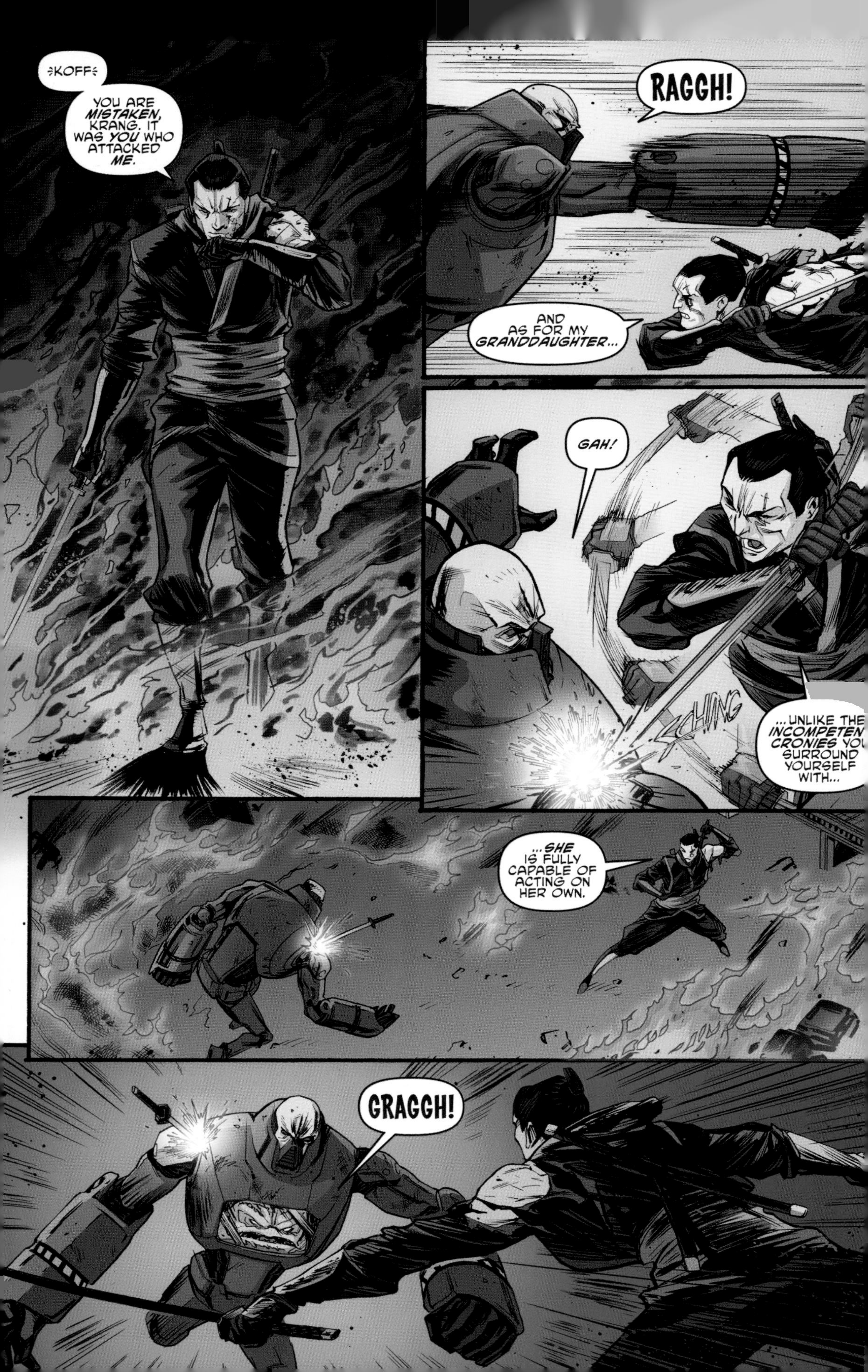

KOFF
YOU ARE MISTAKEN, KRANG. IT WAS YOU WHO ATTACKED ME.
RAGGH!
AND AS FOR MY GRANDDAUGHTER...
GAH!
SCHING
...UNLIKE THE INCOMPETENT CRONIES YOU SURROUND YOURSELF WITH...
...SHE IS FULLY CAPABLE OF ACTING ON HER OWN.
GRAGGH!

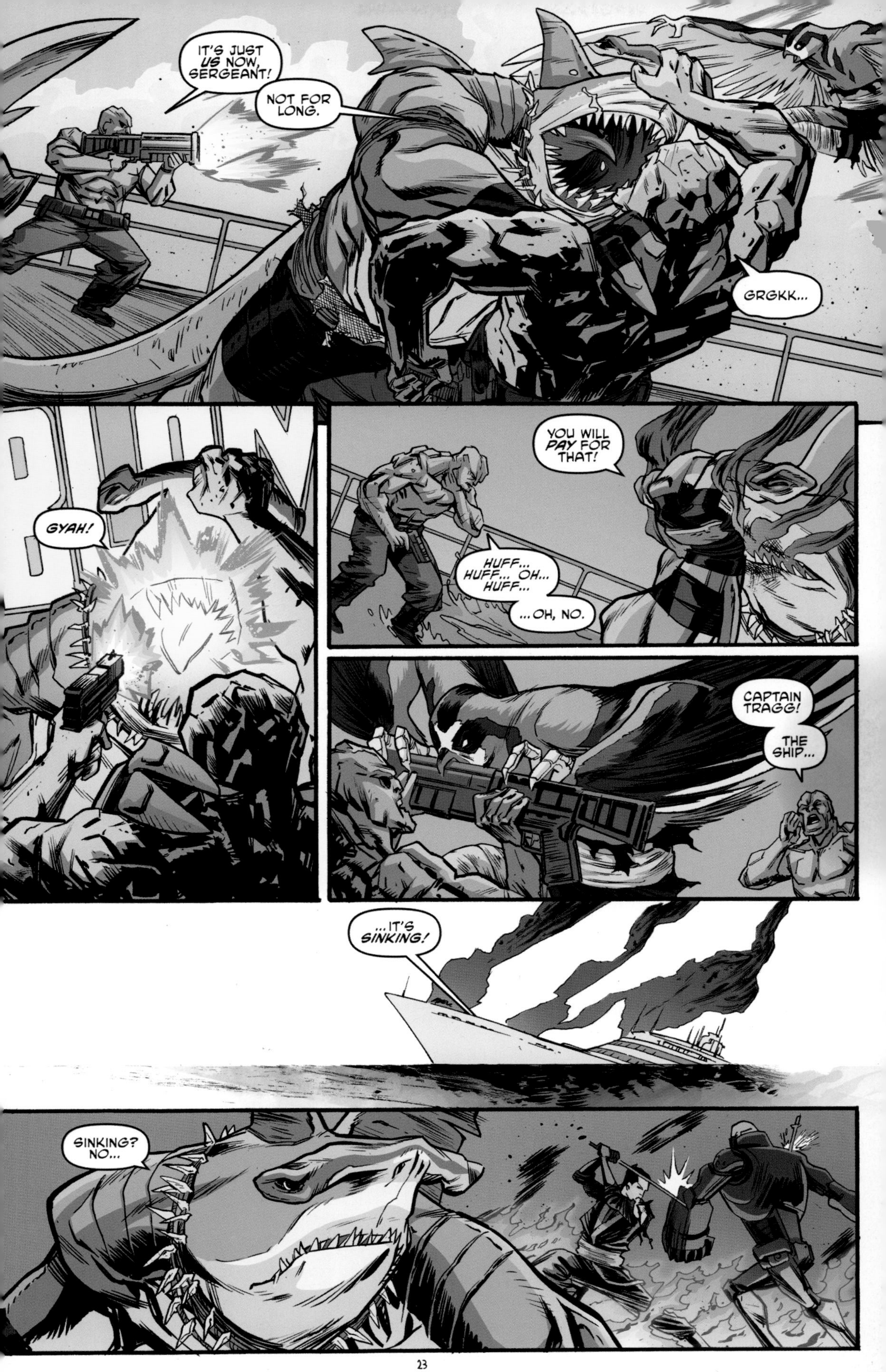
IT'S JUST US NOW, SERGEANT!
NOT FOR LONG.
GRGKK...
GYAH!
YOU WILL PAY FOR THAT!
HUFF... HUFF... OH... HUFF...
...OH, NO.
CAPTAIN TRAGG!
THE SHIP...
...IT'S SINKING!
SINKING? NO...

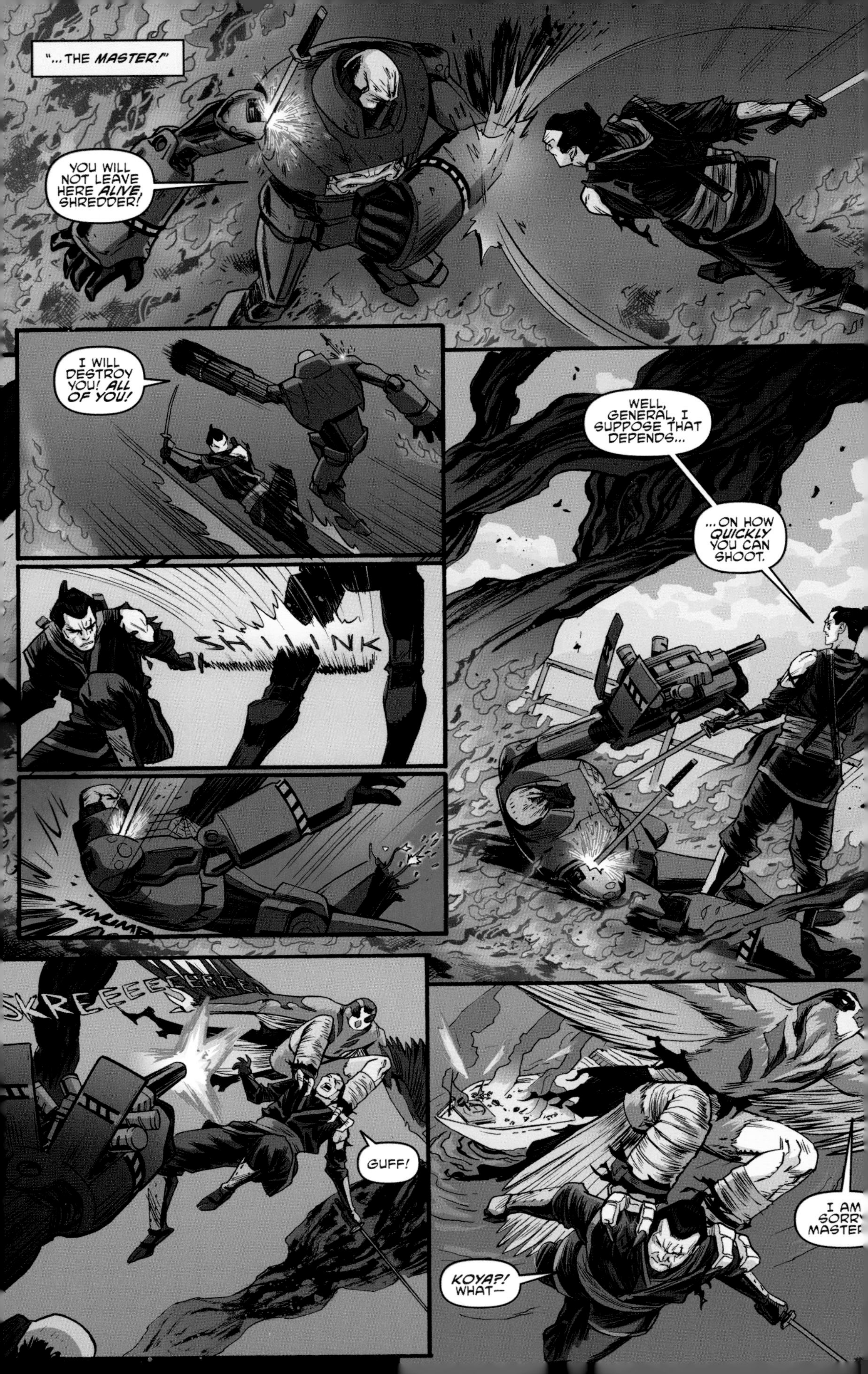
"...THE MASTER!"
YOU WILL NOT LEAVE HERE ALIVE, SHREDDER!
I WILL DESTROY YOU! ALL OF YOU!
WELL, GENERAL, I SUPPOSE THAT DEPENDS...
...ON HOW QUICKLY YOU CAN SHOOT.
SHIIINK
THUMP
SKREEEEEEEEE
GUFF!
I AM SORRY MASTER
KOYA?! WHAT—

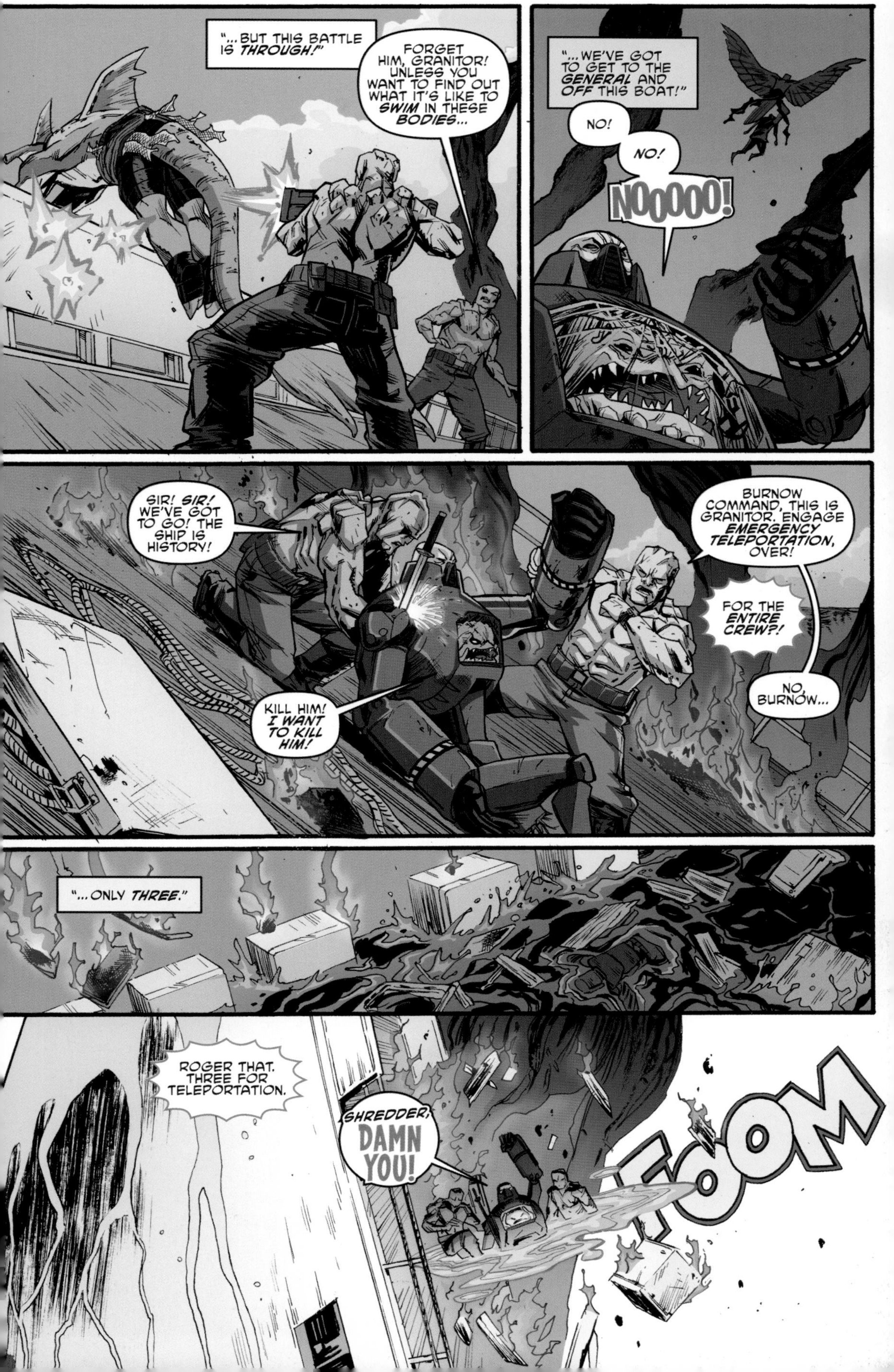
"...BUT THIS BATTLE IS THROUGH!"
FORGET HIM, GRANITOR! UNLESS YOU WANT TO FIND OUT WHAT IT'S LIKE TO SWIM IN THESE BODIES...
"...WE'VE GOT TO GET TO THE GENERAL AND OFF THIS BOAT!"
NO!
NO!
NOOOOO!
SIR! SIR! WE'VE GOT TO GO! THE SHIP IS HISTORY!
KILL HIM! I WANT TO KILL HIM!
BURNOW COMMAND, THIS IS GRANITOR. ENGAGE EMERGENCY TELEPORTATION, OVER!
FOR THE ENTIRE CREW?!
NO, BURNOW...
"...ONLY THREE."
ROGER THAT. THREE FOR TELEPORTATION.
SHREDDER, DAMN YOU!
FOOM

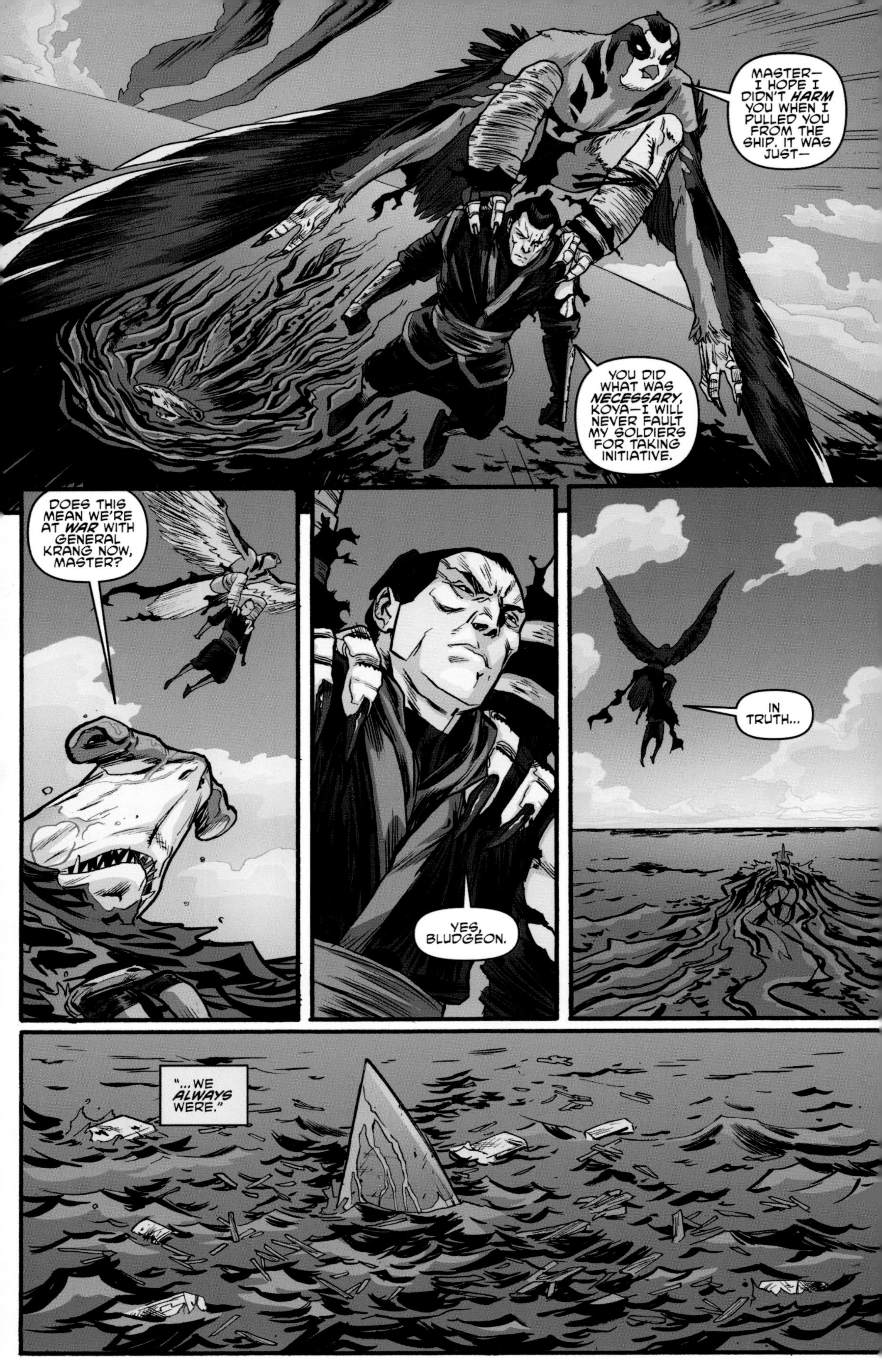
MASTER— I HOPE I DIDN'T HARM YOU WHEN I PULLED YOU FROM THE SHIP. IT WAS JUST—
YOU DID WHAT WAS NECESSARY, KOYA—I WILL NEVER FAULT MY SOLDIERS FOR TAKING INITIATIVE.
DOES THIS MEAN WE'RE AT WAR WITH GENERAL KRANG NOW, MASTER?
YES, BLUDGEON.
IN TRUTH...
"...WE ALWAYS WERE."

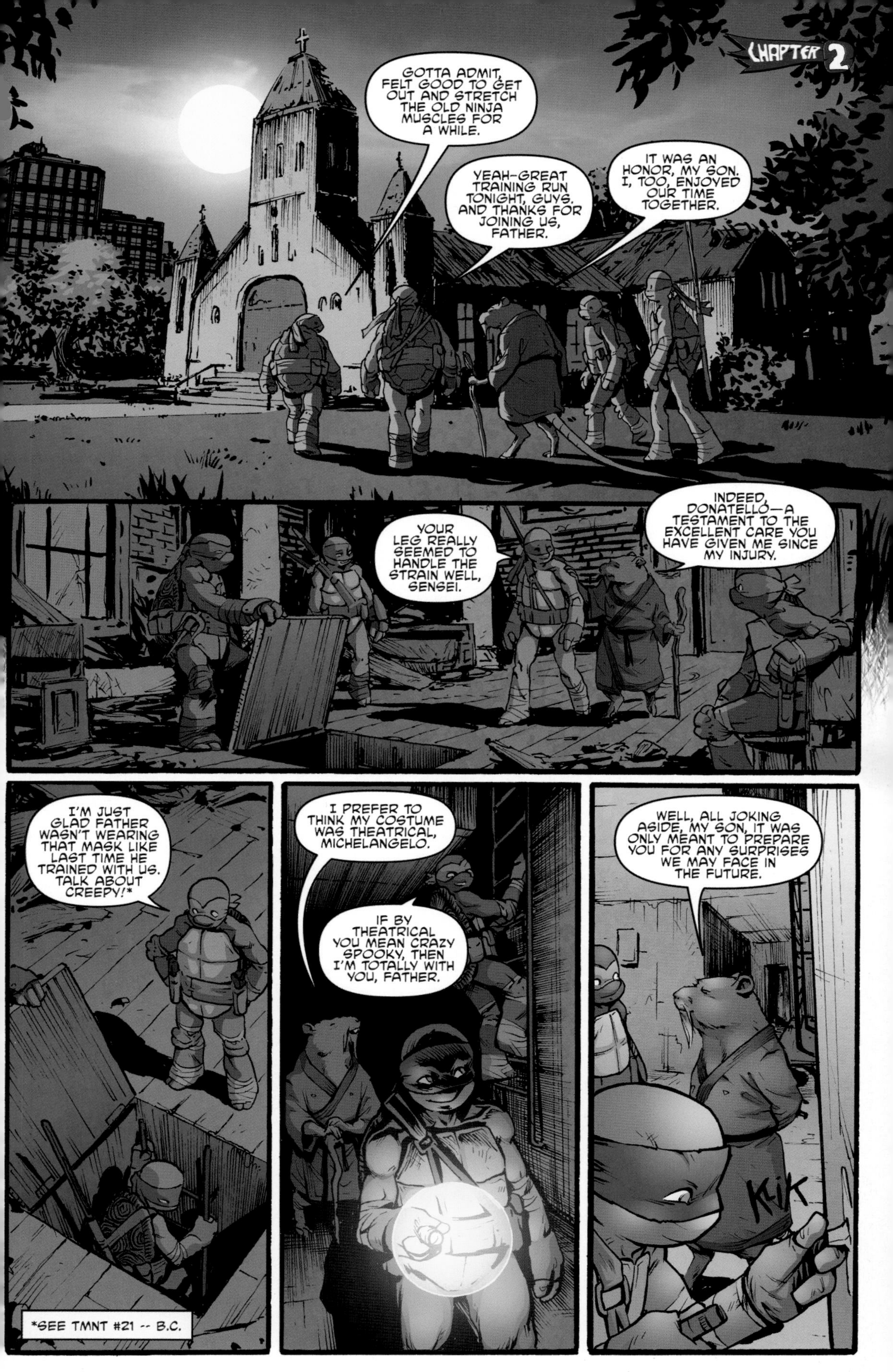
CHAPTER 2
GOTTA ADMIT, FELT GOOD TO GET OUT AND STRETCH THE OLD NINJA MUSCLES FOR A WHILE.
YEAH--GREAT TRAINING RUN TONIGHT, GUYS. AND THANKS FOR JOINING US, FATHER.
IT WAS AN HONOR, MY SON. I, TOO, ENJOYED OUR TIME TOGETHER.
YOUR LEG REALLY SEEMED TO HANDLE THE STRAIN WELL, SENSEI.
INDEED, DONATELLO--A TESTAMENT TO THE EXCELLENT CARE YOU HAVE GIVEN ME SINCE MY INJURY.
I'M JUST GLAD FATHER WASN'T WEARING THAT MASK LIKE LAST TIME HE TRAINED WITH US. TALK ABOUT CREEPY!*
*SEE TMNT #21 -- B.C.
I PREFER TO THINK MY COSTUME WAS THEATRICAL, MICHELANGELO.
IF BY THEATRICAL YOU MEAN CRAZY SPOOKY, THEN I'M TOTALLY WITH YOU, FATHER.
WELL, ALL JOKING ASIDE, MY SON, IT WAS ONLY MEANT TO PREPARE YOU FOR ANY SURPRISES WE MAY FACE IN THE FUTURE.
KLIK

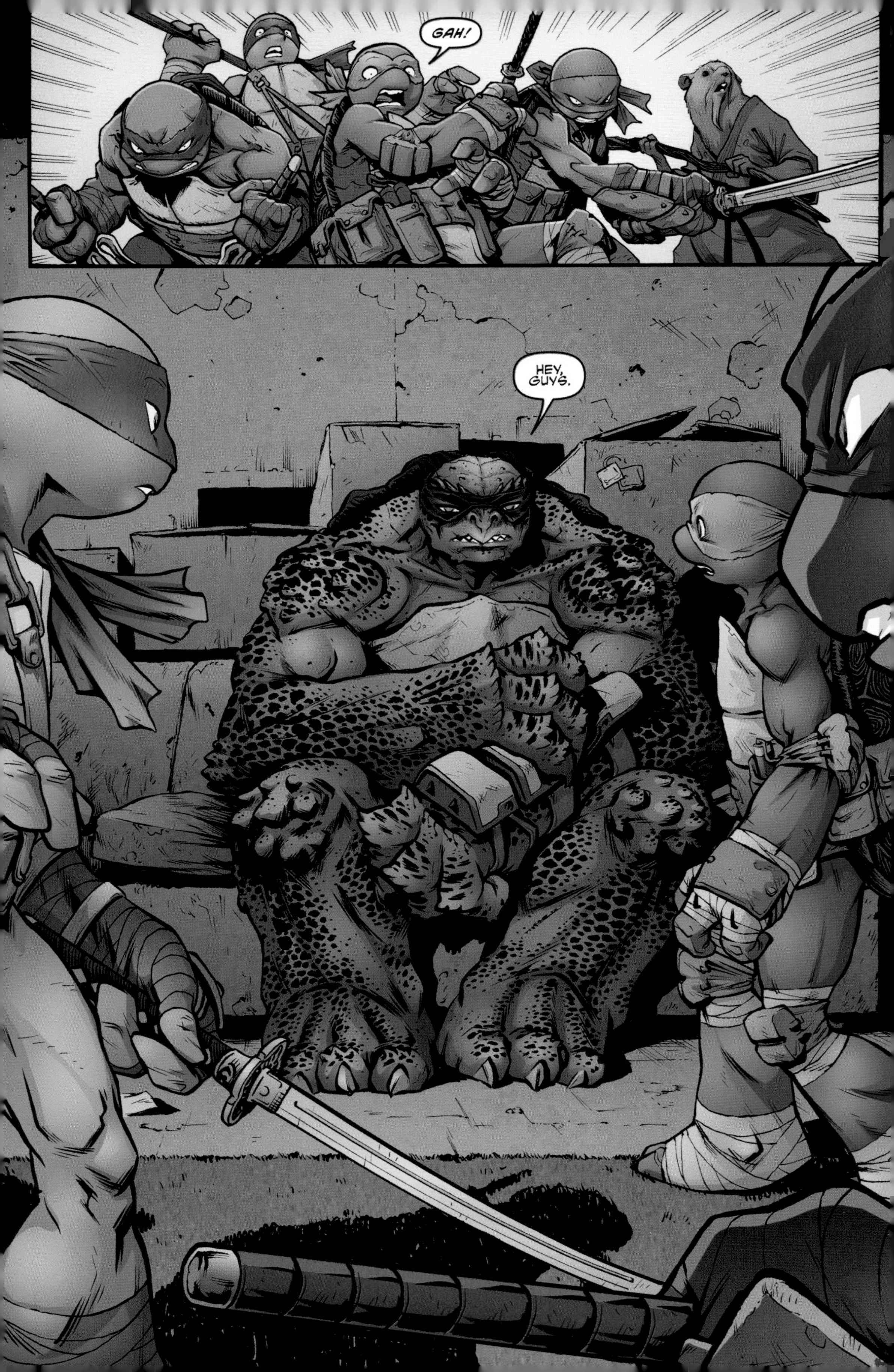
GAH!
HEY, GUYS.

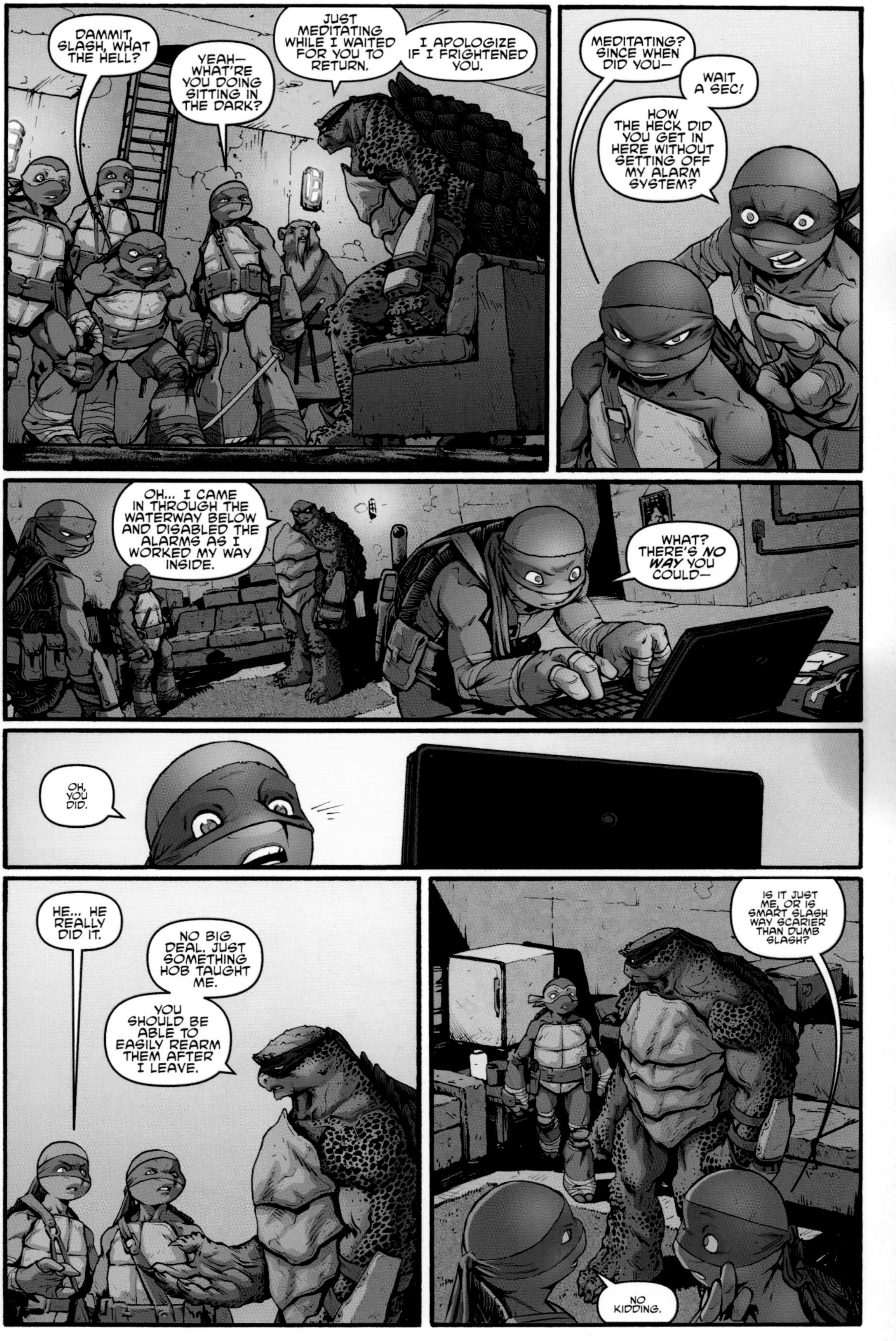
DAMMIT, SLASH, WHAT THE HELL?
YEAH— WHAT'RE YOU DOING SITTING IN THE DARK?
JUST MEDITATING WHILE I WAITED FOR YOU TO RETURN.
I APOLOGIZE IF I FRIGHTENED YOU.
MEDITATING? SINCE WHEN DID YOU—
WAIT A SEC!
HOW THE HECK DID YOU GET IN HERE WITHOUT SETTING OFF MY ALARM SYSTEM?
OH... I CAME IN THROUGH THE WATERWAY BELOW AND DISABLED THE ALARMS AS I WORKED MY WAY INSIDE.
WHAT? THERE'S NO WAY YOU COULD—
OH, YOU DID.
HE... HE REALLY DID IT.
NO BIG DEAL. JUST SOMETHING HOB TAUGHT ME.
YOU SHOULD BE ABLE TO EASILY REARM THEM AFTER I LEAVE.
IS IT JUST ME, OR IS SMART SLASH WAY SCARIER THAN DUMB SLASH?
NO KIDDING.

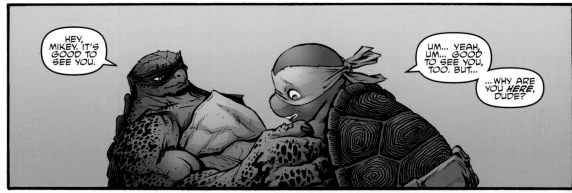

HEY, MIKEY, IT'S GOOD TO SEE YOU.

UM... YEAH, UM... GOOD TO SEE YOU, TOO. BUT...

...WHY ARE YOU *HERE*, DUDE?

HOB SENT ME TO INVITE YOU TO OUR HOME, SPLINTER.

THERE'S SOMETHING IMPORTANT HE WANTS YOU TO SEE.

IT'S *MASTER* SPLINTER, MAN...

...AND LET ME GUESS—THAT FLEA-BITER'S DYIN' TO SHOW OFF SOME *NEW MUTANTS* HE AND THAT FREAKY LINDSEY'S MADE, HUH?

I'M NOT SUPPOSED TO SAY. HOB JUST SAID TO TELL MASTER SPLINTER IT'S TIME TO MAKE GOOD ON HIS PROMISE.

PROMISE? *WHAT* PROMISE, FATHER?

WE WILL SPEAK OF THIS LATER, DONATELLO.

BUT—

LATER, MY SON.

THANKS FOR DELIVERING THE MESSAGE, SLASH. PLEASE LET HOB KNOW WE'LL BE THERE SOON.

WE'VE GOT SOME THINGS TO DISCUSS AS A *FAMILY* FIRST.

OKAY, LEO.

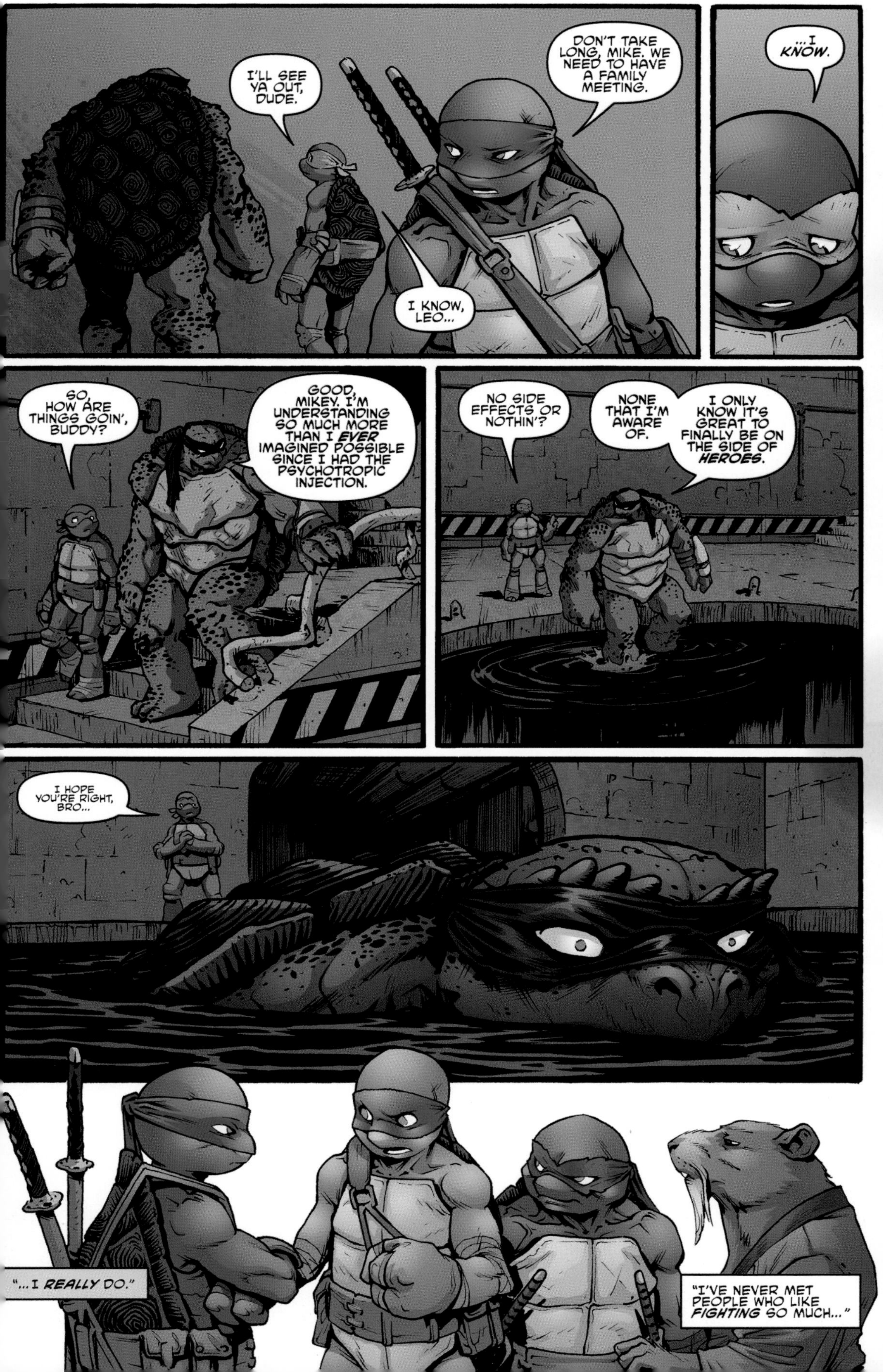
I'LL SEE YA OUT, DUDE.
DON'T TAKE LONG, MIKE. WE NEED TO HAVE A FAMILY MEETING.
I KNOW, LEO...
...I KNOW.
SO, HOW ARE THINGS GOIN', BUDDY?
GOOD, MIKEY. I'M UNDERSTANDING SO MUCH MORE THAN I EVER IMAGINED POSSIBLE SINCE I HAD THE PSYCHOTROPIC INJECTION.
NO SIDE EFFECTS OR NOTHIN'?
NONE THAT I'M AWARE OF.
I ONLY KNOW IT'S GREAT TO FINALLY BE ON THE SIDE OF HEROES.
I HOPE YOU'RE RIGHT, BRO...
"...I REALLY DO."
"I'VE NEVER MET PEOPLE WHO LIKE FIGHTING SO MUCH..."

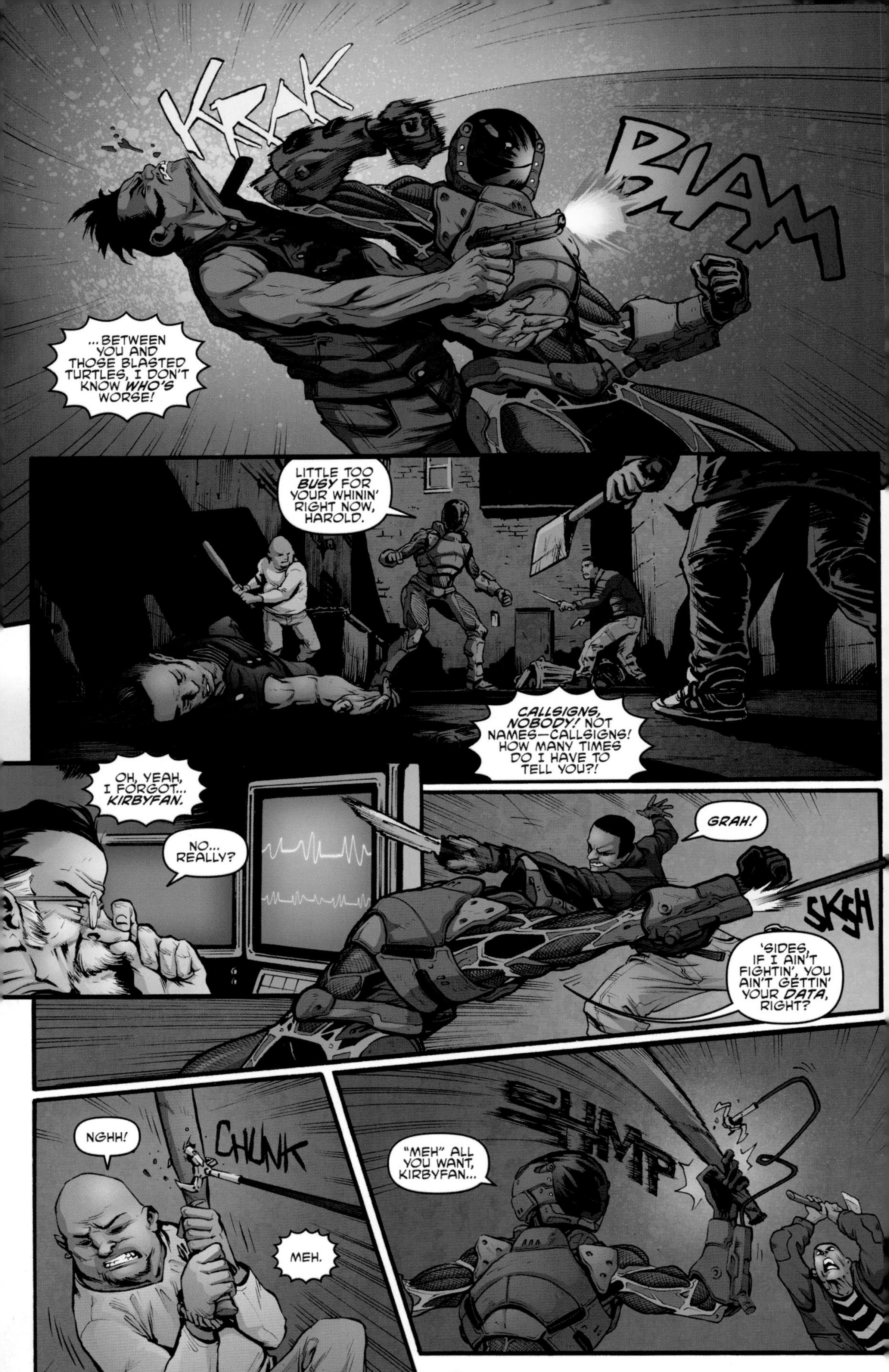
KRAK
BLAM
...BETWEEN YOU AND THOSE BLASTED TURTLES, I DON'T KNOW WHO'S WORSE!
LITTLE TOO BUSY FOR YOUR WHININ' RIGHT NOW, HAROLD.
CALLSIGNS, NOBODY! NOT NAMES—CALLSIGNS! HOW MANY TIMES DO I HAVE TO TELL YOU?!
OH, YEAH, I FORGOT... KIRBYFAN.
NO... REALLY?
GRAH!
SKSH
'SIDES, IF I AIN'T FIGHTIN', YOU AIN'T GETTIN' YOUR DATA, RIGHT?
NGHH!
CHUNK
MEH.
"MEH" ALL YOU WANT, KIRBYFAN...
SHMP

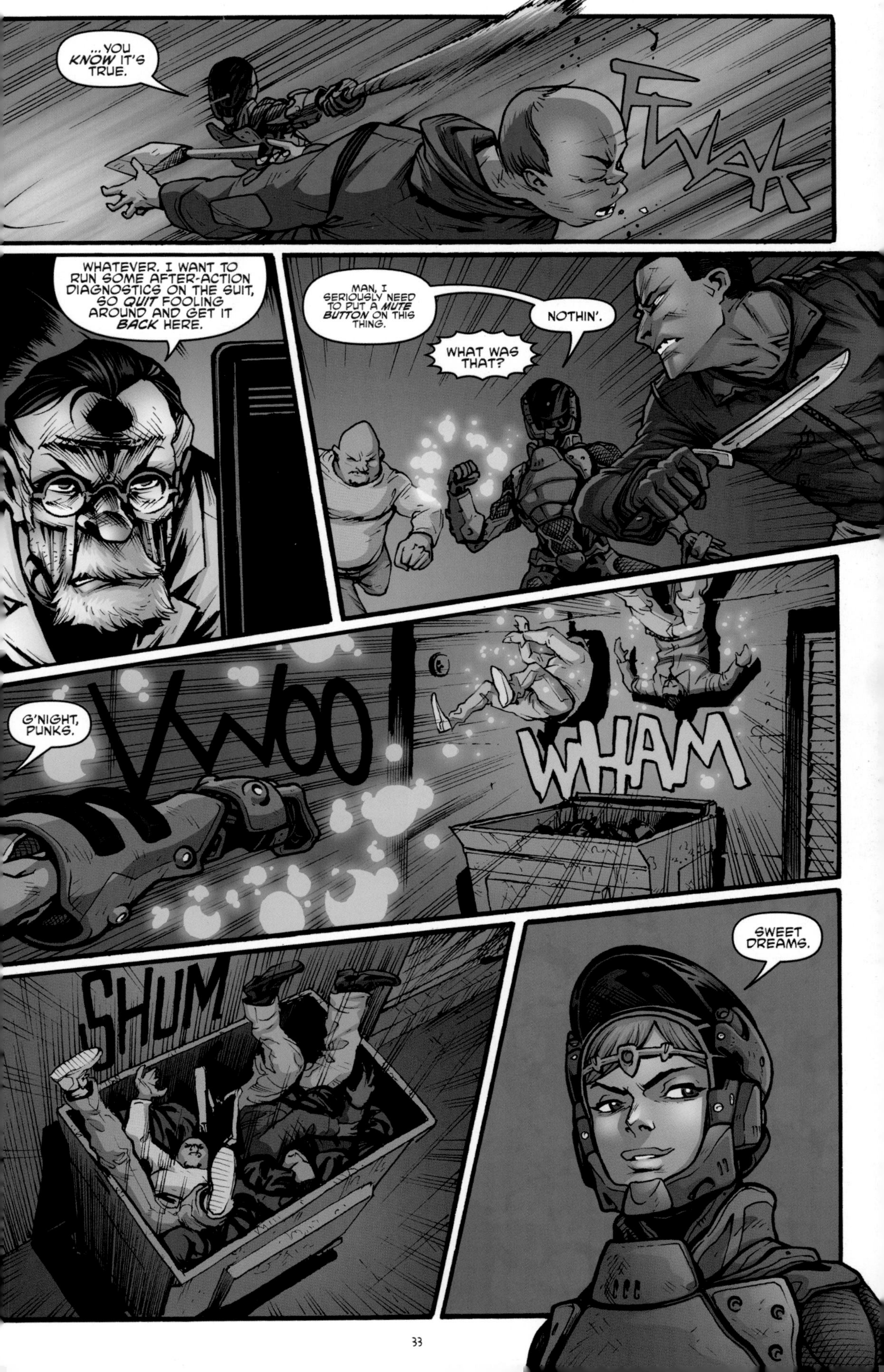
...YOU KNOW IT'S TRUE.
FWAK
WHATEVER. I WANT TO RUN SOME AFTER-ACTION DIAGNOSTICS ON THE SUIT, SO QUIT FOOLING AROUND AND GET IT BACK HERE.
MAN, I SERIOUSLY NEED TO PUT A MUTE BUTTON ON THIS THING.
WHAT WAS THAT?
NOTHIN'.
G'NIGHT, PUNKS.
VWOO!
WHAM
SHUM
SWEET DREAMS.

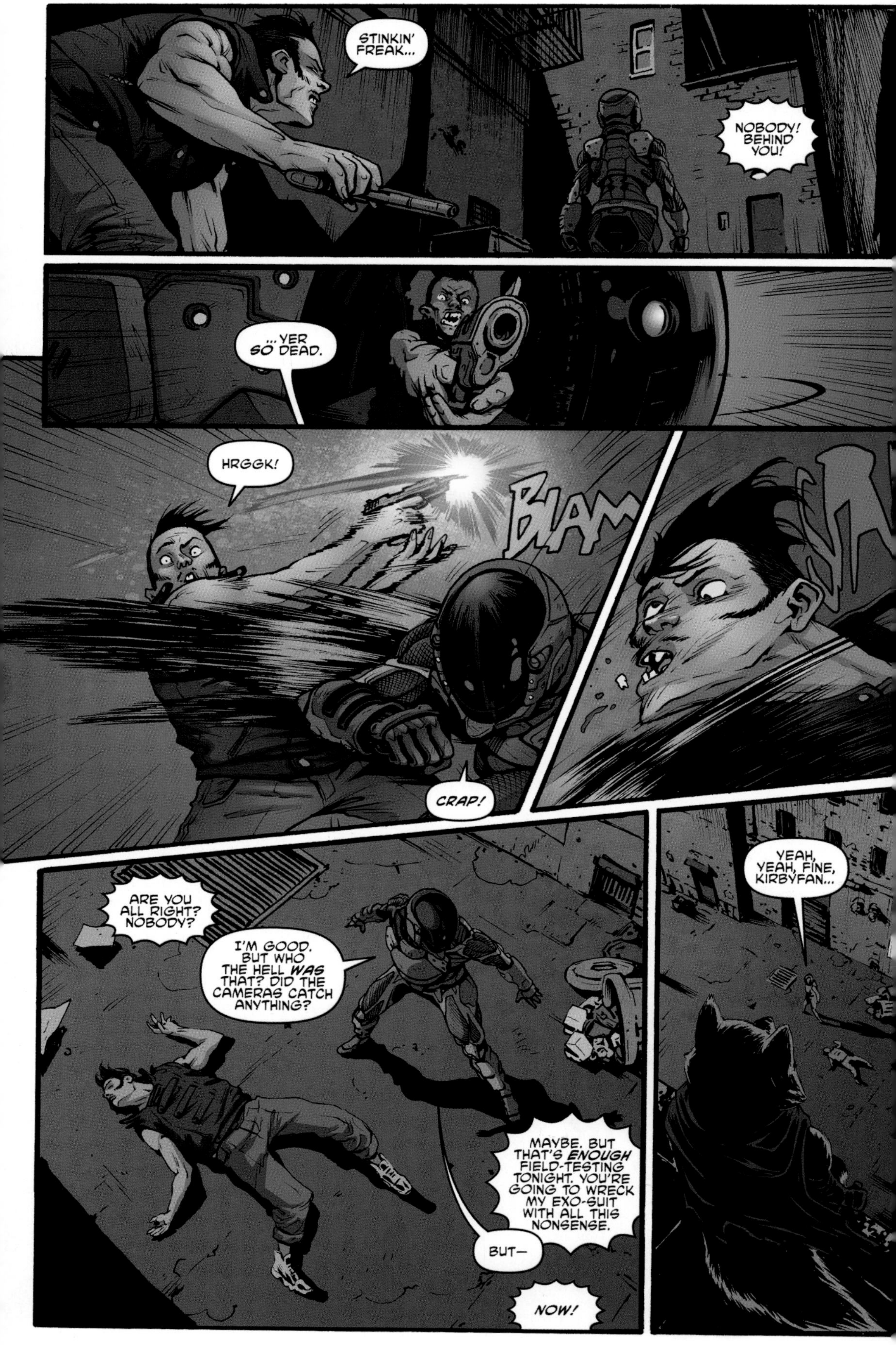
STINKIN' FREAK...
NOBODY! BEHIND YOU!
...YER SO DEAD.
HRGGK!
BLAM
CRAP!
ARE YOU ALL RIGHT? NOBODY?
I'M GOOD. BUT WHO THE HELL WAS THAT? DID THE CAMERAS CATCH ANYTHING?
MAYBE. BUT THAT'S ENOUGH FIELD-TESTING TONIGHT. YOU'RE GOING TO WRECK MY EXO-SUIT WITH ALL THIS NONSENSE.
BUT—
NOW!
YEAH, YEAH, FINE, KIRBYFAN...

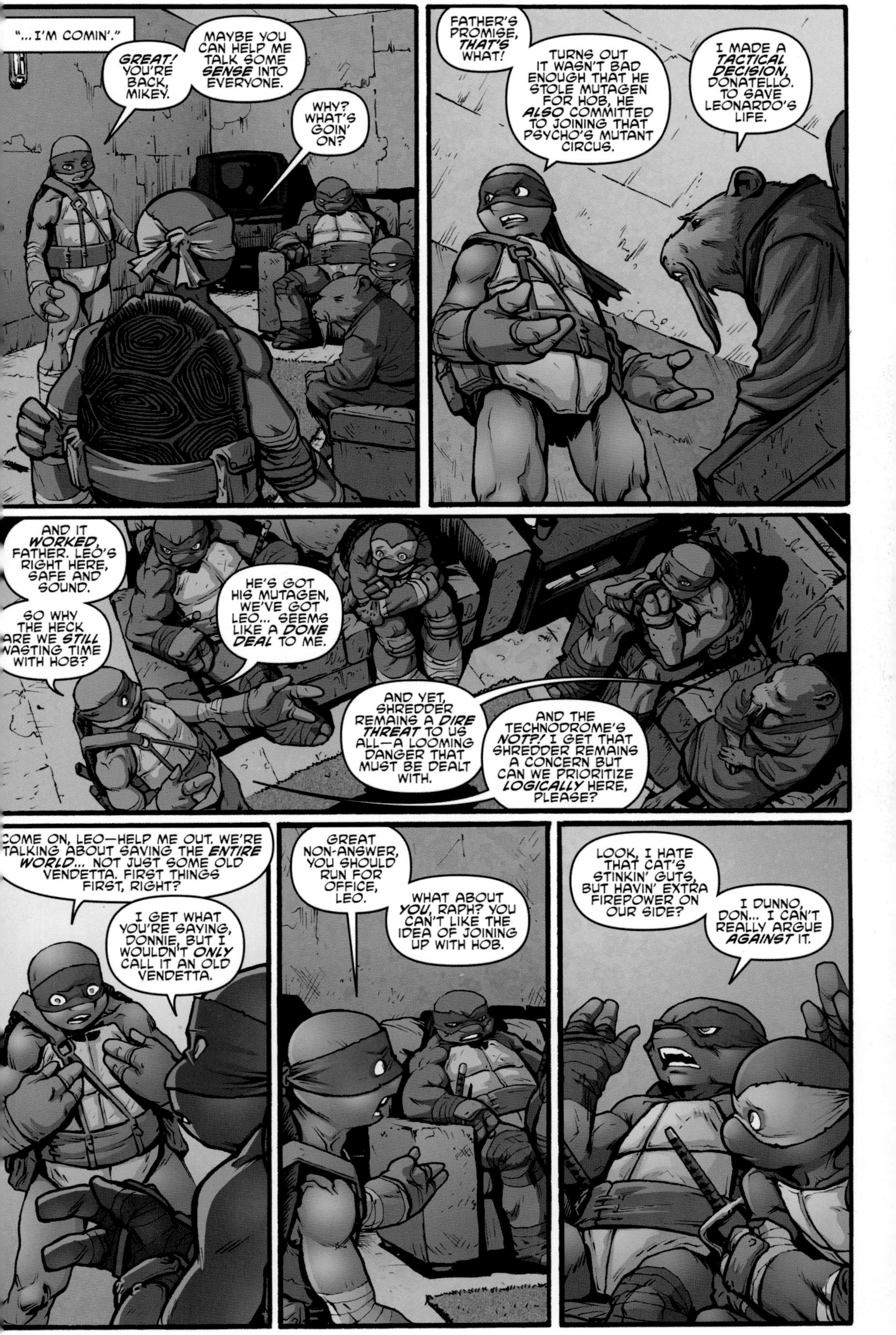
"... I'M COMIN'."
GREAT! YOU'RE BACK, MIKEY.
MAYBE YOU CAN HELP ME TALK SOME SENSE INTO EVERYONE.
WHY? WHAT'S GOIN' ON?
FATHER'S PROMISE, THAT'S WHAT!
TURNS OUT IT WASN'T BAD ENOUGH THAT HE STOLE MUTAGEN FOR HOB, HE ALSO COMMITTED TO JOINING THAT PSYCHO'S MUTANT CIRCUS.
I MADE A TACTICAL DECISION, DONATELLO. TO SAVE LEONARDO'S LIFE.
AND IT WORKED, FATHER. LEO'S RIGHT HERE, SAFE AND SOUND.
SO WHY THE HECK ARE WE STILL WASTING TIME WITH HOB?
HE'S GOT HIS MUTAGEN, WE'VE GOT LEO... SEEMS LIKE A DONE DEAL TO ME.
AND YET, SHREDDER REMAINS A DIRE THREAT TO US ALL—A LOOMING DANGER THAT MUST BE DEALT WITH.
AND THE TECHNODROME'S NOT?! I GET THAT SHREDDER REMAINS A CONCERN BUT CAN WE PRIORITIZE LOGICALLY HERE, PLEASE?
COME ON, LEO—HELP ME OUT. WE'RE TALKING ABOUT SAVING THE ENTIRE WORLD... NOT JUST SOME OLD VENDETTA. FIRST THINGS FIRST, RIGHT?
I GET WHAT YOU'RE SAYING, DONNIE, BUT I WOULDN'T ONLY CALL IT AN OLD VENDETTA.
GREAT NON-ANSWER, YOU SHOULD RUN FOR OFFICE, LEO.
WHAT ABOUT YOU, RAPH? YOU CAN'T LIKE THE IDEA OF JOINING UP WITH HOB.
LOOK, I HATE THAT CAT'S STINKIN' GUTS, BUT HAVIN' EXTRA FIREPOWER ON OUR SIDE?
I DUNNO, DON... I CAN'T REALLY ARGUE AGAINST IT.

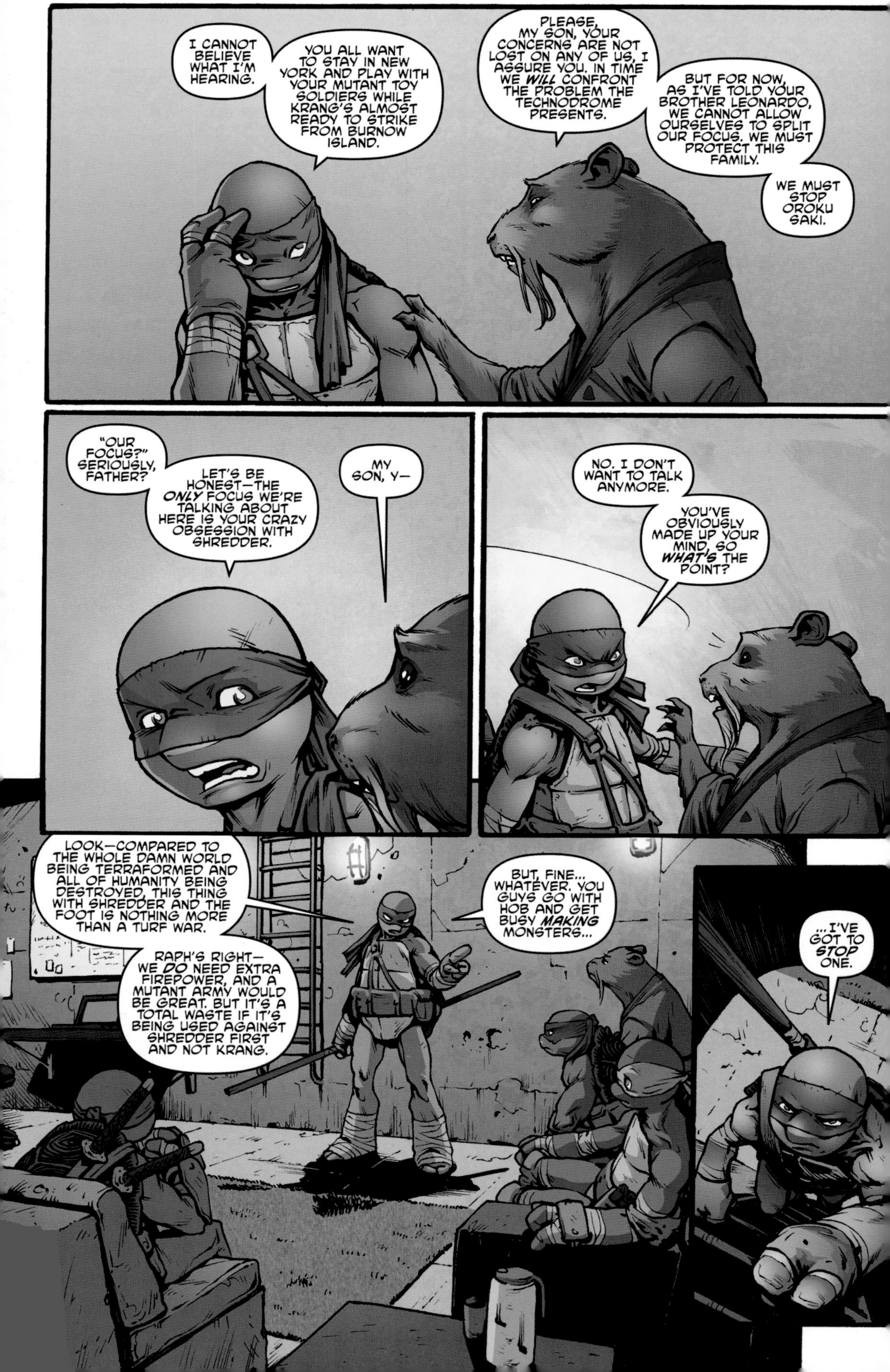

I CANNOT BELIEVE WHAT I'M HEARING.
YOU ALL WANT TO STAY IN NEW YORK AND PLAY WITH YOUR MUTANT TOY SOLDIERS WHILE KRANG'S ALMOST READY TO STRIKE FROM BURNOW ISLAND.
PLEASE, MY SON, YOUR CONCERNS ARE NOT LOST ON ANY OF US, I ASSURE YOU. IN TIME WE *WILL* CONFRONT THE PROBLEM THE TECHNODROME PRESENTS.
BUT FOR NOW, AS I'VE TOLD YOUR BROTHER LEONARDO, WE CANNOT ALLOW OURSELVES TO SPLIT OUR FOCUS. WE MUST PROTECT THIS FAMILY.
WE MUST STOP OROKU SAKI.
"OUR FOCUS?" SERIOUSLY, FATHER?
LET'S BE HONEST—THE *ONLY* FOCUS WE'RE TALKING ABOUT HERE IS YOUR CRAZY OBSESSION WITH SHREDDER.
MY SON, Y—
NO. I DON'T WANT TO TALK ANYMORE.
YOU'VE OBVIOUSLY MADE UP YOUR MIND, SO *WHAT'S* THE POINT?
LOOK—COMPARED TO THE WHOLE DAMN WORLD BEING TERRAFORMED AND ALL OF HUMANITY BEING DESTROYED, THIS THING WITH SHREDDER AND THE FOOT IS NOTHING MORE THAN A TURF WAR.
RAPH'S RIGHT— WE *DO* NEED EXTRA FIREPOWER, AND A MUTANT ARMY WOULD BE GREAT. BUT IT'S A TOTAL WASTE IF IT'S BEING USED AGAINST SHREDDER FIRST AND NOT KRANG.
BUT, FINE... WHATEVER. YOU GUYS GO WITH HOB AND GET BUSY *MAKING* MONSTERS...
...I'VE GOT TO *STOP* ONE.

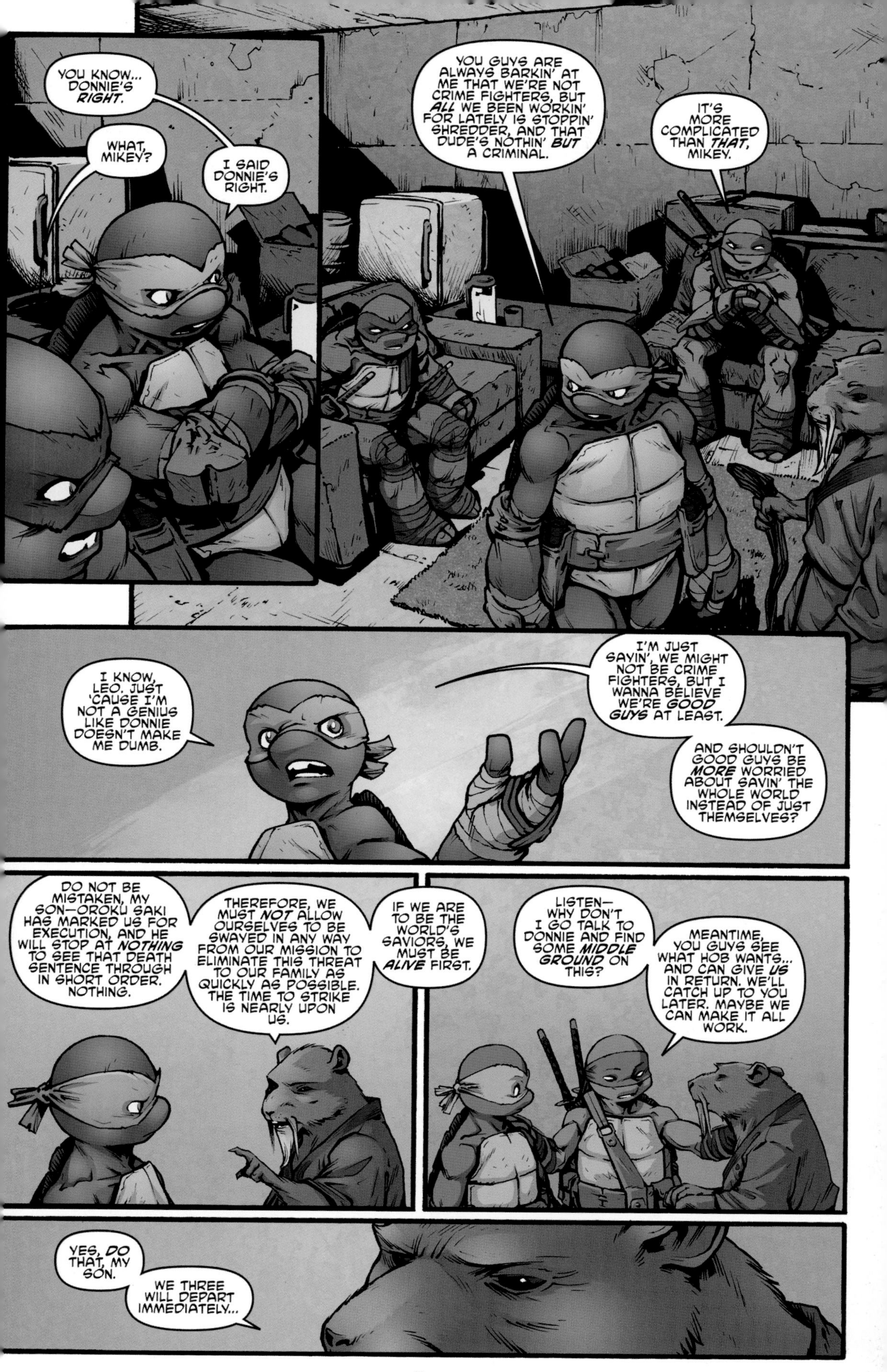

YOU KNOW... DONNIE'S *RIGHT*.
WHAT, MIKEY?
I SAID DONNIE'S RIGHT.
YOU GUYS ARE ALWAYS BARKIN' AT ME THAT WE'RE NOT CRIME FIGHTERS, BUT *ALL* WE BEEN WORKIN' FOR LATELY IS STOPPIN' SHREDDER, AND THAT DUDE'S NOTHIN' *BUT* A CRIMINAL.
IT'S MORE COMPLICATED THAN *THAT*, MIKEY.
I KNOW, LEO. JUST 'CAUSE I'M NOT A GENIUS LIKE DONNIE DOESN'T MAKE ME DUMB.
I'M JUST SAYIN', WE MIGHT NOT BE CRIME FIGHTERS, BUT I WANNA BELIEVE WE'RE *GOOD GUYS* AT LEAST.
AND SHOULDN'T GOOD GUYS BE *MORE* WORRIED ABOUT SAVIN' THE WHOLE WORLD INSTEAD OF JUST THEMSELVES?
DO NOT BE MISTAKEN, MY SON—OROKU SAKI HAS MARKED US FOR EXECUTION, AND HE WILL STOP AT *NOTHING* TO SEE THAT DEATH SENTENCE THROUGH IN SHORT ORDER. NOTHING.
THEREFORE, WE MUST *NOT* ALLOW OURSELVES TO BE SWAYED IN ANY WAY FROM OUR MISSION TO ELIMINATE THIS THREAT TO OUR FAMILY AS QUICKLY AS POSSIBLE. THE TIME TO STRIKE IS NEARLY UPON US.
IF WE ARE TO BE THE WORLD'S SAVIORS, WE MUST BE *ALIVE* FIRST.
LISTEN— WHY DON'T I GO TALK TO DONNIE AND FIND SOME *MIDDLE GROUND* ON THIS?
MEANTIME, YOU GUYS SEE WHAT HOB WANTS... AND CAN GIVE *US* IN RETURN. WE'LL CATCH UP TO YOU LATER. MAYBE WE CAN MAKE IT ALL WORK.
YES, *DO* THAT, MY SON.
WE THREE WILL DEPART IMMEDIATELY...

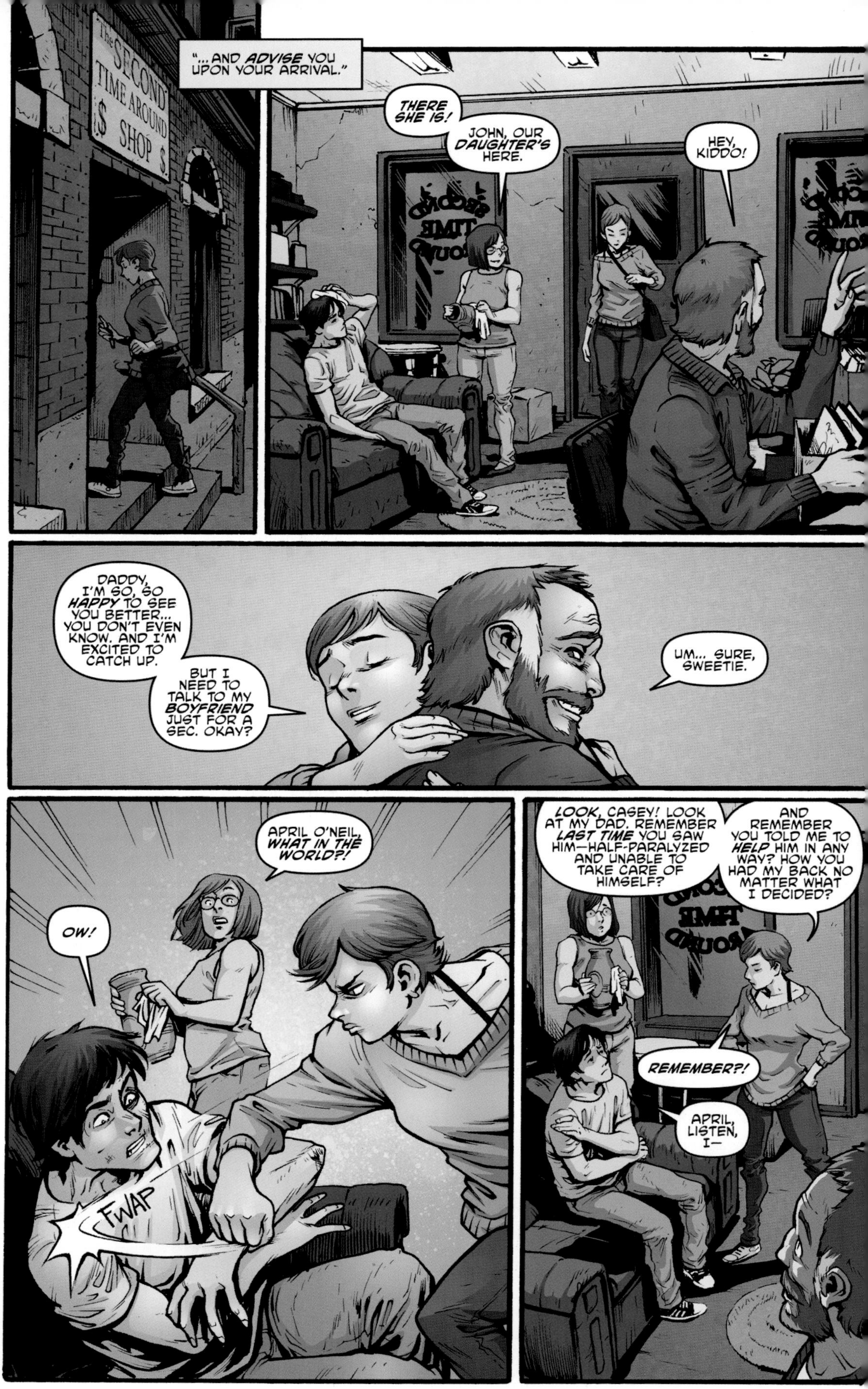
"...AND *ADVISE* YOU UPON YOUR ARRIVAL."
The SECOND TIME AROUND $ SHOP $.
THERE SHE IS!
JOHN, OUR *DAUGHTER'S* HERE.
HEY, KIDDO!
DADDY, I'M SO, SO *HAPPY* TO SEE YOU BETTER... YOU DON'T EVEN KNOW. AND I'M EXCITED TO CATCH UP.
BUT I NEED TO TALK TO MY *BOYFRIEND* JUST FOR A SEC. OKAY?
UM... SURE, SWEETIE.
APRIL O'NEIL, *WHAT IN THE WORLD?!*
OW!
FWAP
LOOK, CASEY! LOOK AT MY DAD. REMEMBER *LAST TIME* YOU SAW HIM—HALF-PARALYZED AND UNABLE TO TAKE CARE OF HIMSELF?
AND REMEMBER YOU TOLD ME TO *HELP* HIM IN ANY WAY? HOW YOU HAD MY BACK NO MATTER WHAT I DECIDED?
REMEMBER?!
APRIL, LISTEN, I—

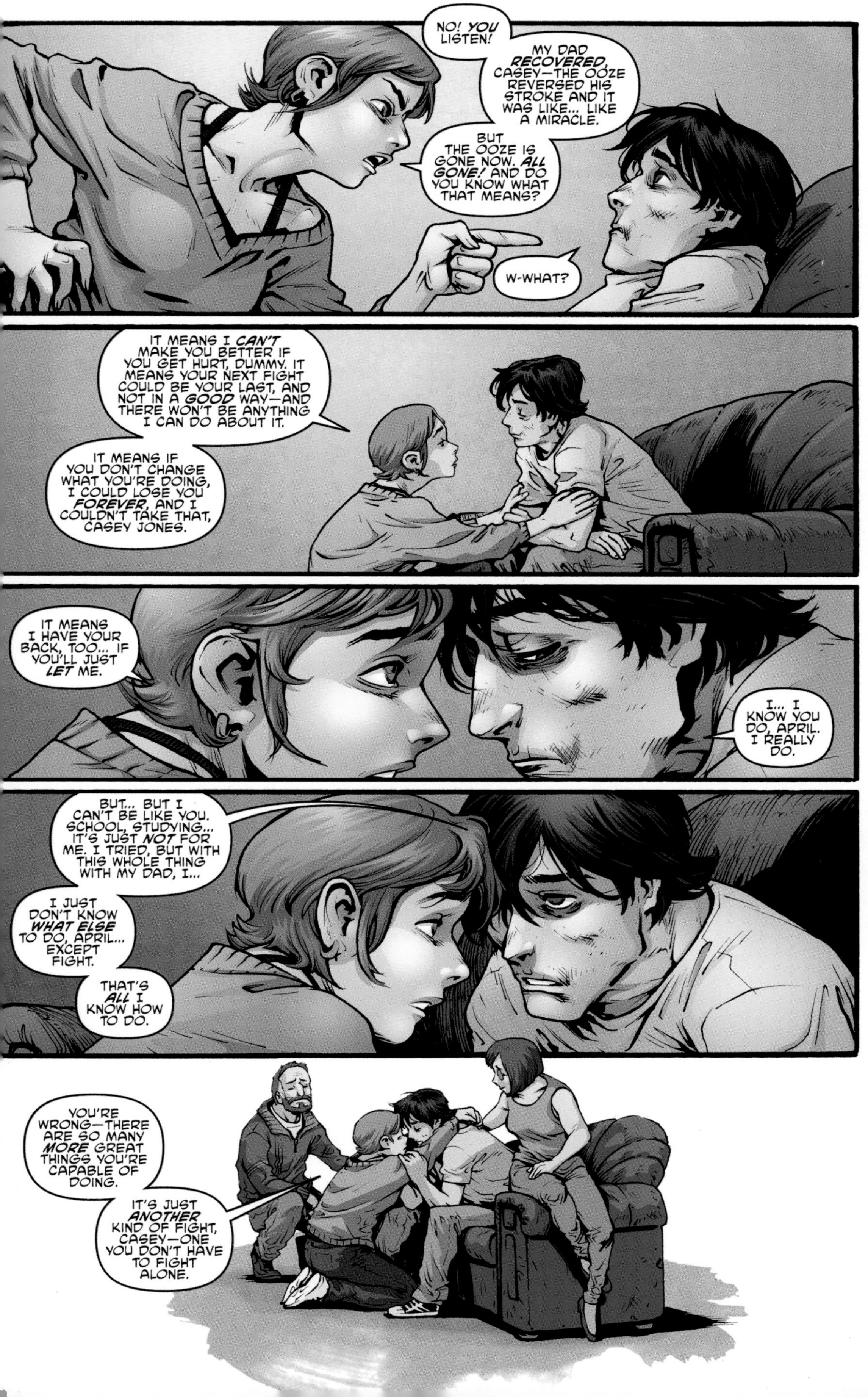
NO! YOU LISTEN!
MY DAD RECOVERED, CASEY—THE OOZE REVERSED HIS STROKE AND IT WAS LIKE... LIKE A MIRACLE.
BUT THE OOZE IS GONE NOW. ALL GONE! AND DO YOU KNOW WHAT THAT MEANS?
W-WHAT?
IT MEANS I CAN'T MAKE YOU BETTER IF YOU GET HURT, DUMMY. IT MEANS YOUR NEXT FIGHT COULD BE YOUR LAST, AND NOT IN A GOOD WAY—AND THERE WON'T BE ANYTHING I CAN DO ABOUT IT.
IT MEANS IF YOU DON'T CHANGE WHAT YOU'RE DOING, I COULD LOSE YOU FOREVER, AND I COULDN'T TAKE THAT, CASEY JONES.
IT MEANS I HAVE YOUR BACK, TOO... IF YOU'LL JUST LET ME.
I... I KNOW YOU DO, APRIL. I REALLY DO.
BUT... BUT I CAN'T BE LIKE YOU. SCHOOL, STUDYING... IT'S JUST NOT FOR ME. I TRIED, BUT WITH THIS WHOLE THING WITH MY DAD, I...
I JUST DON'T KNOW WHAT ELSE TO DO, APRIL... EXCEPT FIGHT.
THAT'S ALL I KNOW HOW TO DO.
YOU'RE WRONG—THERE ARE SO MANY MORE GREAT THINGS YOU'RE CAPABLE OF DOING.
IT'S JUST ANOTHER KIND OF FIGHT, CASEY—ONE YOU DON'T HAVE TO FIGHT ALONE.

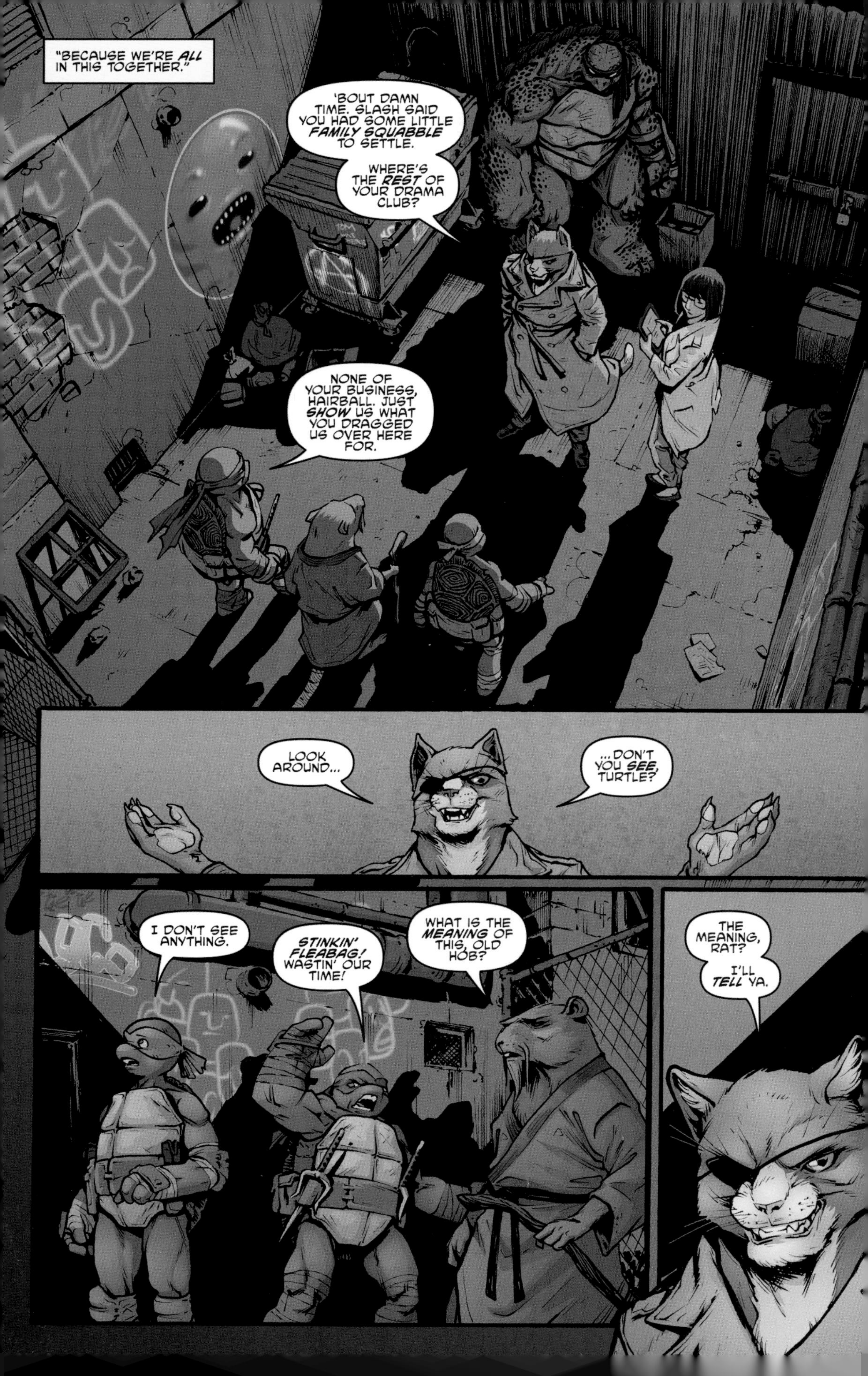
"BECAUSE WE'RE *ALL* IN THIS TOGETHER."
'BOUT DAMN TIME. SLASH SAID YOU HAD SOME LITTLE *FAMILY SQUABBLE* TO SETTLE.
WHERE'S THE *REST* OF YOUR DRAMA CLUB?
NONE OF YOUR BUSINESS, HAIRBALL. JUST *SHOW* US WHAT YOU DRAGGED US OVER HERE FOR.
LOOK AROUND...
...DON'T YOU *SEE*, TURTLE?
I DON'T SEE ANYTHING.
STINKIN' FLEABAG! WASTIN' OUR TIME!
WHAT IS THE *MEANING* OF THIS, OLD HOB?
THE MEANING, RAT?
I'LL *TELL* YA.

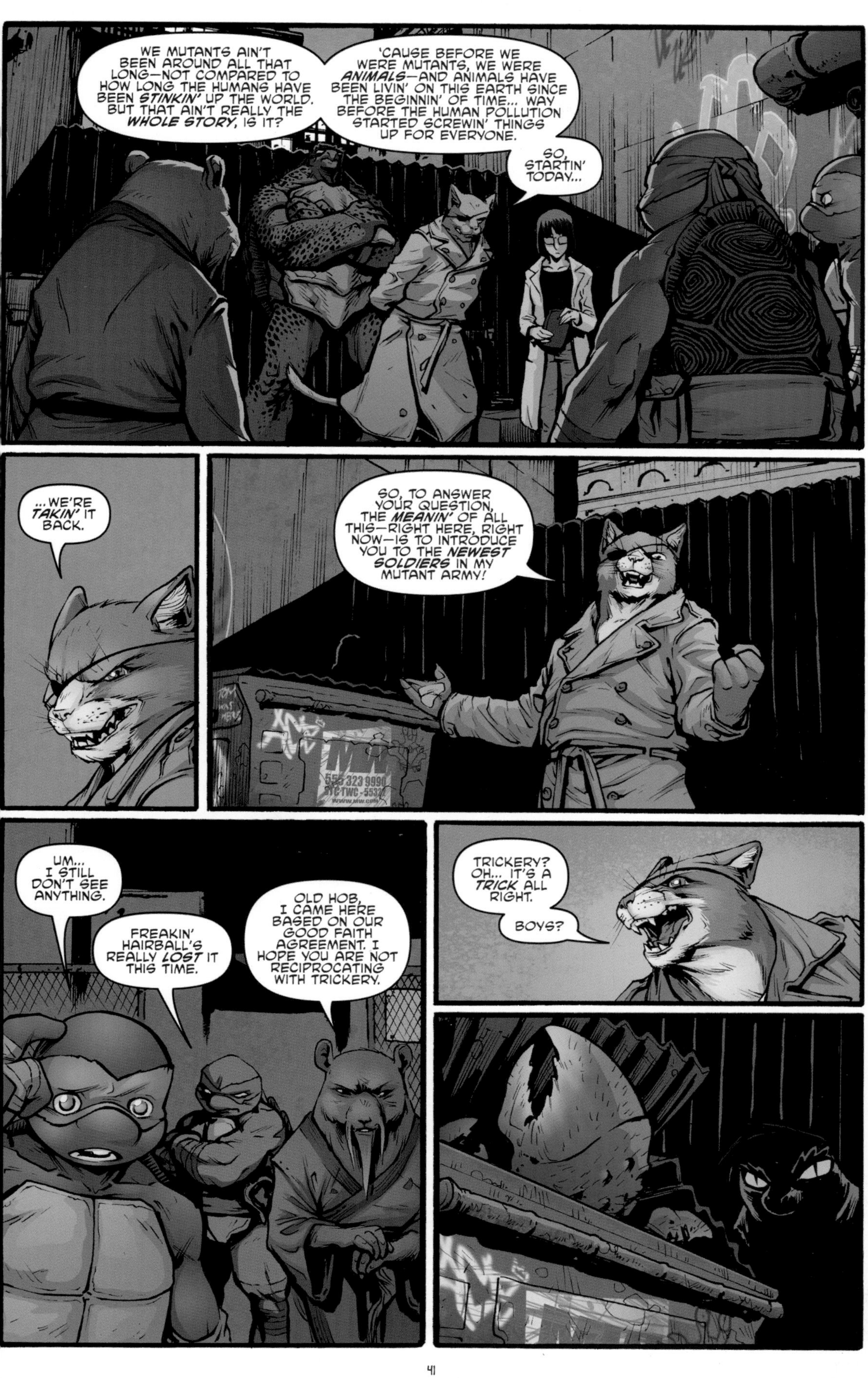

WE MUTANTS AIN'T BEEN AROUND ALL THAT LONG—NOT COMPARED TO HOW LONG THE HUMANS HAVE BEEN STINKIN' UP THE WORLD. BUT THAT AIN'T REALLY THE WHOLE STORY, IS IT?
'CAUSE BEFORE WE WERE MUTANTS, WE WERE ANIMALS—AND ANIMALS HAVE BEEN LIVIN' ON THIS EARTH SINCE THE BEGINNIN' OF TIME... WAY BEFORE THE HUMAN POLLUTION STARTED SCREWIN' THINGS UP FOR EVERYONE.
SO, STARTIN' TODAY...
...WE'RE TAKIN' IT BACK.
SO, TO ANSWER YOUR QUESTION, THE MEANIN' OF ALL THIS—RIGHT HERE, RIGHT NOW—IS TO INTRODUCE YOU TO THE NEWEST SOLDIERS IN MY MUTANT ARMY!
UM... I STILL DON'T SEE ANYTHING.
FREAKIN' HAIRBALL'S REALLY LOST IT THIS TIME.
OLD HOB, I CAME HERE BASED ON OUR GOOD FAITH AGREEMENT. I HOPE YOU ARE NOT RECIPROCATING WITH TRICKERY.
TRICKERY? OH... IT'S A TRICK ALL RIGHT.
BOYS?

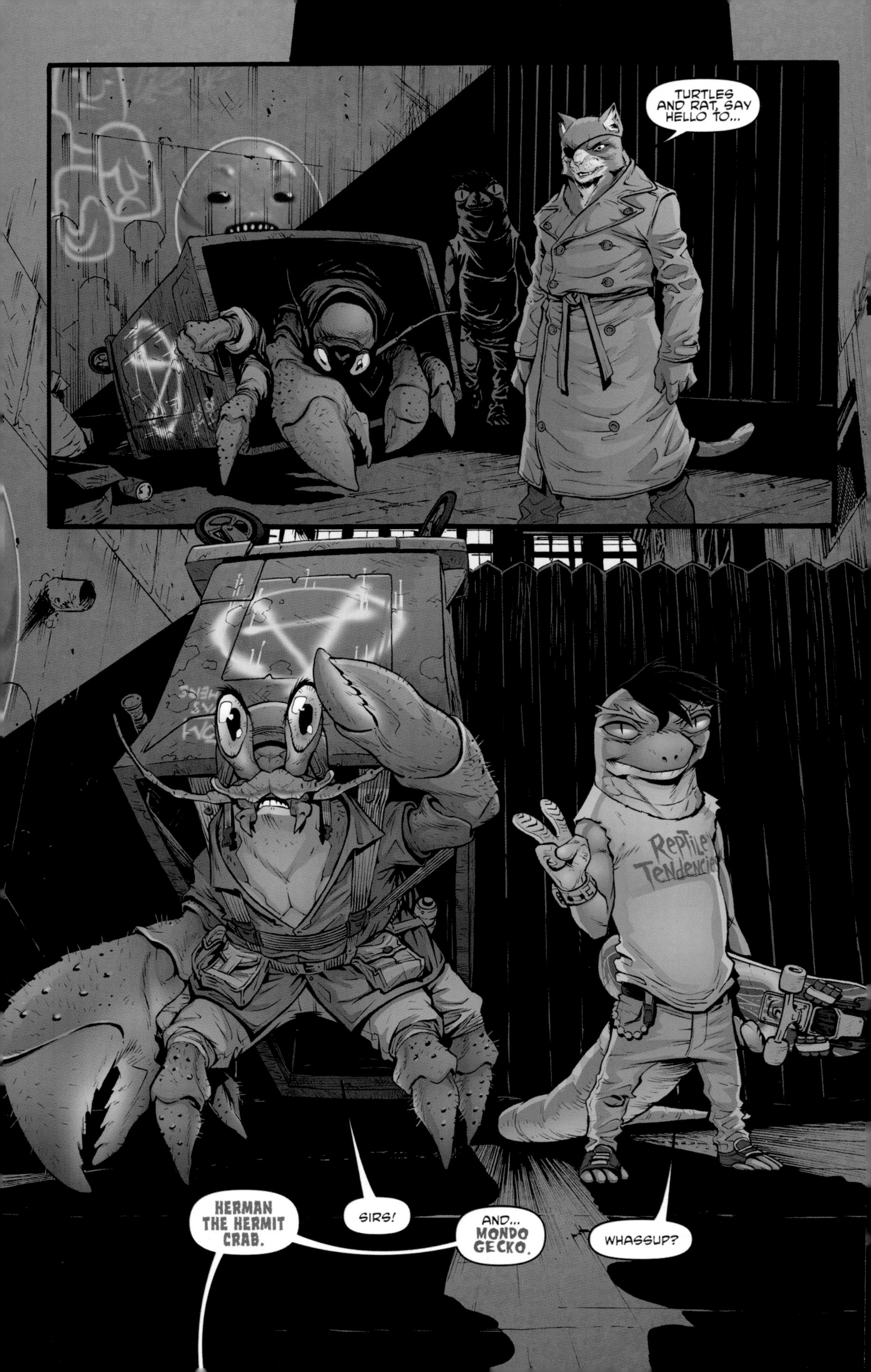
TURTLES AND RAT, SAY HELLO TO...
REPTILE TENDENCIES
HERMAN THE HERMIT CRAB.
SIRS!
AND... MONDO GECKO.
WHASSUP?

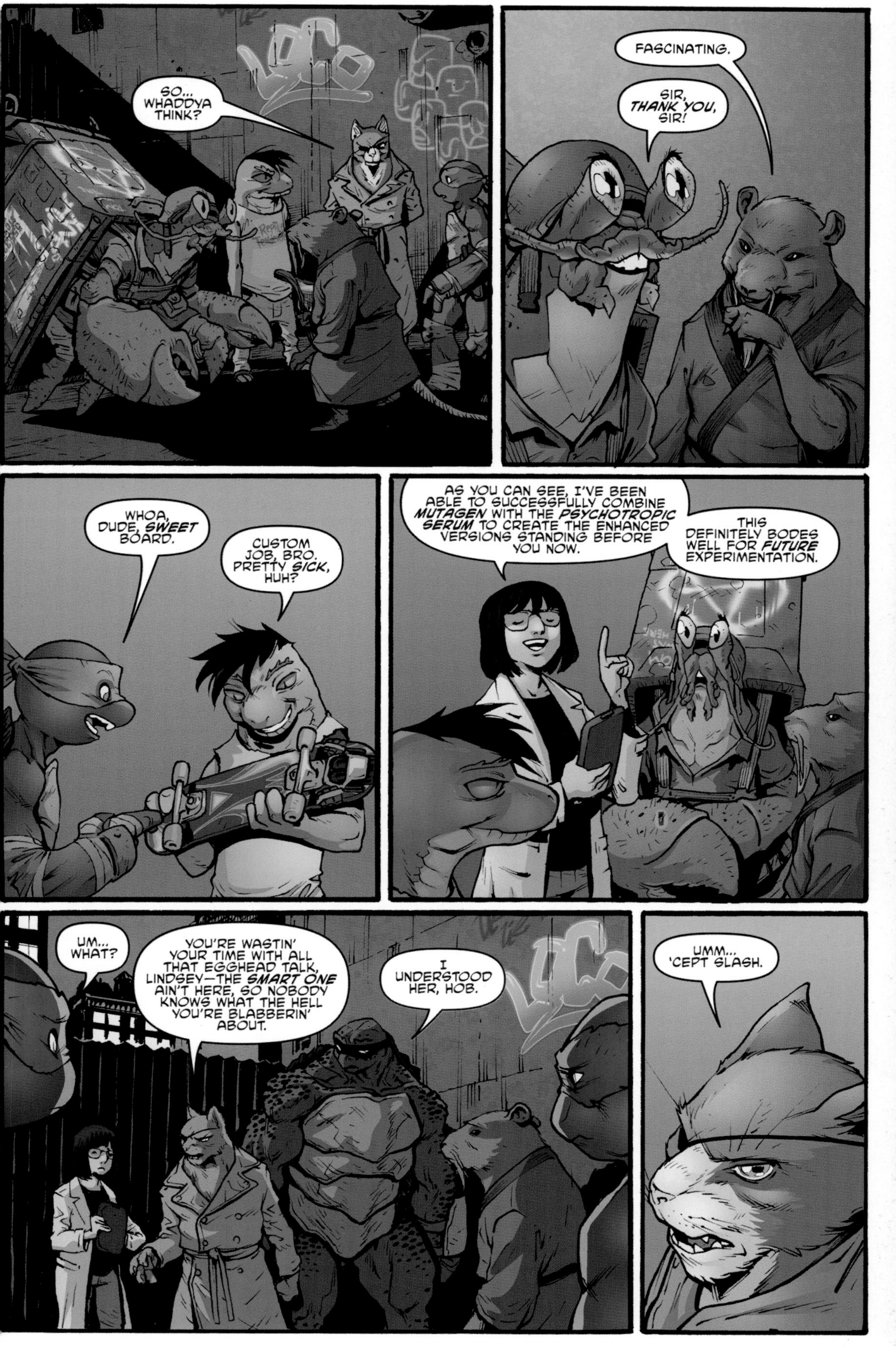
SO... WHADDYA THINK?
FASCINATING.
SIR, THANK YOU, SIR!
WHOA, DUDE, SWEET BOARD.
CUSTOM JOB, BRO. PRETTY SICK, HUH?
AS YOU CAN SEE, I'VE BEEN ABLE TO SUCCESSFULLY COMBINE MUTAGEN WITH THE PSYCHOTROPIC SERUM TO CREATE THE ENHANCED VERSIONS STANDING BEFORE YOU NOW.
THIS DEFINITELY BODES WELL FOR FUTURE EXPERIMENTATION.
UM... WHAT?
YOU'RE WASTIN' YOUR TIME WITH ALL THAT EGGHEAD TALK, LINDSEY—THE SMART ONE AIN'T HERE, SO NOBODY KNOWS WHAT THE HELL YOU'RE BLABBERIN' ABOUT.
I UNDERSTOOD HER, HOB.
UMM... 'CEPT SLASH.

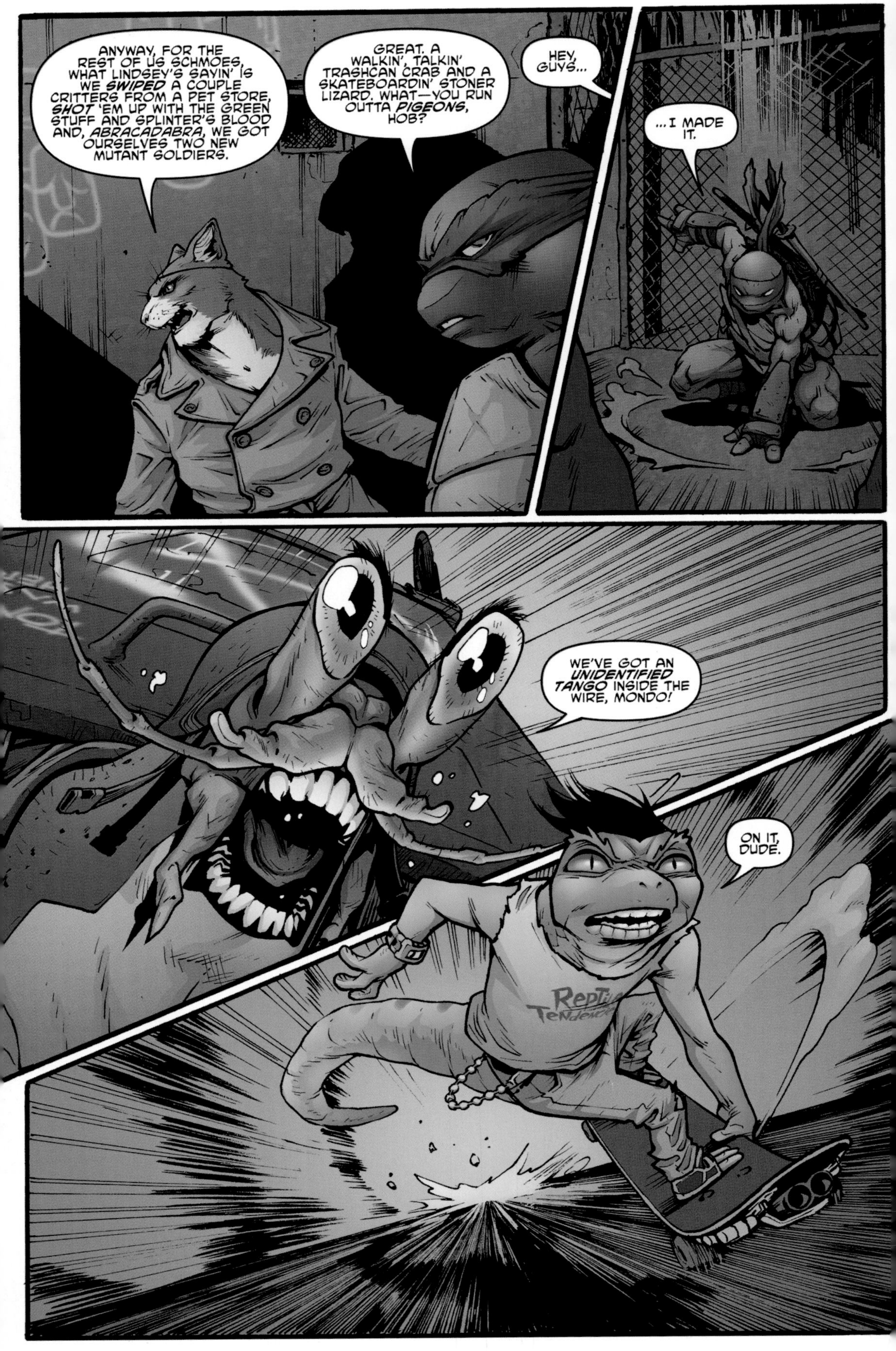

ANYWAY, FOR THE REST OF US SCHMOES, WHAT LINDSEY'S SAYIN' IS WE SWIPED A COUPLE CRITTERS FROM A PET STORE, SHOT 'EM UP WITH THE GREEN STUFF AND SPLINTER'S BLOOD AND, ABRACADABRA, WE GOT OURSELVES TWO NEW MUTANT SOLDIERS.
GREAT. A WALKIN', TALKIN' TRASHCAN CRAB AND A SKATEBOARDIN' STONER LIZARD. WHAT—YOU RUN OUTTA PIGEONS, HOB?
HEY, GUYS...
...I MADE IT.
WE'VE GOT AN UNIDENTIFIED TANGO INSIDE THE WIRE, MONDO!
ON IT, DUDE.

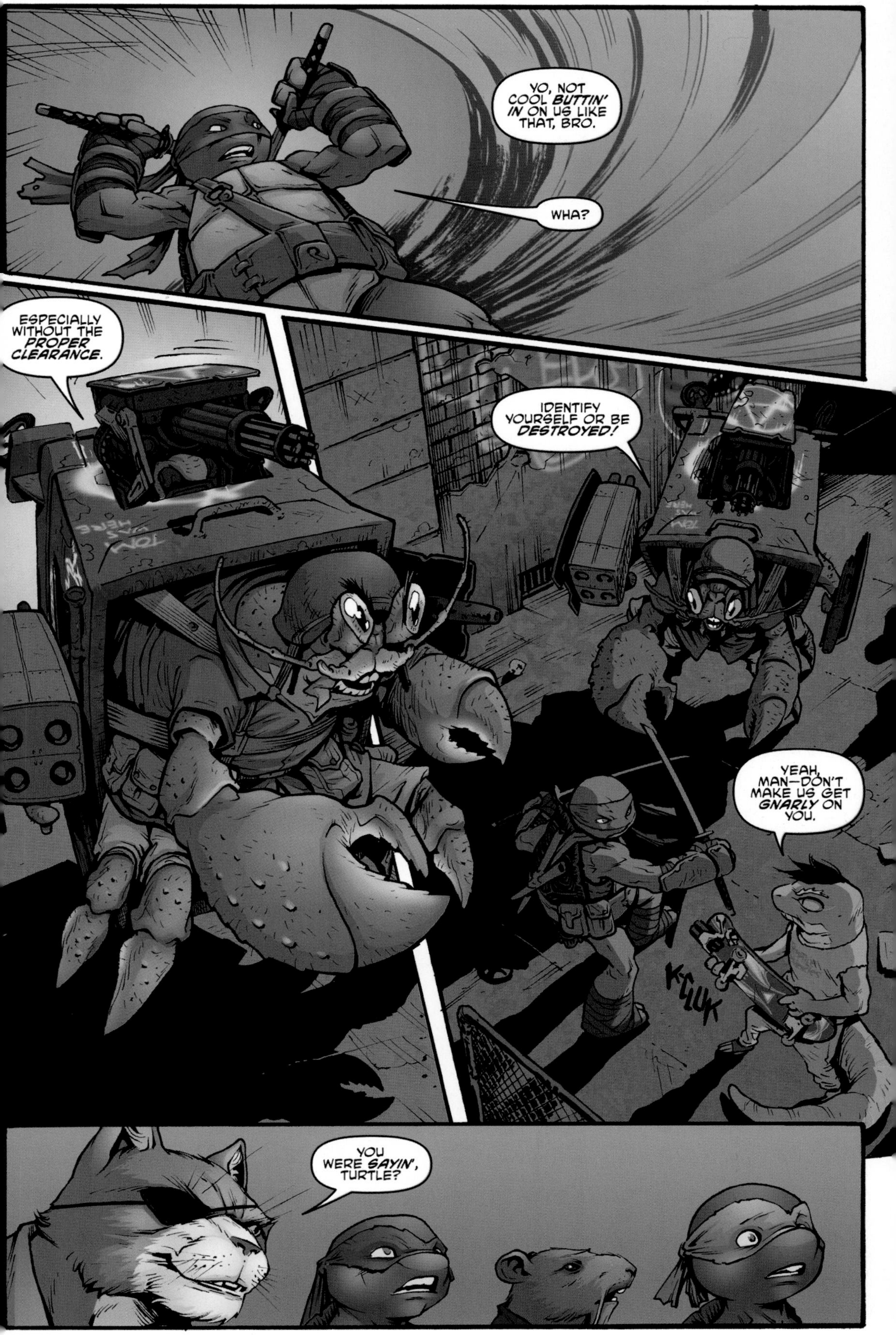
YO, NOT COOL BUTTIN' IN ON US LIKE THAT, BRO.
WHA?
ESPECIALLY WITHOUT THE PROPER CLEARANCE.
IDENTIFY YOURSELF OR BE DESTROYED!
YEAH, MAN—DON'T MAKE US GET GNARLY ON YOU.
K-CLUK
YOU WERE SAYIN', TURTLE?

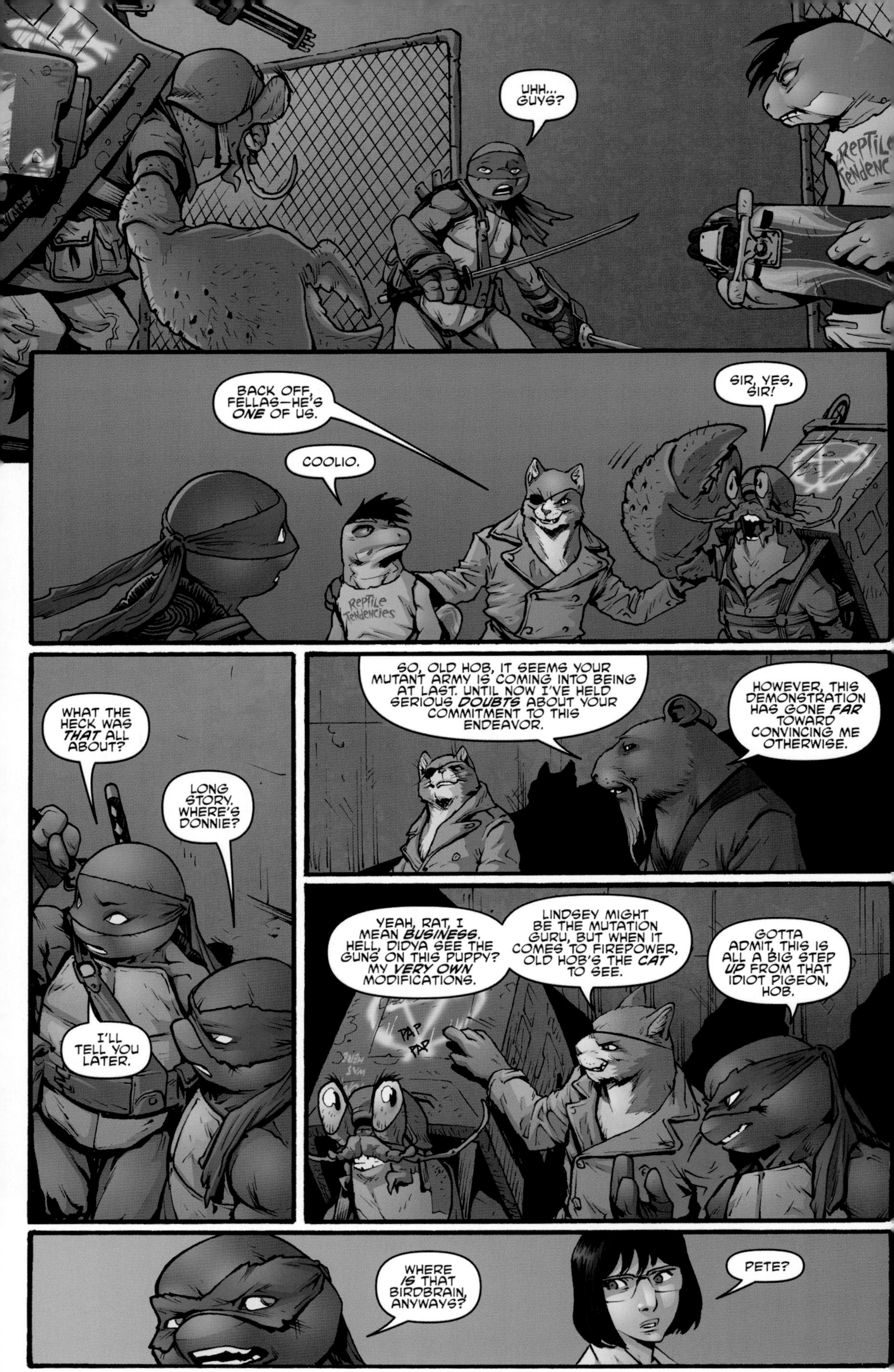
UHH... GUYS?
BACK OFF, FELLAS—HE'S ONE OF US.
SIR, YES, SIR!
COOLIO.
REPTILE TENDENCIES
WHAT THE HECK WAS THAT ALL ABOUT?
LONG STORY. WHERE'S DONNIE?
I'LL TELL YOU LATER.
SO, OLD HOB, IT SEEMS YOUR MUTANT ARMY IS COMING INTO BEING AT LAST. UNTIL NOW I'VE HELD SERIOUS DOUBTS ABOUT YOUR COMMITMENT TO THIS ENDEAVOR.
HOWEVER, THIS DEMONSTRATION HAS GONE FAR TOWARD CONVINCING ME OTHERWISE.
YEAH, RAT, I MEAN BUSINESS. HELL, DIDYA SEE THE GUNS ON THIS PUPPY? MY VERY OWN MODIFICATIONS.
LINDSEY MIGHT BE THE MUTATION GURU, BUT WHEN IT COMES TO FIREPOWER, OLD HOB'S THE CAT TO SEE.
GOTTA ADMIT, THIS IS ALL A BIG STEP UP FROM THAT IDIOT PIGEON, HOB.
PAP PAP
WHERE IS THAT BIRDBRAIN, ANYWAYS?
PETE?

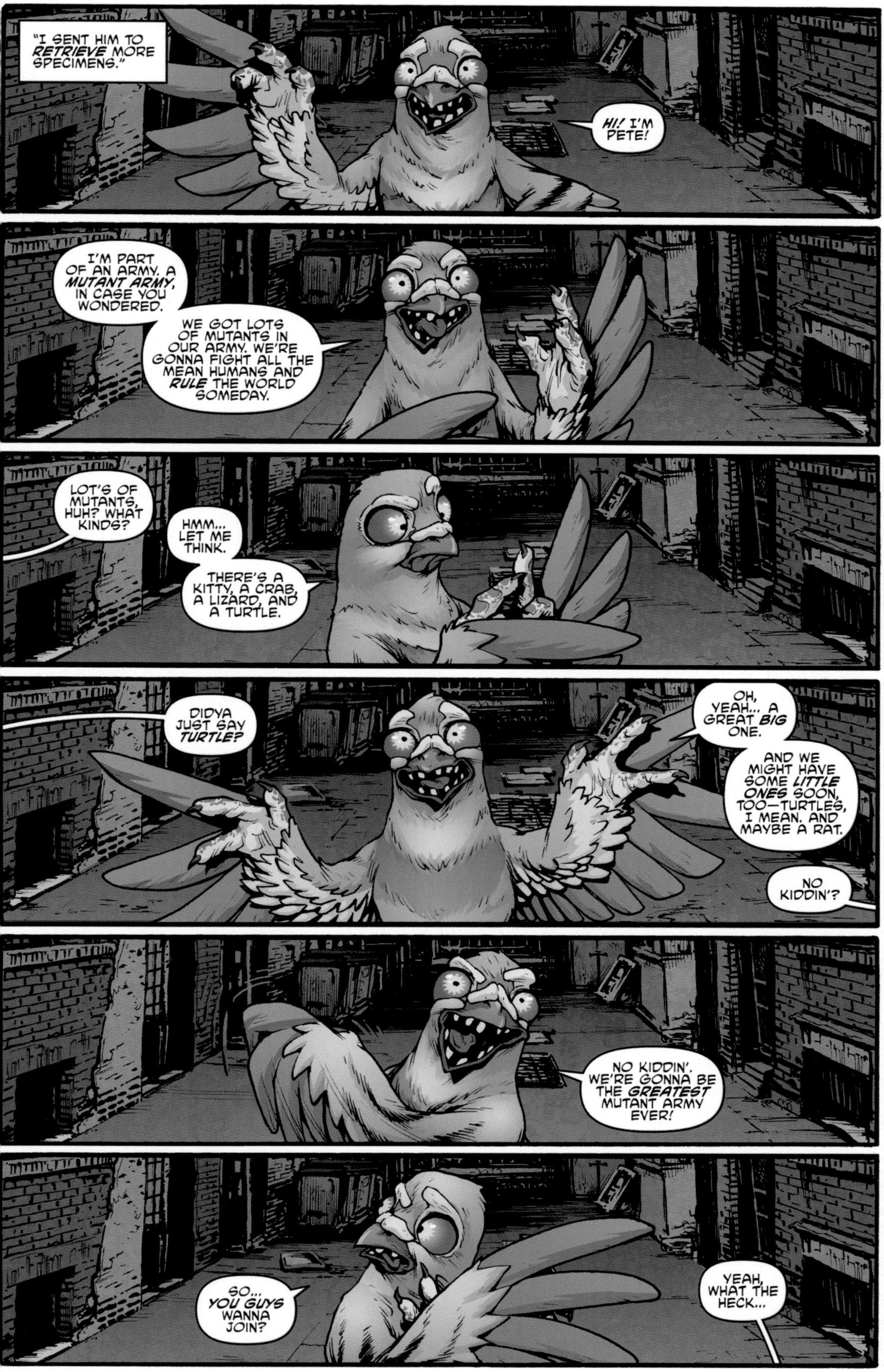
"I SENT HIM TO RETRIEVE MORE SPECIMENS."
HI! I'M PETE!
I'M PART OF AN ARMY. A MUTANT ARMY, IN CASE YOU WONDERED.
WE GOT LOTS OF MUTANTS IN OUR ARMY. WE'RE GONNA FIGHT ALL THE MEAN HUMANS AND RULE THE WORLD SOMEDAY.
LOT'S OF MUTANTS, HUH? WHAT KINDS?
HMM... LET ME THINK.
THERE'S A KITTY, A CRAB, A LIZARD, AND A TURTLE.
DIDYA JUST SAY TURTLE?
OH, YEAH... A GREAT BIG ONE.
AND WE MIGHT HAVE SOME LITTLE ONES SOON, TOO—TURTLES, I MEAN. AND MAYBE A RAT.
NO KIDDIN'?
NO KIDDIN'. WE'RE GONNA BE THE GREATEST MUTANT ARMY EVER!
SO... YOU GUYS WANNA JOIN?
YEAH, WHAT THE HECK...

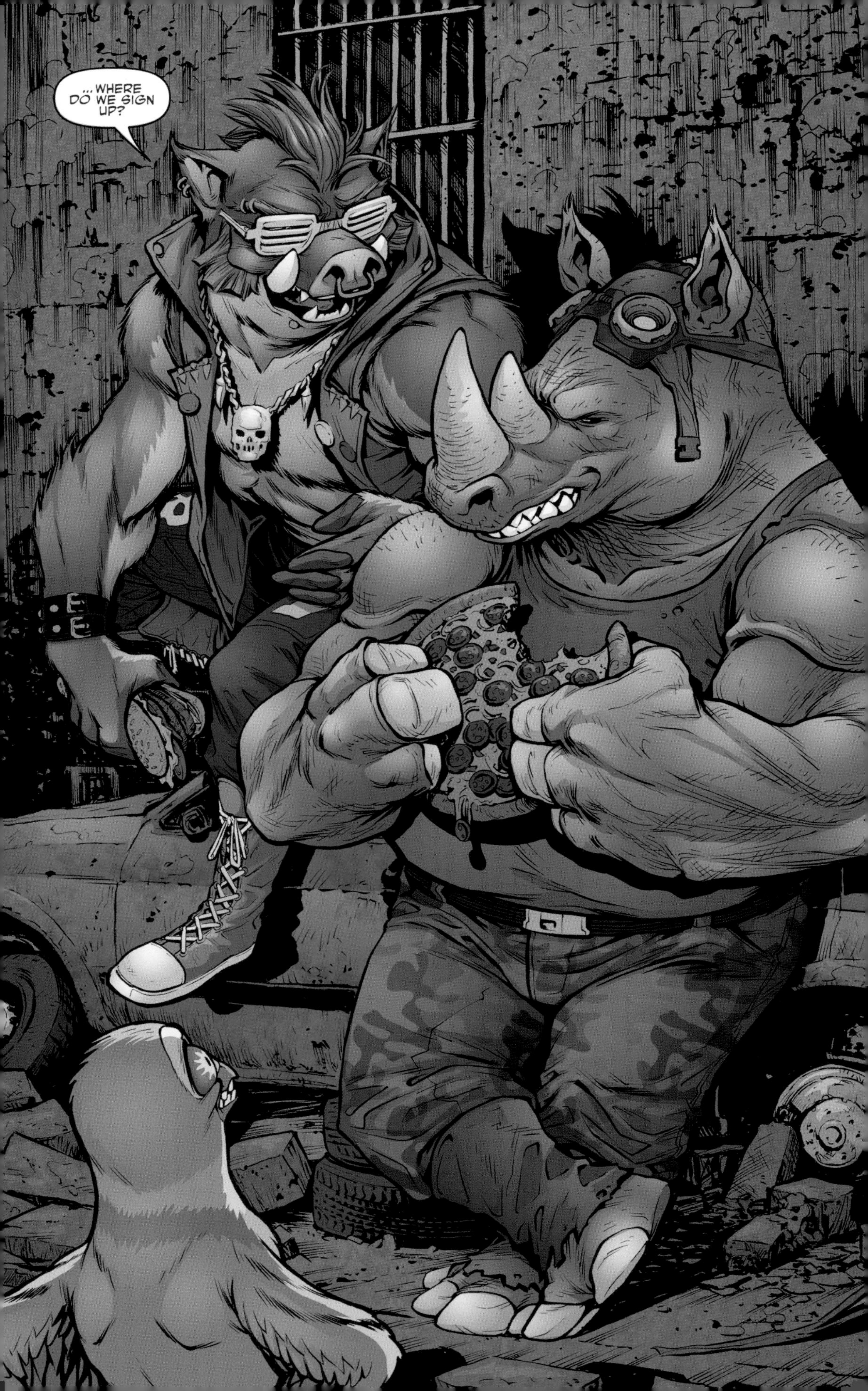
...WHERE DO WE SIGN UP?

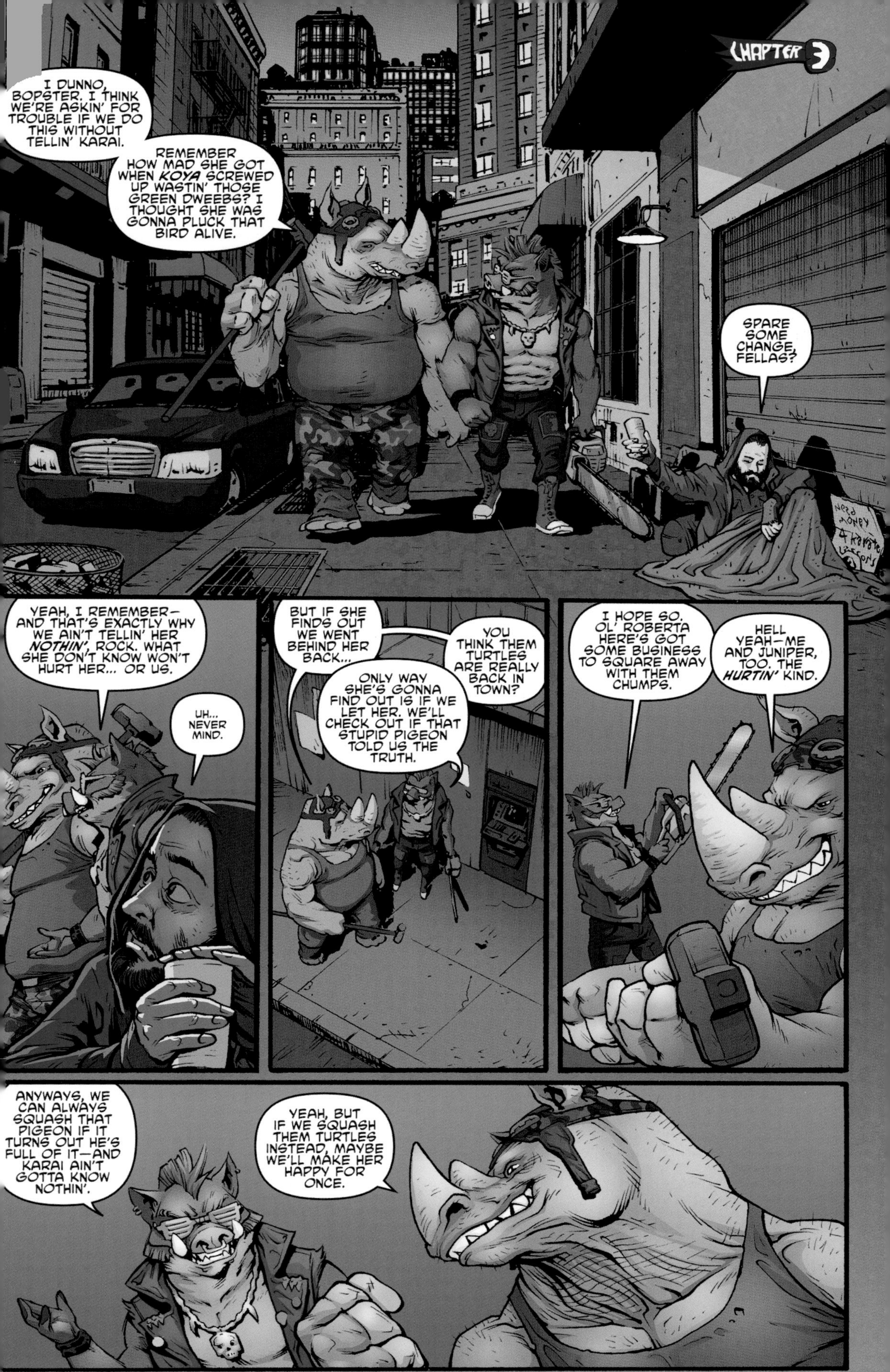
CHAPTER 3
I DUNNO, BOPSTER. I THINK WE'RE ASKIN' FOR TROUBLE IF WE DO THIS WITHOUT TELLIN' KARAI.
REMEMBER HOW MAD SHE GOT WHEN KOYA SCREWED UP WASTIN' THOSE GREEN DWEEBS? I THOUGHT SHE WAS GONNA PLUCK THAT BIRD ALIVE.
SPARE SOME CHANGE, FELLAS?
YEAH, I REMEMBER—AND THAT'S EXACTLY WHY WE AIN'T TELLIN' HER NOTHIN', ROCK. WHAT SHE DON'T KNOW WON'T HURT HER... OR US.
UH... NEVER MIND.
BUT IF SHE FINDS OUT WE WENT BEHIND HER BACK...
ONLY WAY SHE'S GONNA FIND OUT IS IF WE LET HER. WE'LL CHECK OUT IF THAT STUPID PIGEON TOLD US THE TRUTH.
YOU THINK THEM TURTLES ARE REALLY BACK IN TOWN?
I HOPE SO. OL' ROBERTA HERE'S GOT SOME BUSINESS TO SQUARE AWAY WITH THEM CHUMPS.
HELL YEAH—ME AND JUNIPER, TOO. THE HURTIN' KIND.
ANYWAYS, WE CAN ALWAYS SQUASH THAT PIGEON IF IT TURNS OUT HE'S FULL OF IT—AND KARAI AIN'T GOTTA KNOW NOTHIN'.
YEAH, BUT IF WE SQUASH THEM TURTLES INSTEAD, MAYBE WE'LL MAKE HER HAPPY FOR ONCE.

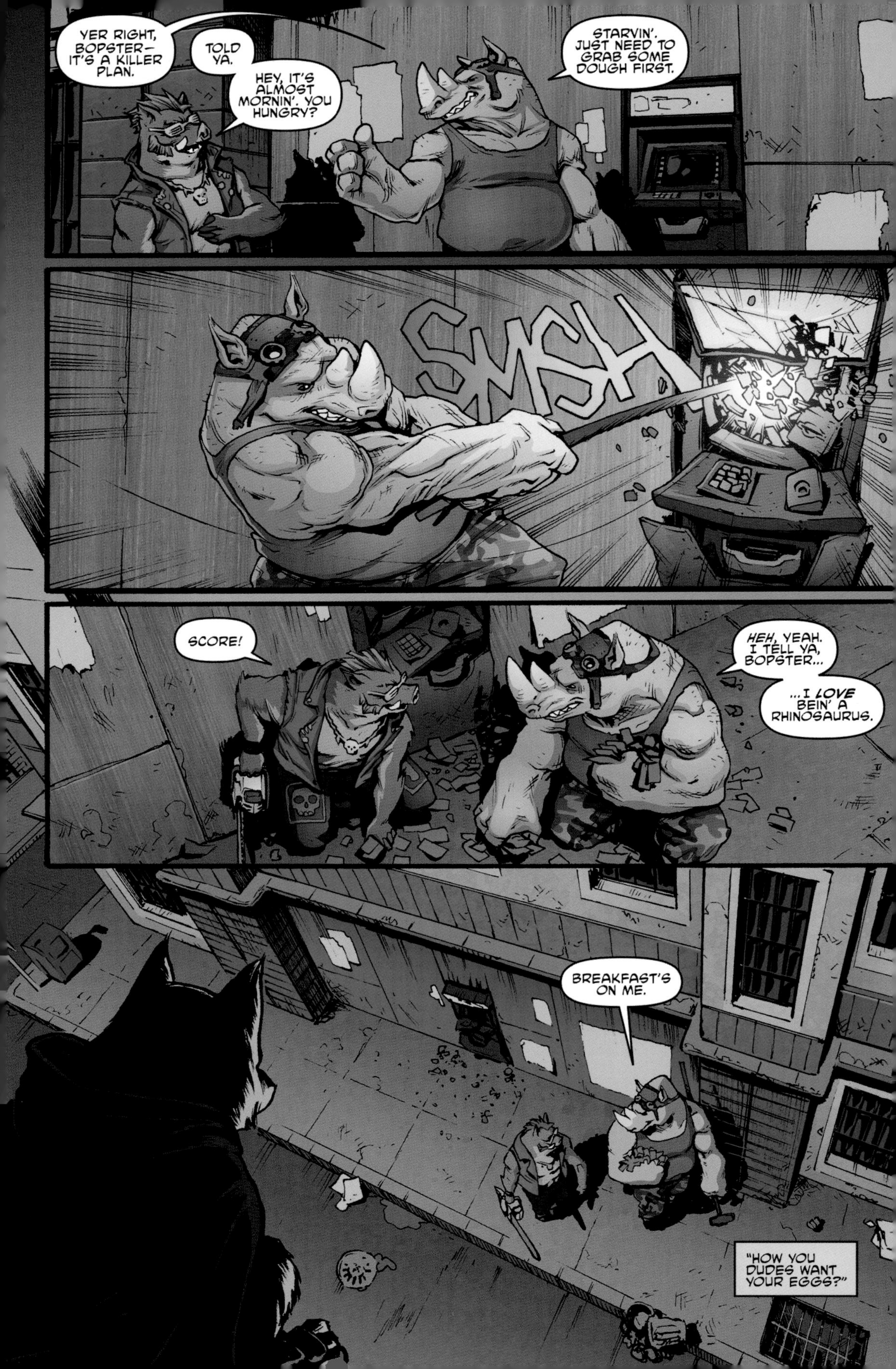
YER RIGHT, BOPSTER— IT'S A KILLER PLAN.
TOLD YA.
HEY, IT'S ALMOST MORNIN'. YOU HUNGRY?
STARVIN'. JUST NEED TO GRAB SOME DOUGH FIRST.
SMSH
SCORE!
HEH, YEAH. I TELL YA, BOPSTER...
...I LOVE BEIN' A RHINOSAURUS.
BREAKFAST'S ON ME.
"HOW YOU DUDES WANT YOUR EGGS?"

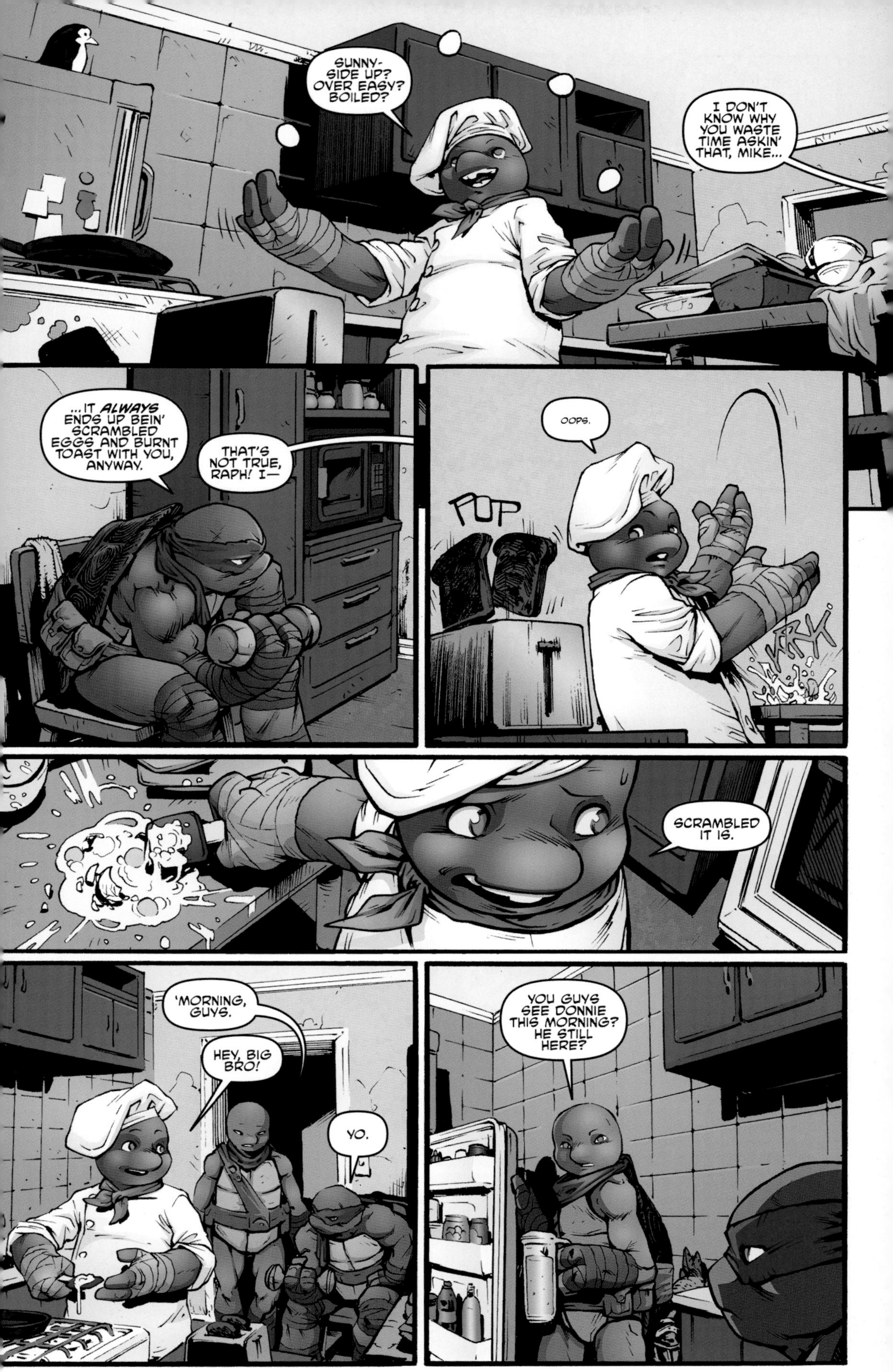
SUNNY-SIDE UP? OVER EASY? BOILED?
I DON'T KNOW WHY YOU WASTE TIME ASKIN' THAT, MIKE...
...IT ALWAYS ENDS UP BEIN' SCRAMBLED EGGS AND BURNT TOAST WITH YOU, ANYWAY.
THAT'S NOT TRUE, RAPH! I—
OOPS.
POP
SCRAMBLED IT IS.
'MORNING, GUYS.
HEY, BIG BRO!
YO.
YOU GUYS SEE DONNIE THIS MORNING? HE STILL HERE?

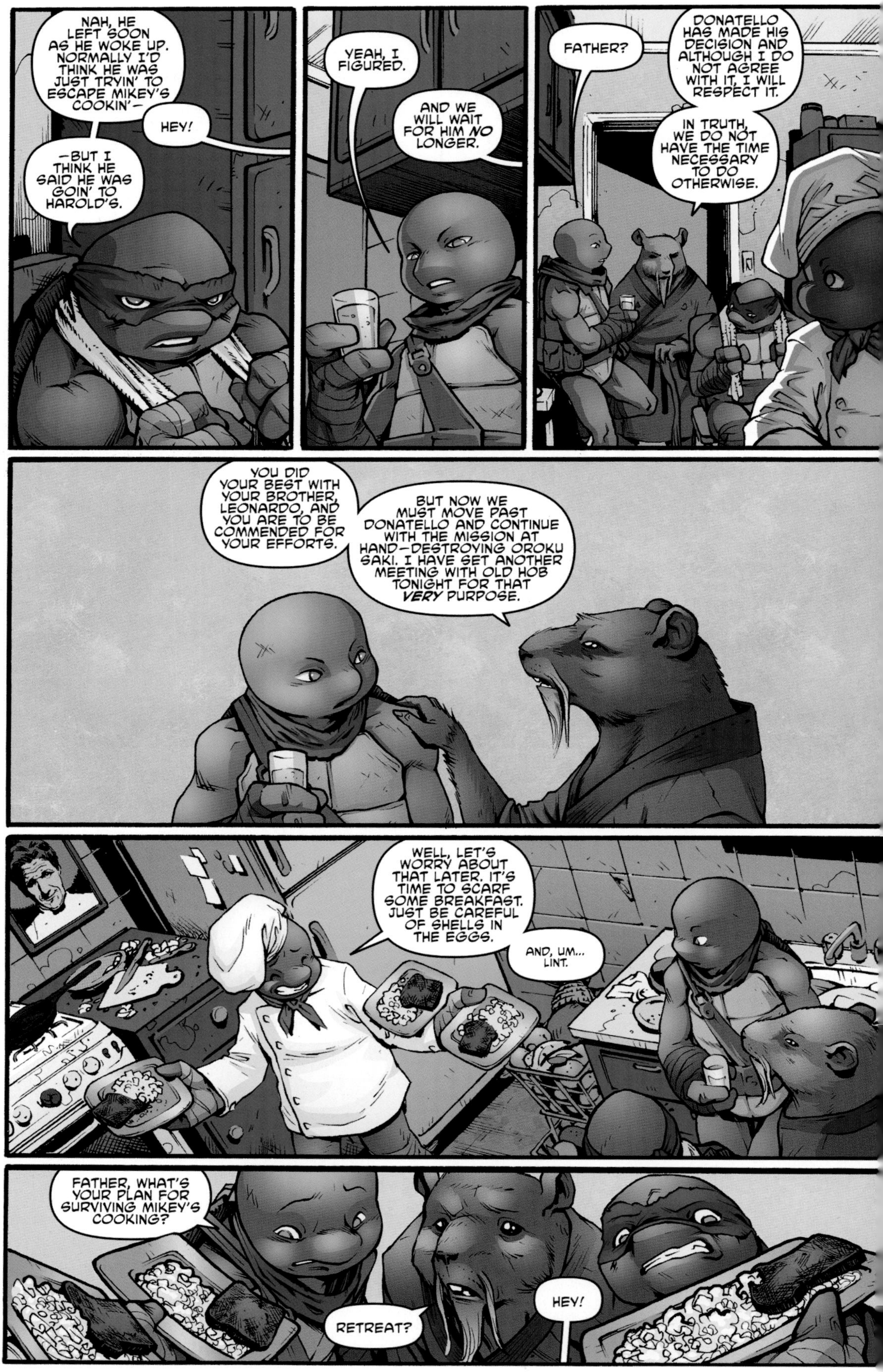
NAH, HE LEFT SOON AS HE WOKE UP. NORMALLY I'D THINK HE WAS JUST TRYIN' TO ESCAPE MIKEY'S COOKIN'—
HEY!
—BUT I THINK HE SAID HE WAS GOIN' TO HAROLD'S.
YEAH, I FIGURED.
AND WE WILL WAIT FOR HIM NO LONGER.
FATHER?
DONATELLO HAS MADE HIS DECISION AND ALTHOUGH I DO NOT AGREE WITH IT, I WILL RESPECT IT.
IN TRUTH, WE DO NOT HAVE THE TIME NECESSARY TO DO OTHERWISE.
YOU DID YOUR BEST WITH YOUR BROTHER, LEONARDO, AND YOU ARE TO BE COMMENDED FOR YOUR EFFORTS.
BUT NOW WE MUST MOVE PAST DONATELLO AND CONTINUE WITH THE MISSION AT HAND—DESTROYING OROKU SAKI. I HAVE SET ANOTHER MEETING WITH OLD HOB TONIGHT FOR THAT VERY PURPOSE.
WELL, LET'S WORRY ABOUT THAT LATER. IT'S TIME TO SCARF SOME BREAKFAST. JUST BE CAREFUL OF SHELLS IN THE EGGS.
AND, UM... LINT.
FATHER, WHAT'S YOUR PLAN FOR SURVIVING MIKEY'S COOKING?
RETREAT?
HEY!

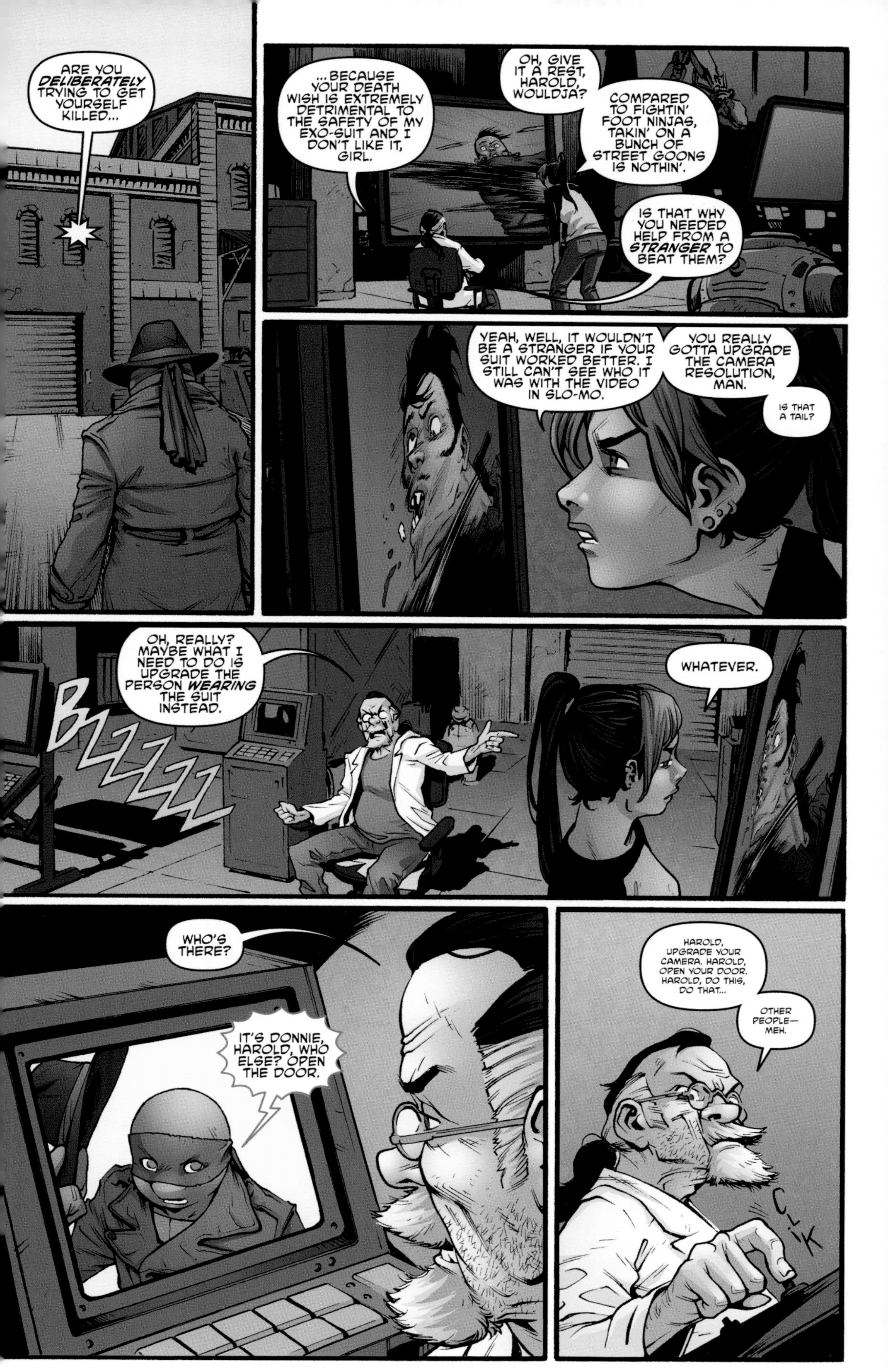
ARE YOU DELIBERATELY TRYING TO GET YOURSELF KILLED...
...BECAUSE YOUR DEATH WISH IS EXTREMELY DETRIMENTAL TO THE SAFETY OF MY EXO-SUIT AND I DON'T LIKE IT, GIRL.
OH, GIVE IT A REST, HAROLD, WOULDJA?
COMPARED TO FIGHTIN' FOOT NINJAS, TAKIN' ON A BUNCH OF STREET GOONS IS NOTHIN'.
IS THAT WHY YOU NEEDED HELP FROM A STRANGER TO BEAT THEM?
YEAH, WELL, IT WOULDN'T BE A STRANGER IF YOUR SUIT WORKED BETTER. I STILL CAN'T SEE WHO IT WAS WITH THE VIDEO IN SLO-MO.
YOU REALLY GOTTA UPGRADE THE CAMERA RESOLUTION, MAN.
IS THAT A TAIL?
OH, REALLY? MAYBE WHAT I NEED TO DO IS UPGRADE THE PERSON WEARING THE SUIT INSTEAD.
WHATEVER.
BZZZZZ
WHO'S THERE?
IT'S DONNIE, HAROLD, WHO ELSE? OPEN THE DOOR.
HAROLD, UPGRADE YOUR CAMERA. HAROLD, OPEN YOUR DOOR. HAROLD, DO THIS, DO THAT...
OTHER PEOPLE— MEH.
CLIK

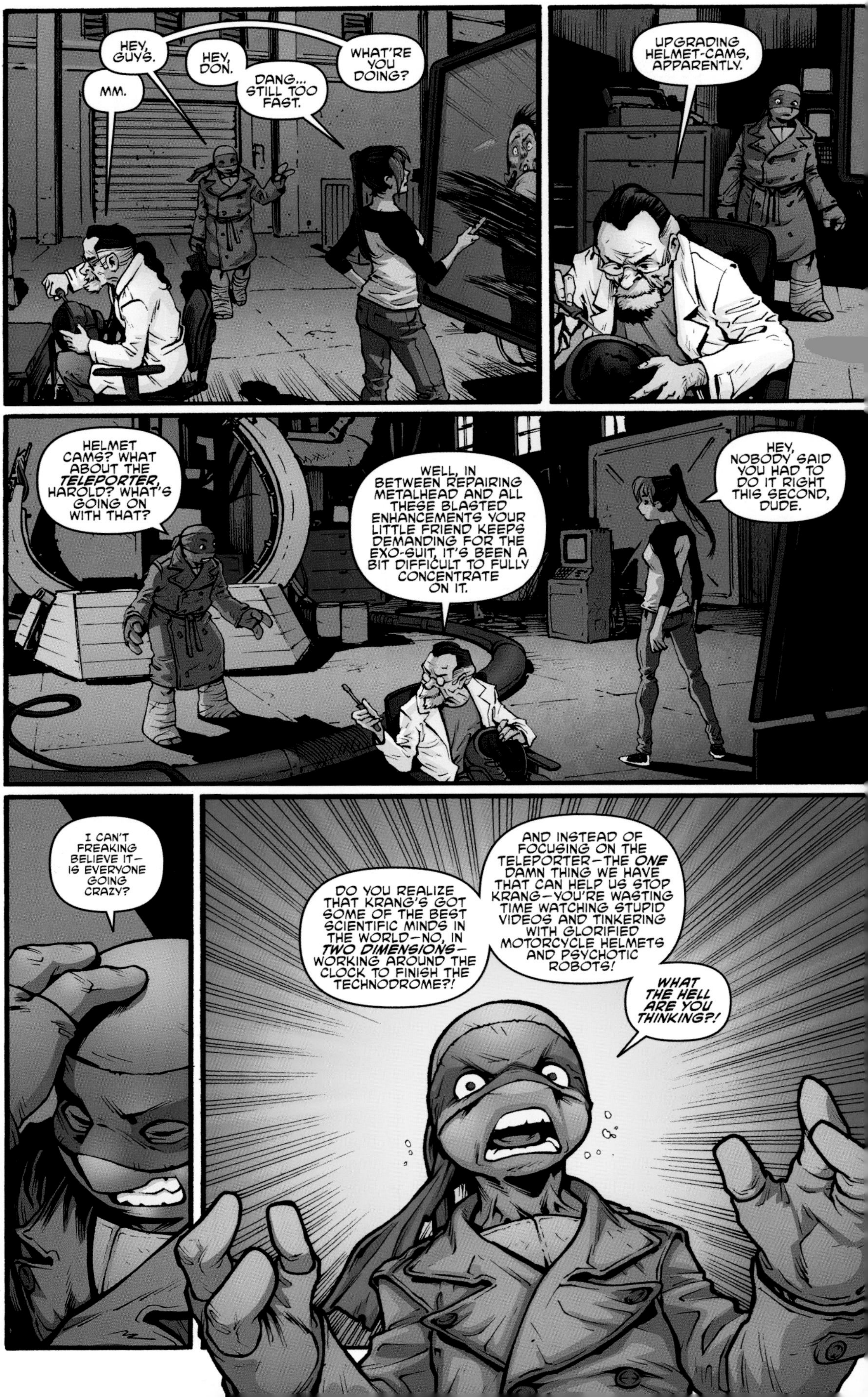
HEY, GUYS.
MM.
HEY, DON.
DANG... STILL TOO FAST.
WHAT'RE YOU DOING?
UPGRADING HELMET-CAMS, APPARENTLY.
HELMET CAMS? WHAT ABOUT THE *TELEPORTER*, HAROLD? WHAT'S GOING ON WITH THAT?
WELL, IN BETWEEN REPAIRING METALHEAD AND ALL THESE BLASTED ENHANCEMENTS YOUR LITTLE FRIEND KEEPS DEMANDING FOR THE EXO-SUIT, IT'S BEEN A BIT DIFFICULT TO FULLY CONCENTRATE ON IT.
HEY, NOBODY SAID YOU HAD TO DO IT RIGHT THIS SECOND, DUDE.
I CAN'T FREAKING BELIEVE IT— IS EVERYONE GOING CRAZY?
DO YOU REALIZE THAT KRANG'S GOT SOME OF THE BEST SCIENTIFIC MINDS IN THE WORLD—NO, IN *TWO DIMENSIONS*— WORKING AROUND THE CLOCK TO FINISH THE TECHNODROME?!
AND INSTEAD OF FOCUSING ON THE TELEPORTER—THE *ONE* DAMN THING WE HAVE THAT CAN HELP US STOP KRANG—YOU'RE WASTING TIME WATCHING STUPID VIDEOS AND TINKERING WITH GLORIFIED MOTORCYCLE HELMETS AND PSYCHOTIC ROBOTS!
WHAT THE HELL ARE YOU THINKING?!

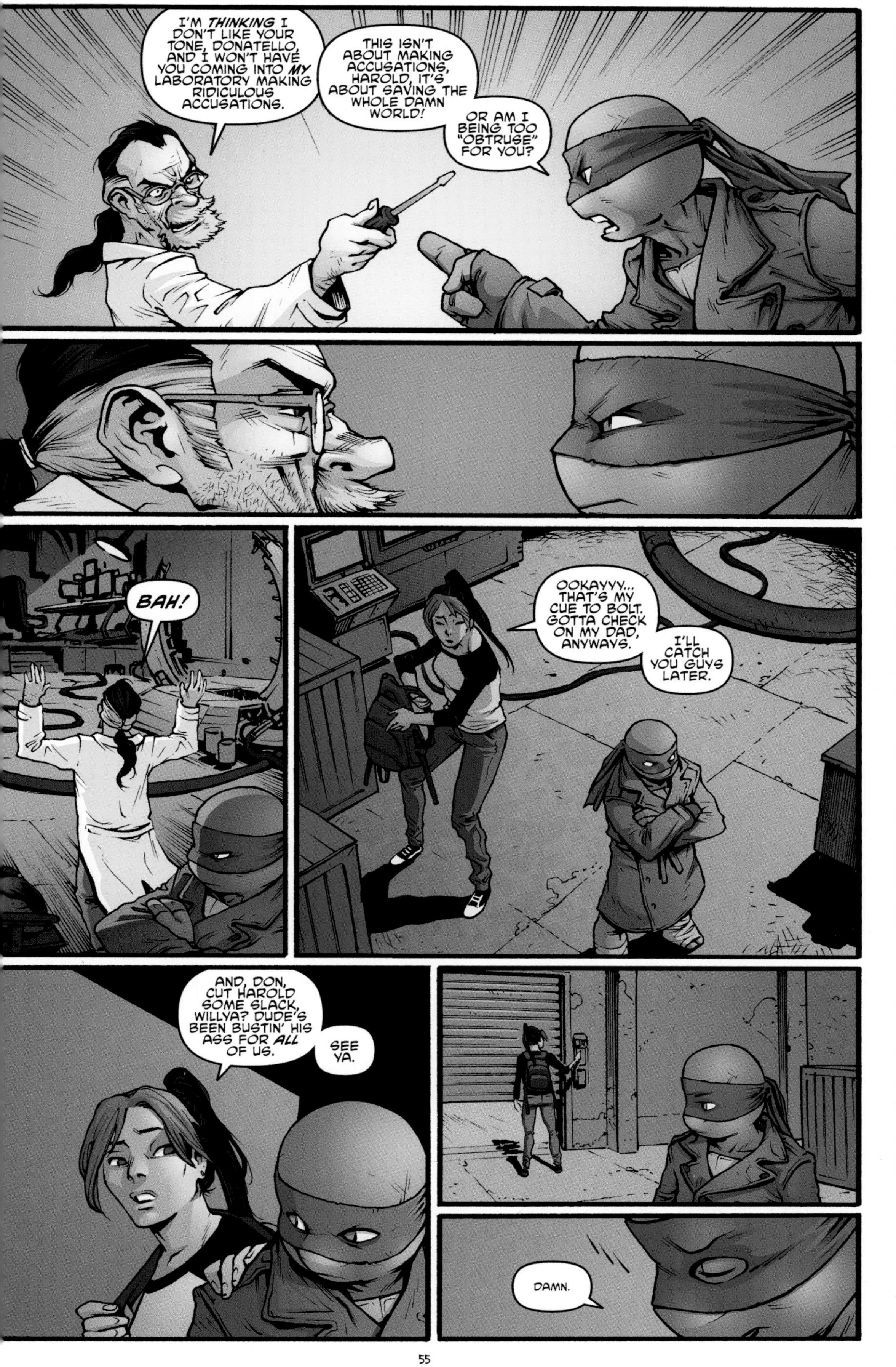
I'M *THINKING* I DON'T LIKE YOUR TONE, DONATELLO, AND I WON'T HAVE YOU COMING INTO *MY* LABORATORY MAKING RIDICULOUS ACCUSATIONS.
THIS ISN'T ABOUT MAKING ACCUSATIONS, HAROLD, IT'S ABOUT SAVING THE WHOLE DAMN WORLD!
OR AM I BEING TOO "OBTRUSE" FOR YOU?
BAH!
OOKAYYY... THAT'S MY CUE TO BOLT. GOTTA CHECK ON MY DAD, ANYWAYS.
I'LL CATCH YOU GUYS LATER.
AND, DON, CUT HAROLD SOME SLACK, WILLYA? DUDE'S BEEN BUSTIN' HIS ASS FOR *ALL* OF US.
SEE YA.
DAMN.

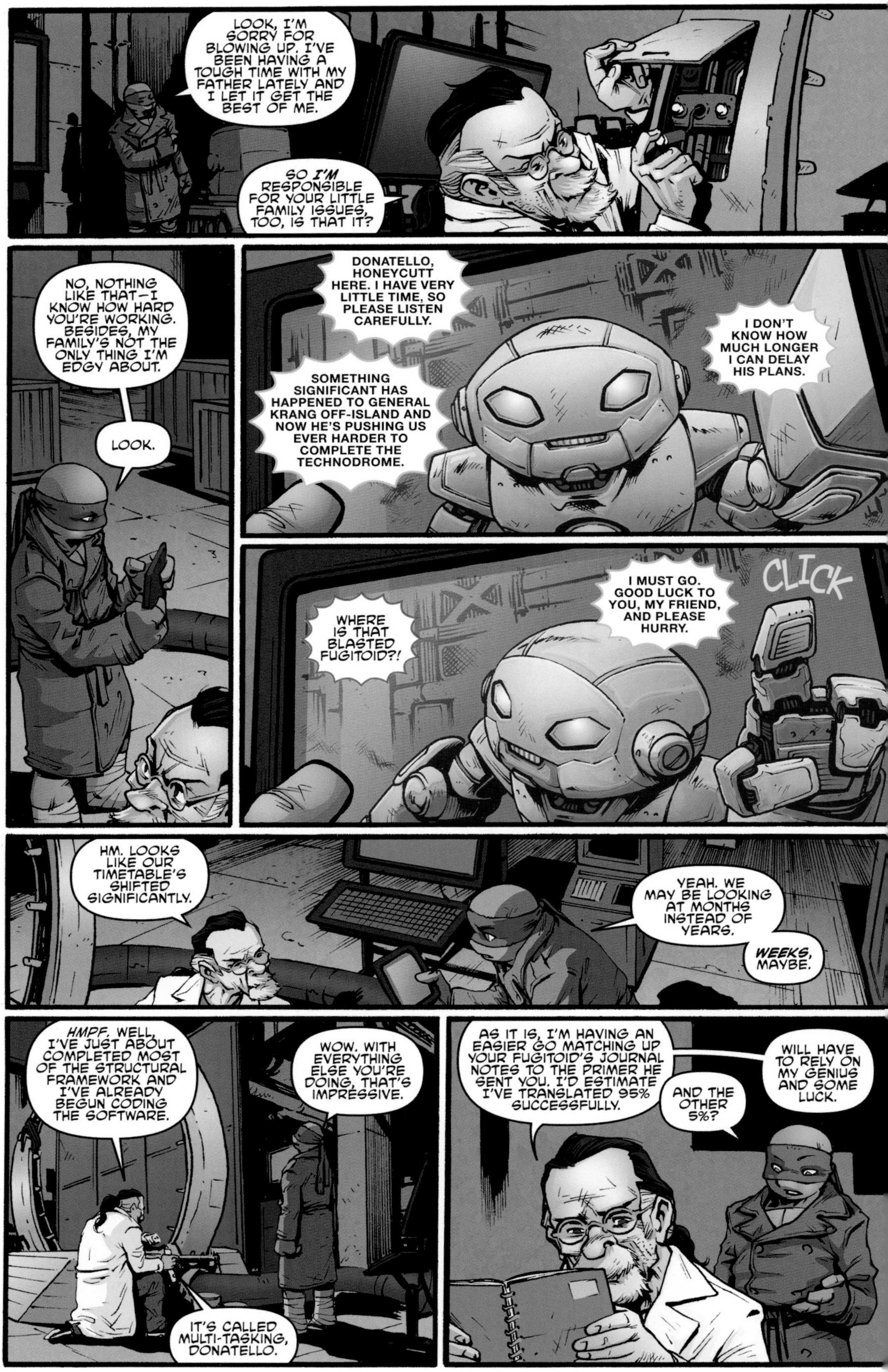
LOOK, I'M SORRY FOR BLOWING UP. I'VE BEEN HAVING A TOUGH TIME WITH MY FATHER LATELY AND I LET IT GET THE BEST OF ME.
SO *I'M* RESPONSIBLE FOR YOUR LITTLE FAMILY ISSUES, TOO, IS THAT IT?
NO, NOTHING LIKE THAT—I KNOW HOW HARD YOU'RE WORKING. BESIDES, MY FAMILY'S NOT THE ONLY THING I'M EDGY ABOUT.
LOOK.
DONATELLO, HONEYCUTT HERE. I HAVE VERY LITTLE TIME, SO PLEASE LISTEN CAREFULLY.
SOMETHING SIGNIFICANT HAS HAPPENED TO GENERAL KRANG OFF-ISLAND AND NOW HE'S PUSHING US EVER HARDER TO COMPLETE THE TECHNODROME.
I DON'T KNOW HOW MUCH LONGER I CAN DELAY HIS PLANS.
WHERE IS THAT BLASTED FUGITOID?!
I MUST GO. GOOD LUCK TO YOU, MY FRIEND, AND PLEASE HURRY.
CLICK
HM. LOOKS LIKE OUR TIMETABLE'S SHIFTED SIGNIFICANTLY.
YEAH. WE MAY BE LOOKING AT MONTHS INSTEAD OF YEARS.
WEEKS, MAYBE.
HMPF. WELL, I'VE JUST ABOUT COMPLETED MOST OF THE STRUCTURAL FRAMEWORK AND I'VE ALREADY BEGUN CODING THE SOFTWARE.
WOW. WITH EVERYTHING ELSE YOU'RE DOING, THAT'S IMPRESSIVE.
IT'S CALLED MULTI-TASKING, DONATELLO.
AS IT IS, I'M HAVING AN EASIER GO MATCHING UP YOUR FUGITOID'S JOURNAL NOTES TO THE PRIMER HE SENT YOU. I'D ESTIMATE I'VE TRANSLATED 95% SUCCESSFULLY.
AND THE OTHER 5%?
WILL HAVE TO RELY ON MY GENIUS AND SOME LUCK.

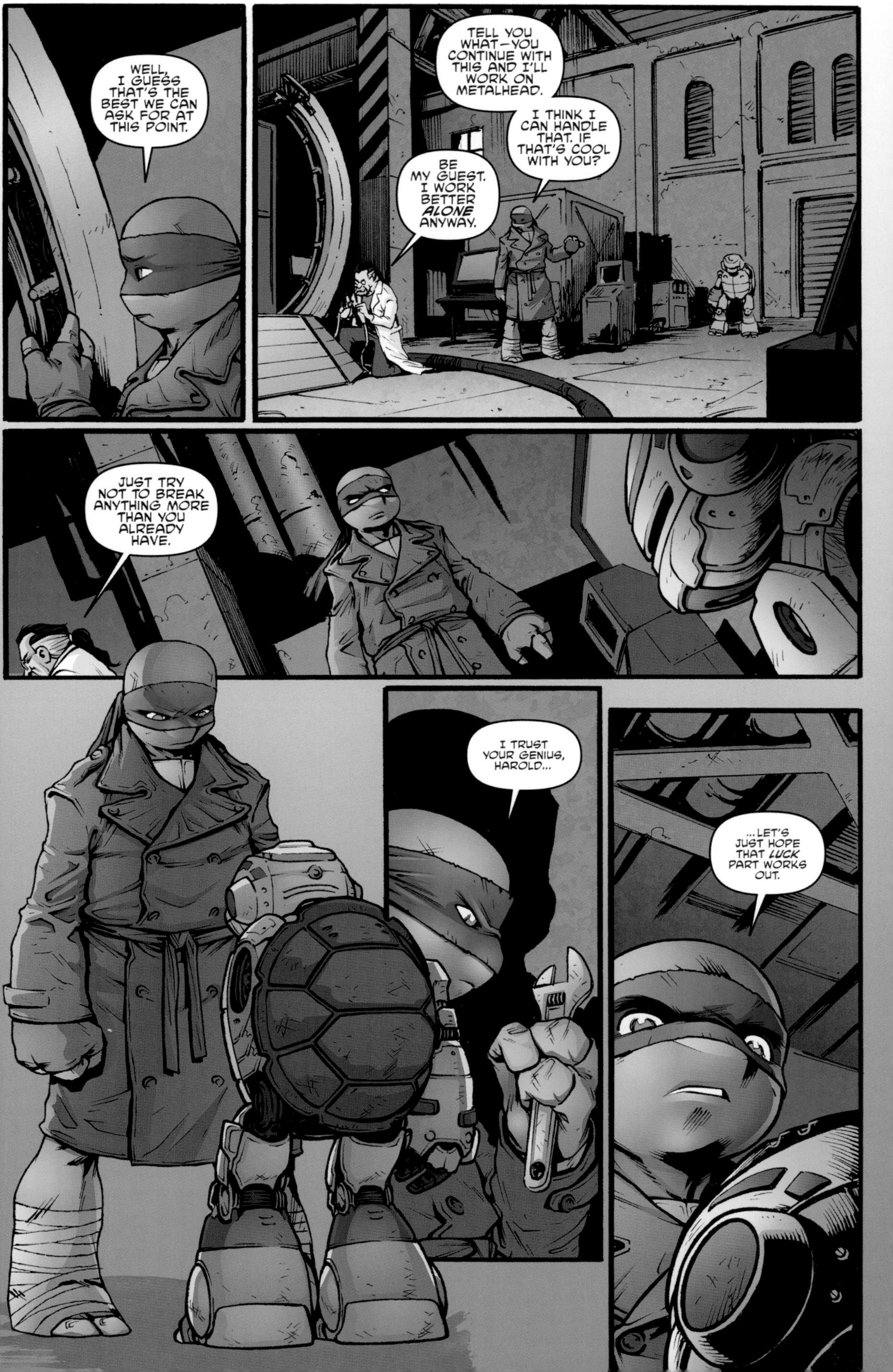
WELL, I GUESS THAT'S THE BEST WE CAN ASK FOR AT THIS POINT.
TELL YOU WHAT—YOU CONTINUE WITH THIS AND I'LL WORK ON METALHEAD.
I THINK I CAN HANDLE THAT. IF THAT'S COOL WITH YOU?
BE MY GUEST. I WORK BETTER ALONE ANYWAY.
JUST TRY NOT TO BREAK ANYTHING MORE THAN YOU ALREADY HAVE.
I TRUST YOUR GENIUS, HAROLD...
...LET'S JUST HOPE THAT LUCK PART WORKS OUT.

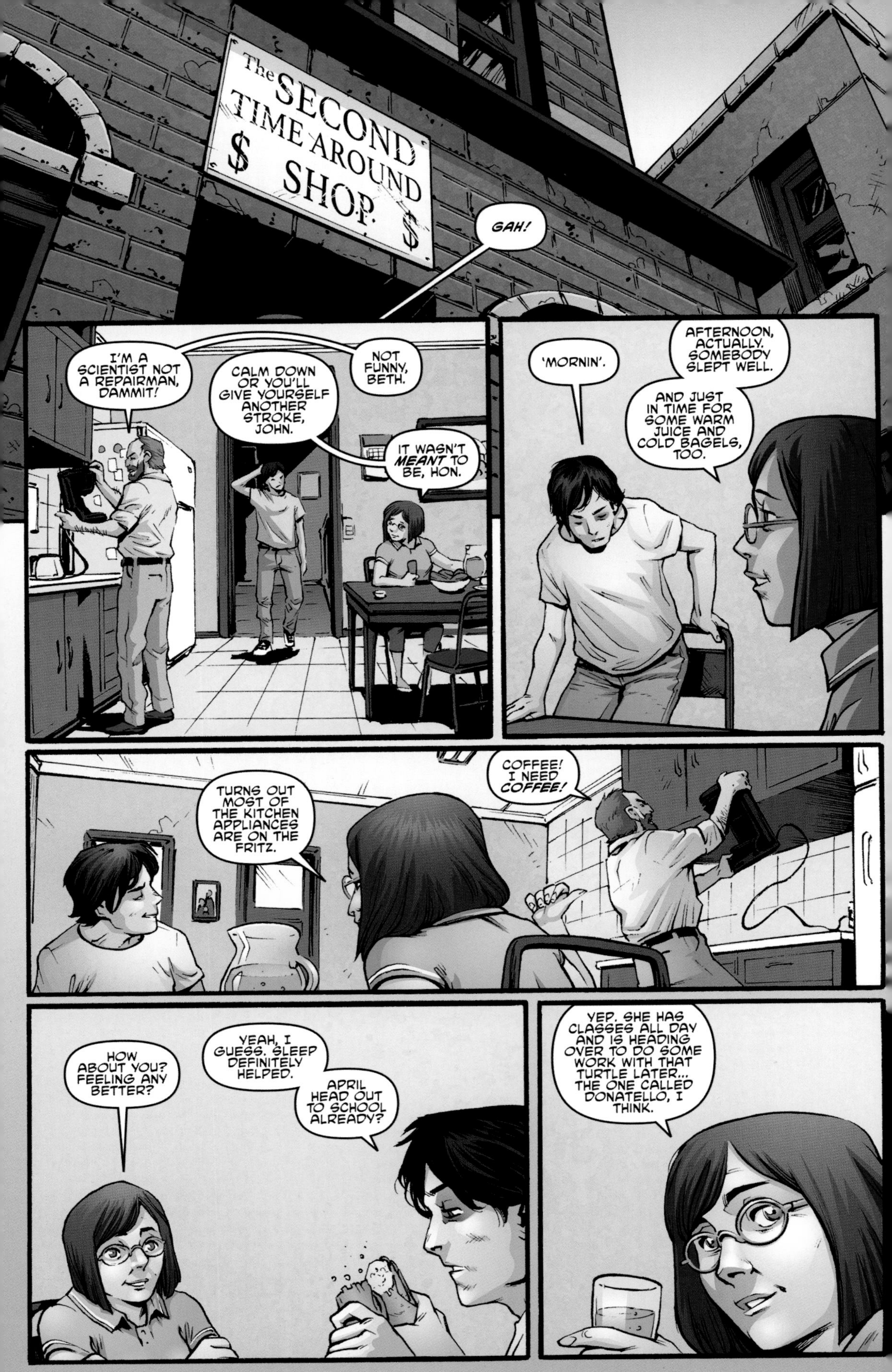
The
SECOND
TIME AROUND
$ SHOP $
GAH!
I'M A SCIENTIST NOT A REPAIRMAN, DAMMIT!
CALM DOWN OR YOU'LL GIVE YOURSELF ANOTHER STROKE, JOHN.
NOT FUNNY, BETH.
IT WASN'T *MEANT* TO BE, HON.
'MORNIN'.
AFTERNOON, ACTUALLY. SOMEBODY SLEPT WELL.
AND JUST IN TIME FOR SOME WARM JUICE AND COLD BAGELS, TOO.
TURNS OUT MOST OF THE KITCHEN APPLIANCES ARE ON THE FRITZ.
COFFEE! I NEED *COFFEE!*
HOW ABOUT YOU? FEELING ANY BETTER?
YEAH, I GUESS. SLEEP DEFINITELY HELPED.
APRIL HEAD OUT TO SCHOOL ALREADY?
YEP. SHE HAS CLASSES ALL DAY AND IS HEADING OVER TO DO SOME WORK WITH THAT TURTLE LATER... THE ONE CALLED DONATELLO, I THINK.

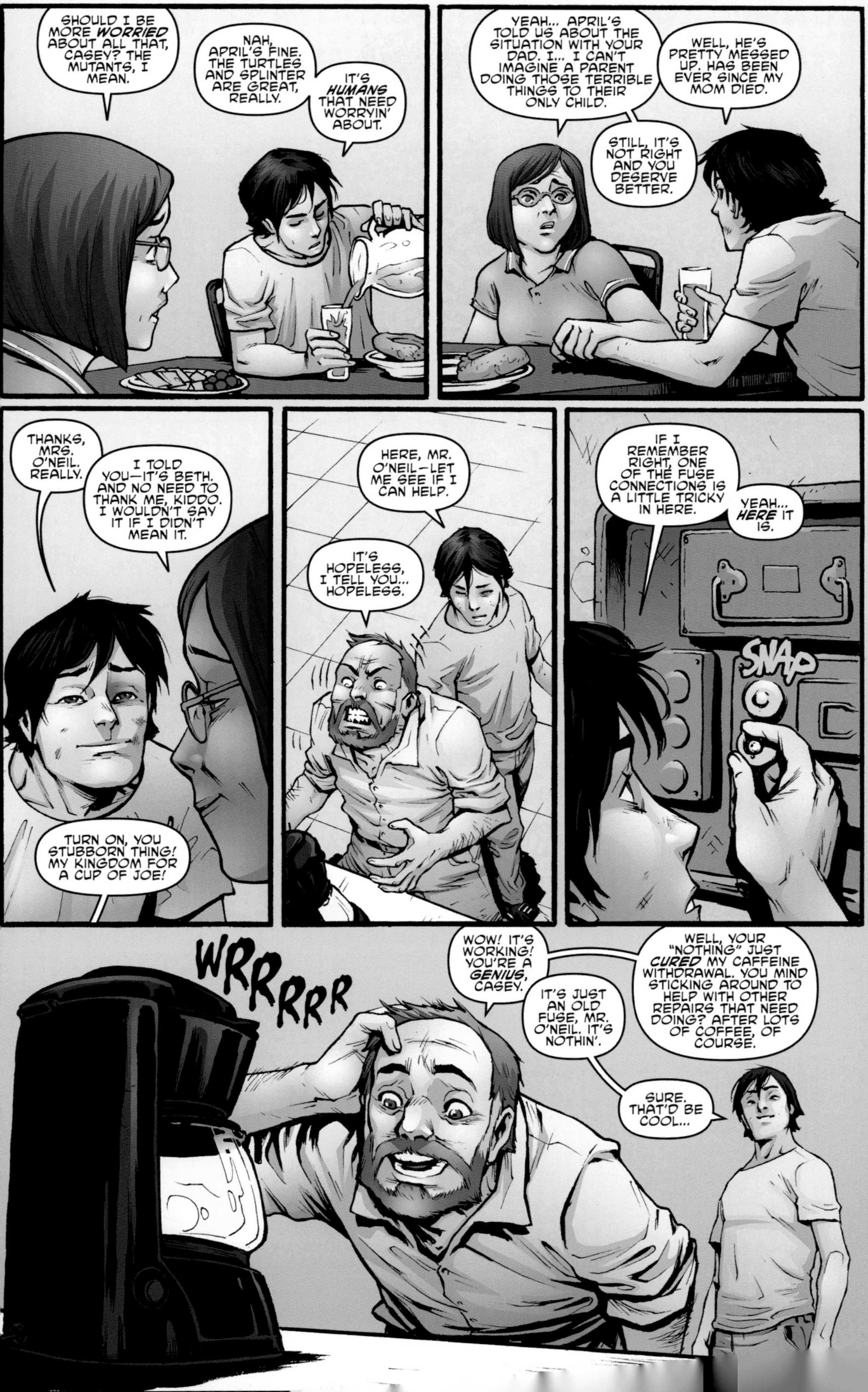
SHOULD I BE MORE WORRIED ABOUT ALL THAT, CASEY? THE MUTANTS, I MEAN.
NAH, APRIL'S FINE. THE TURTLES AND SPLINTER ARE GREAT, REALLY.
IT'S HUMANS THAT NEED WORRYIN' ABOUT.
YEAH... APRIL'S TOLD US ABOUT THE SITUATION WITH YOUR DAD. I... I CAN'T IMAGINE A PARENT DOING THOSE TERRIBLE THINGS TO THEIR ONLY CHILD.
WELL, HE'S PRETTY MESSED UP. HAS BEEN EVER SINCE MY MOM DIED.
STILL, IT'S NOT RIGHT AND YOU DESERVE BETTER.
THANKS, MRS. O'NEIL. REALLY.
I TOLD YOU—IT'S BETH. AND NO NEED TO THANK ME, KIDDO. I WOULDN'T SAY IT IF I DIDN'T MEAN IT.
TURN ON, YOU STUBBORN THING! MY KINGDOM FOR A CUP OF JOE!
HERE, MR. O'NEIL—LET ME SEE IF I CAN HELP.
IT'S HOPELESS, I TELL YOU... HOPELESS.
IF I REMEMBER RIGHT, ONE OF THE FUSE CONNECTIONS IS A LITTLE TRICKY IN HERE.
YEAH... HERE IT IS.
SNAP
WRRRRRR
WOW! IT'S WORKING! YOU'RE A GENIUS, CASEY.
IT'S JUST AN OLD FUSE, MR. O'NEIL. IT'S NOTHIN'.
WELL, YOUR "NOTHING" JUST CURED MY CAFFEINE WITHDRAWAL. YOU MIND STICKING AROUND TO HELP WITH OTHER REPAIRS THAT NEED DOING? AFTER LOTS OF COFFEE, OF COURSE.
SURE. THAT'D BE COOL...

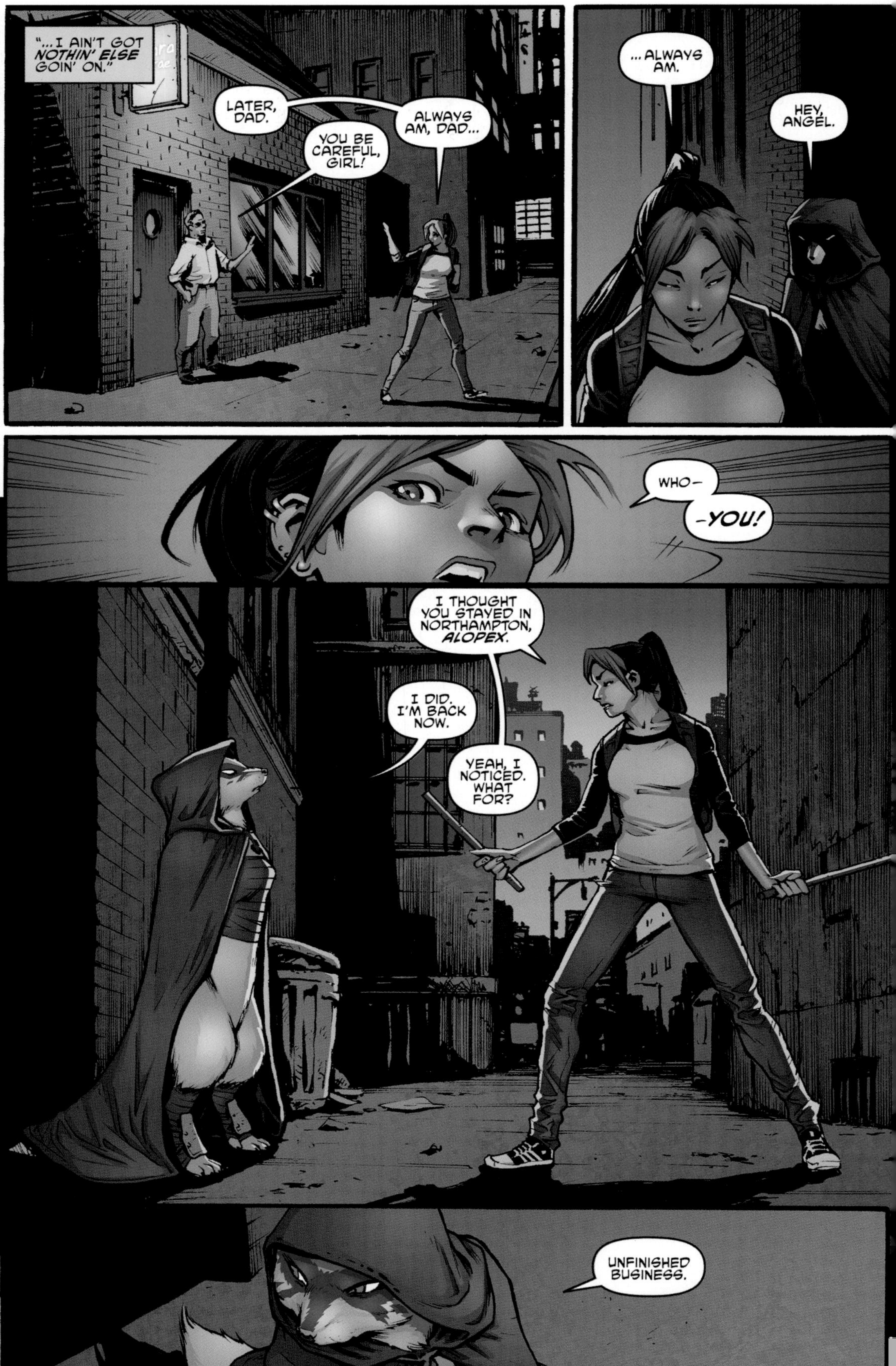
"...I AIN'T GOT *NOTHIN' ELSE* GOIN' ON."
LATER, DAD.
YOU BE CAREFUL, GIRL!
ALWAYS AM, DAD...
...ALWAYS AM.
HEY, ANGEL.
WHO-
-*YOU!*
I THOUGHT YOU STAYED IN NORTHAMPTON, *ALOPEX*.
I DID. I'M BACK NOW.
YEAH, I NOTICED. WHAT FOR?
UNFINISHED BUSINESS.

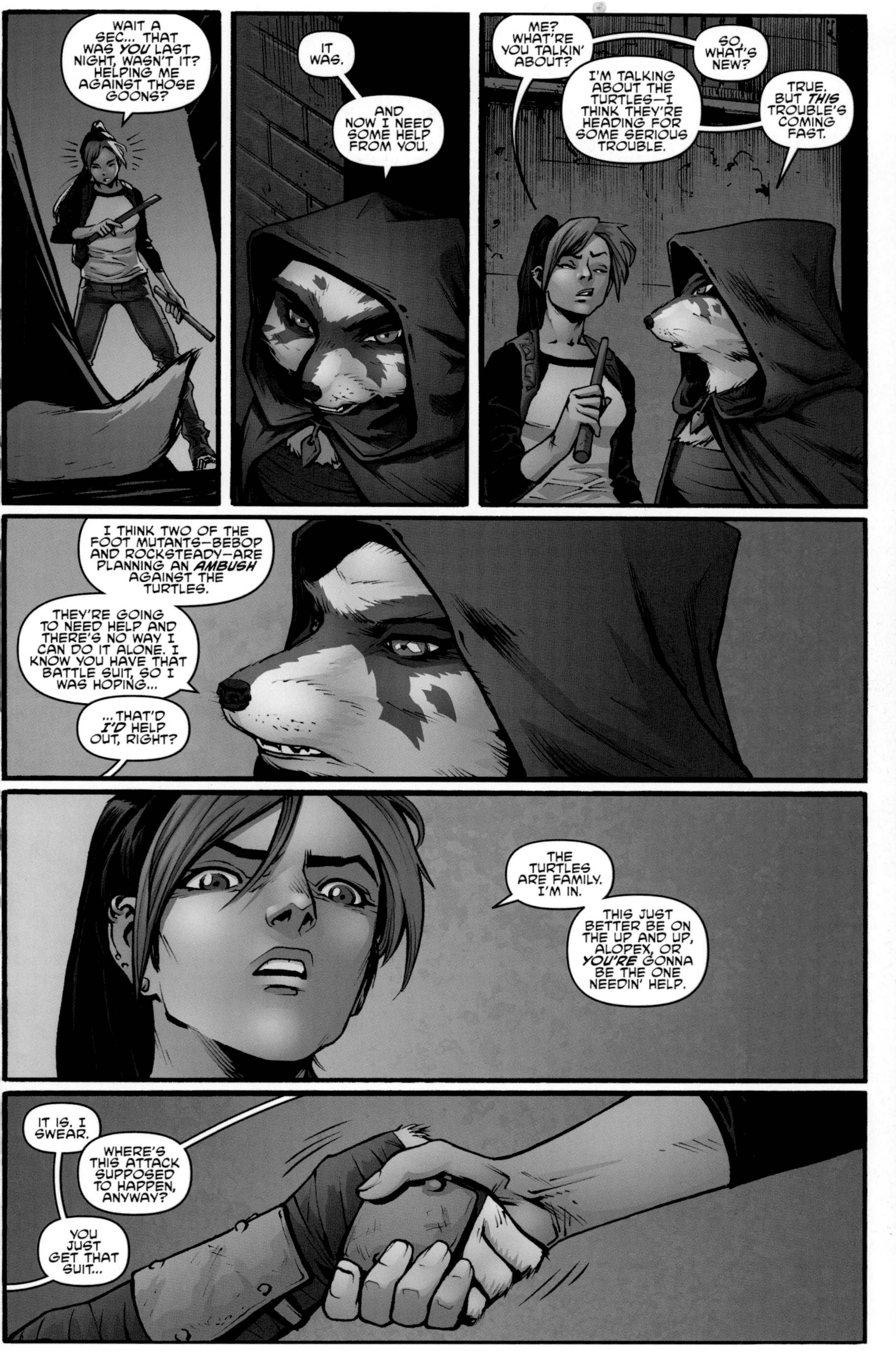
WAIT A SEC... THAT WAS YOU LAST NIGHT, WASN'T IT? HELPING ME AGAINST THOSE GOONS?
IT WAS.
AND NOW I NEED SOME HELP FROM YOU.
ME? WHAT'RE YOU TALKIN' ABOUT?
I'M TALKING ABOUT THE TURTLES—I THINK THEY'RE HEADING FOR SOME SERIOUS TROUBLE.
SO, WHAT'S NEW?
TRUE. BUT THIS TROUBLE'S COMING FAST.
I THINK TWO OF THE FOOT MUTANTS—BEBOP AND ROCKSTEADY—ARE PLANNING AN AMBUSH AGAINST THE TURTLES.
THEY'RE GOING TO NEED HELP AND THERE'S NO WAY I CAN DO IT ALONE. I KNOW YOU HAVE THAT BATTLE SUIT, SO I WAS HOPING...
...THAT'D I'D HELP OUT, RIGHT?
THE TURTLES ARE FAMILY. I'M IN.
THIS JUST BETTER BE ON THE UP AND UP, ALOPEX, OR YOU'RE GONNA BE THE ONE NEEDIN' HELP.
IT IS. I SWEAR.
WHERE'S THIS ATTACK SUPPOSED TO HAPPEN, ANYWAY?
YOU JUST GET THAT SUIT...

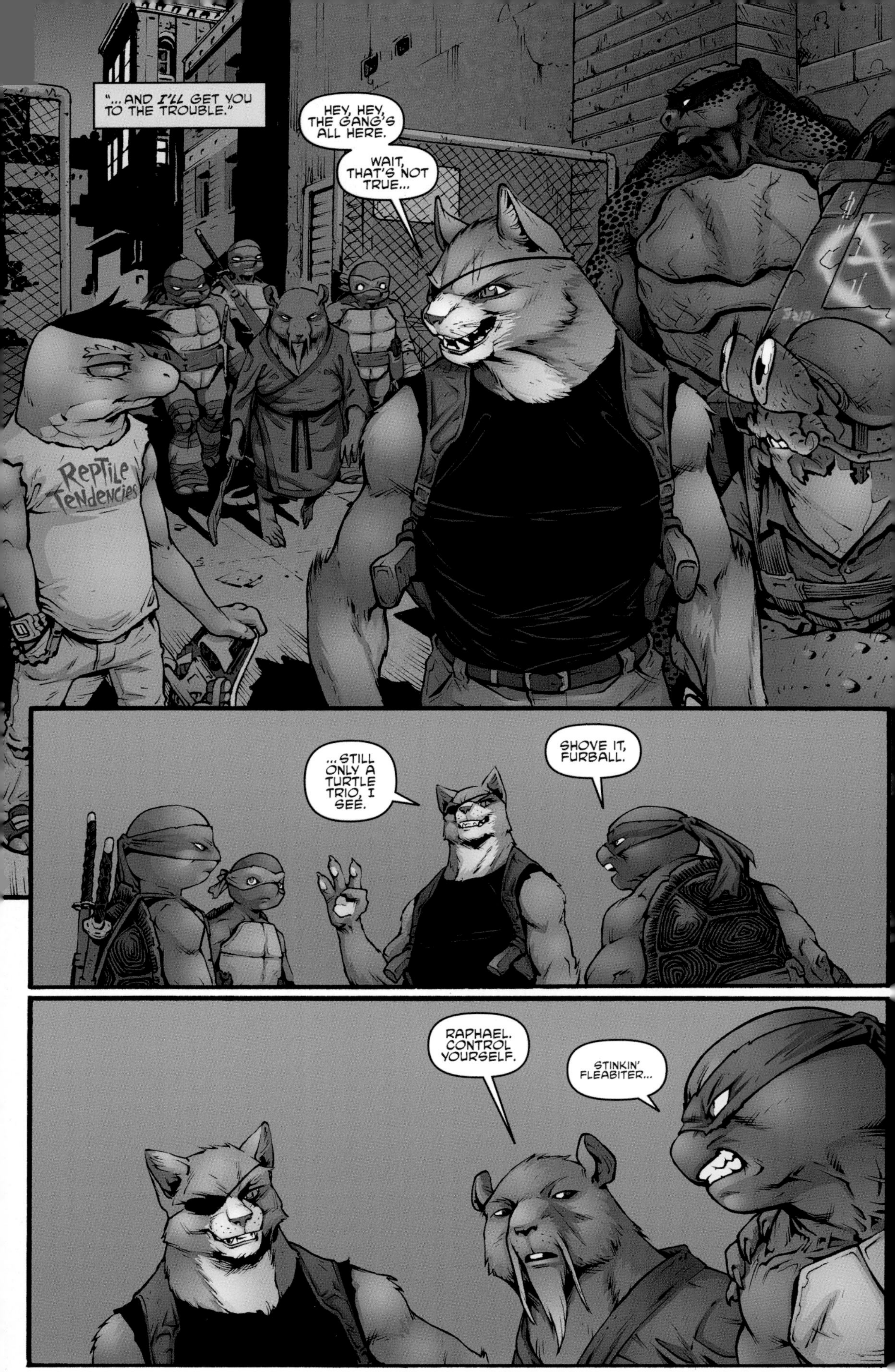
"...AND I'LL GET YOU TO THE TROUBLE."
HEY, HEY, THE GANG'S ALL HERE.
WAIT, THAT'S NOT TRUE...
Reptile Tendencies
...STILL ONLY A TURTLE TRIO, I SEE.
SHOVE IT, FURBALL.
RAPHAEL. CONTROL YOURSELF.
STINKIN' FLEABITER...

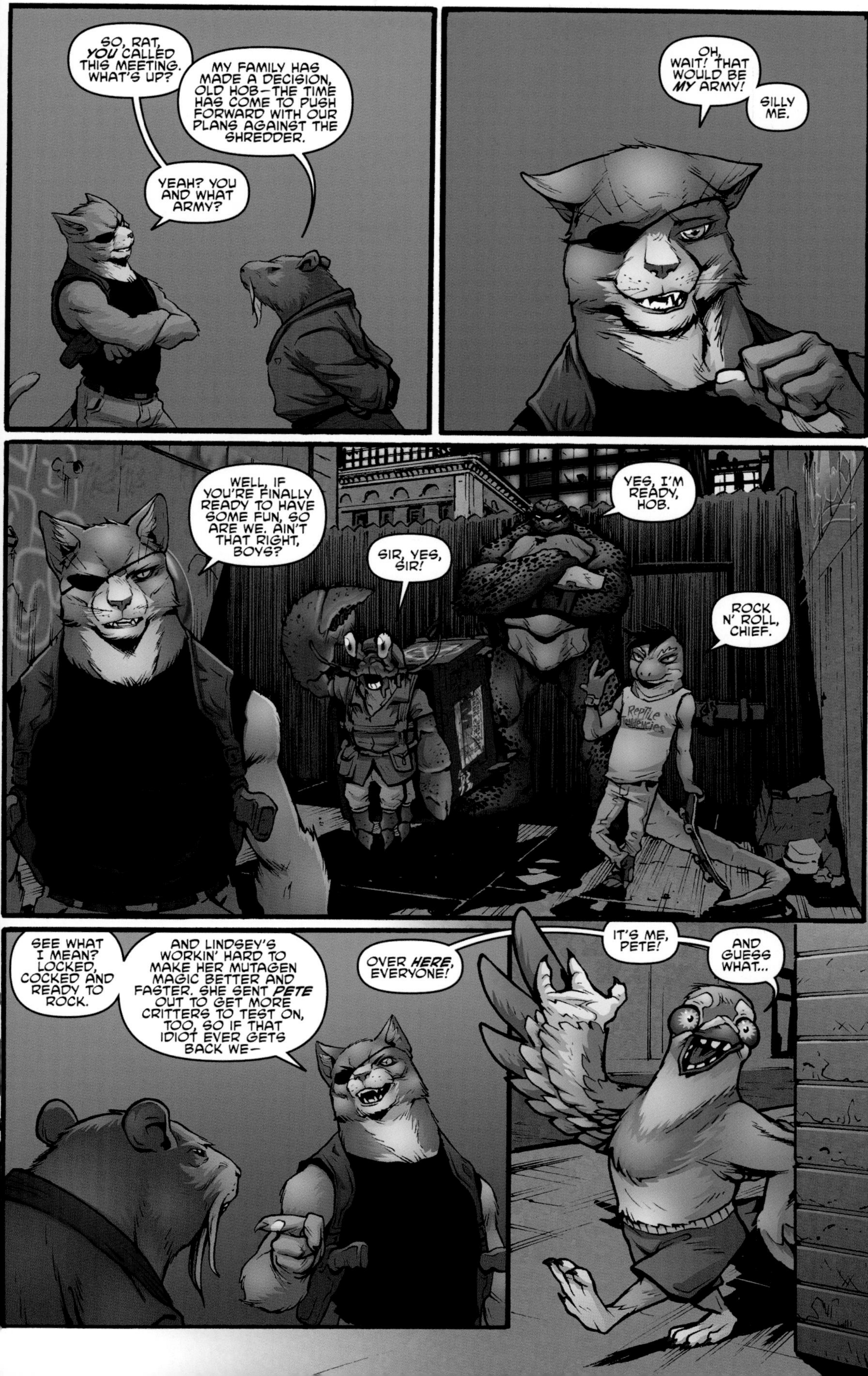
SO, RAT, YOU CALLED THIS MEETING. WHAT'S UP?
MY FAMILY HAS MADE A DECISION, OLD HOB—THE TIME HAS COME TO PUSH FORWARD WITH OUR PLANS AGAINST THE SHREDDER.
YEAH? YOU AND WHAT ARMY?
OH, WAIT! THAT WOULD BE MY ARMY!
SILLY ME.
WELL, IF YOU'RE FINALLY READY TO HAVE SOME FUN, SO ARE WE. AIN'T THAT RIGHT, BOYS?
SIR, YES, SIR!
YES, I'M READY, HOB.
ROCK N' ROLL, CHIEF.
Reptile Tendencies
SEE WHAT I MEAN? LOCKED, COCKED AND READY TO ROCK.
AND LINDSEY'S WORKIN' HARD TO MAKE HER MUTAGEN MAGIC BETTER AND FASTER. SHE SENT PETE OUT TO GET MORE CRITTERS TO TEST ON, TOO, SO IF THAT IDIOT EVER GETS BACK WE—
OVER HERE, EVERYONE!
IT'S ME, PETE!
AND GUESS WHAT...

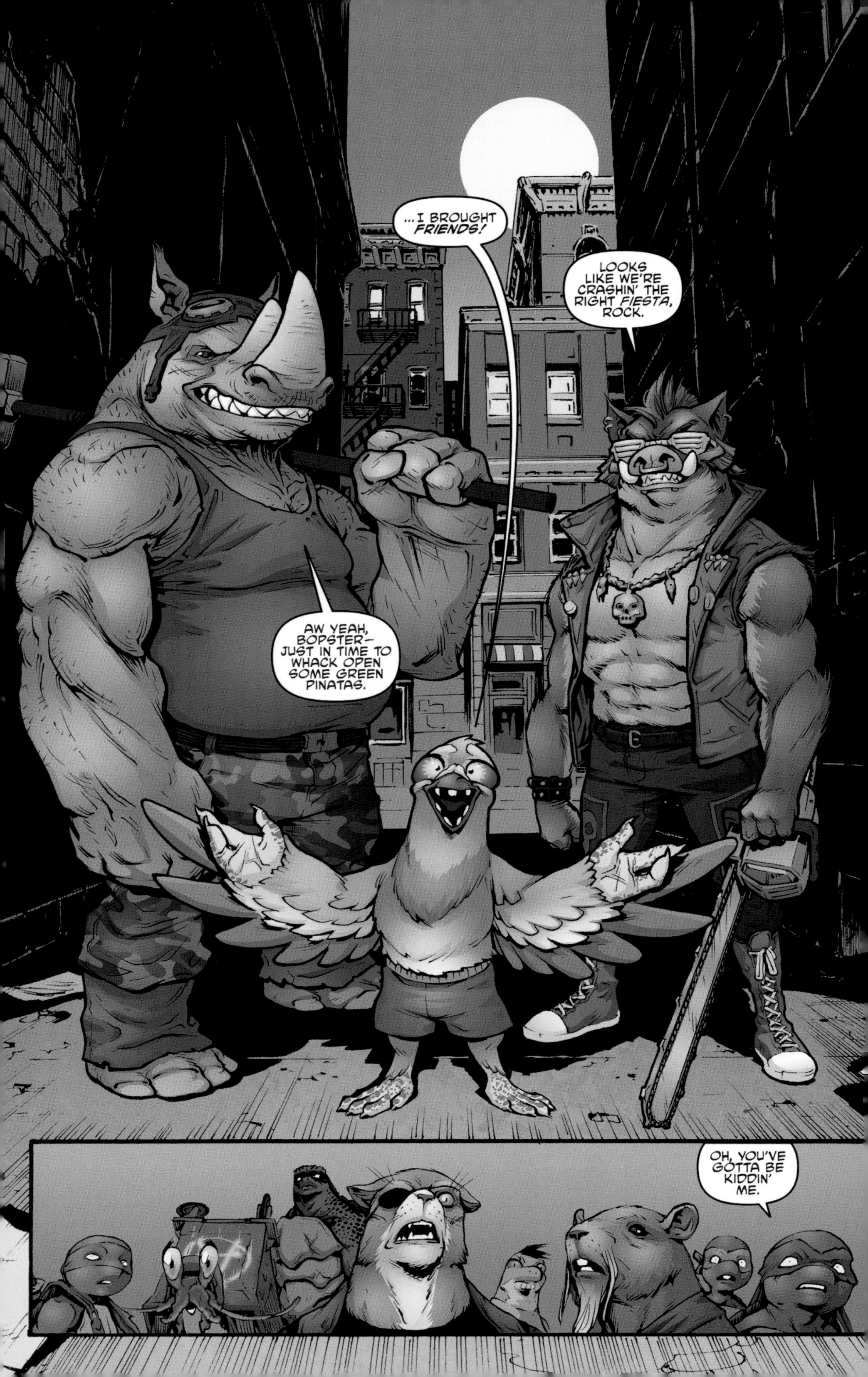
...I BROUGHT *FRIENDS!*
LOOKS LIKE WE'RE CRASHIN' THE RIGHT *FIESTA*, ROCK.
AW YEAH, BOPSTER– JUST IN TIME TO WHACK OPEN SOME GREEN PINATAS.
OH, YOU'VE GOTTA BE KIDDIN' ME.

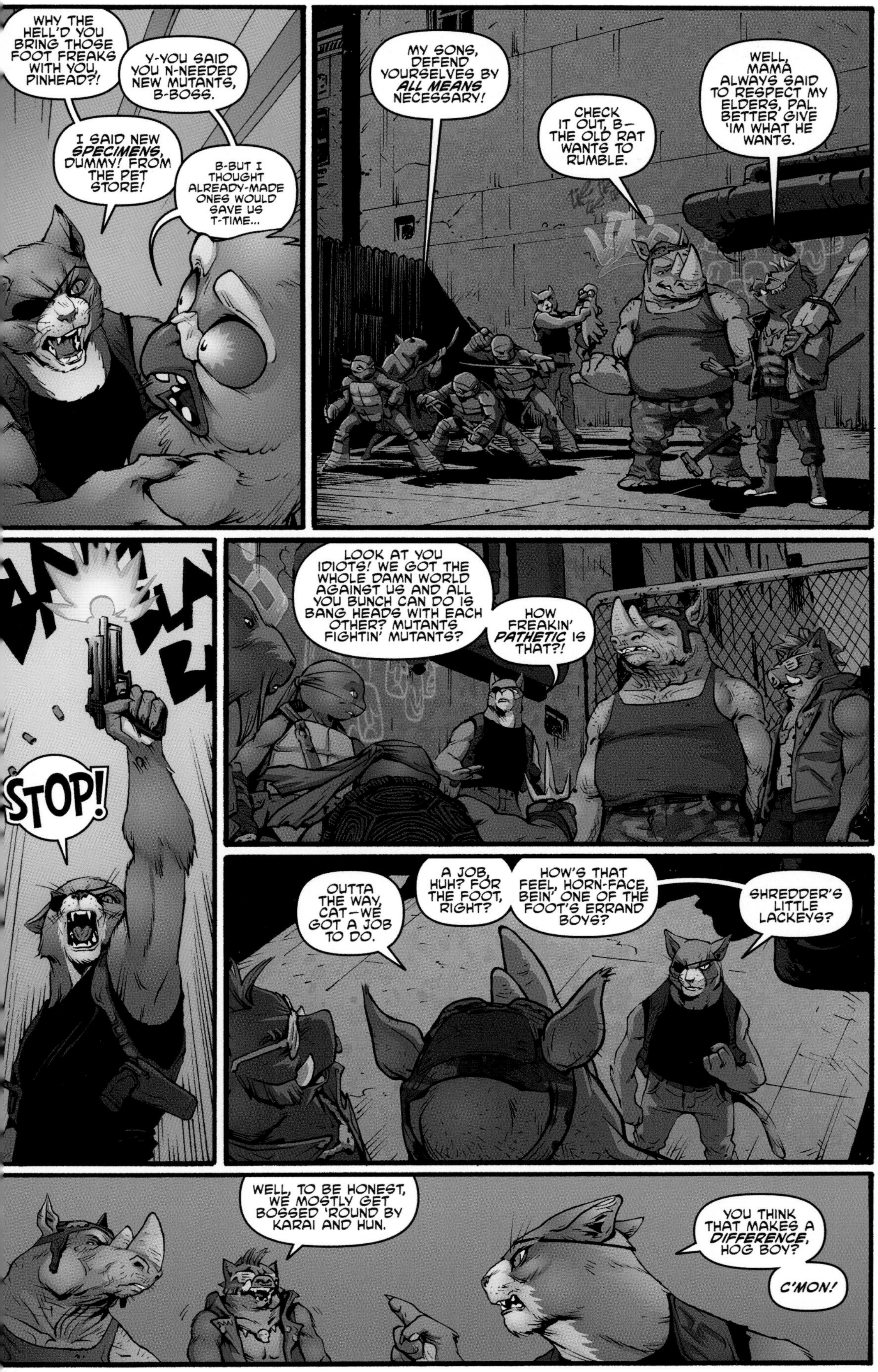
WHY THE HELL'D YOU BRING THOSE FOOT FREAKS WITH YOU, PINHEAD?!
Y-YOU SAID YOU N-NEEDED NEW MUTANTS, B-BOSS.
I SAID NEW *SPECIMENS*, DUMMY! FROM THE PET STORE!
B-BUT I THOUGHT ALREADY-MADE ONES WOULD SAVE US T-TIME...
MY SONS, DEFEND YOURSELVES BY *ALL MEANS* NECESSARY!
CHECK IT OUT, B— THE OLD RAT WANTS TO RUMBLE.
WELL, MAMA ALWAYS SAID TO RESPECT MY ELDERS, PAL. BETTER GIVE 'IM WHAT HE WANTS.
STOP!
LOOK AT YOU IDIOTS! WE GOT THE WHOLE DAMN WORLD AGAINST US AND ALL YOU BUNCH CAN DO IS BANG HEADS WITH EACH OTHER? MUTANTS FIGHTIN' MUTANTS?
HOW FREAKIN' *PATHETIC* IS THAT?!
OUTTA THE WAY, CAT—WE GOT A JOB TO DO.
A JOB, HUH? FOR THE FOOT, RIGHT?
HOW'S THAT FEEL, HORN-FACE, BEIN' ONE OF THE FOOT'S ERRAND BOYS?
SHREDDER'S LITTLE LACKEYS?
WELL, TO BE HONEST, WE MOSTLY GET BOSSED 'ROUND BY KARAI AND HUN.
YOU THINK THAT MAKES A *DIFFERENCE*, HOG BOY?
C'MON!

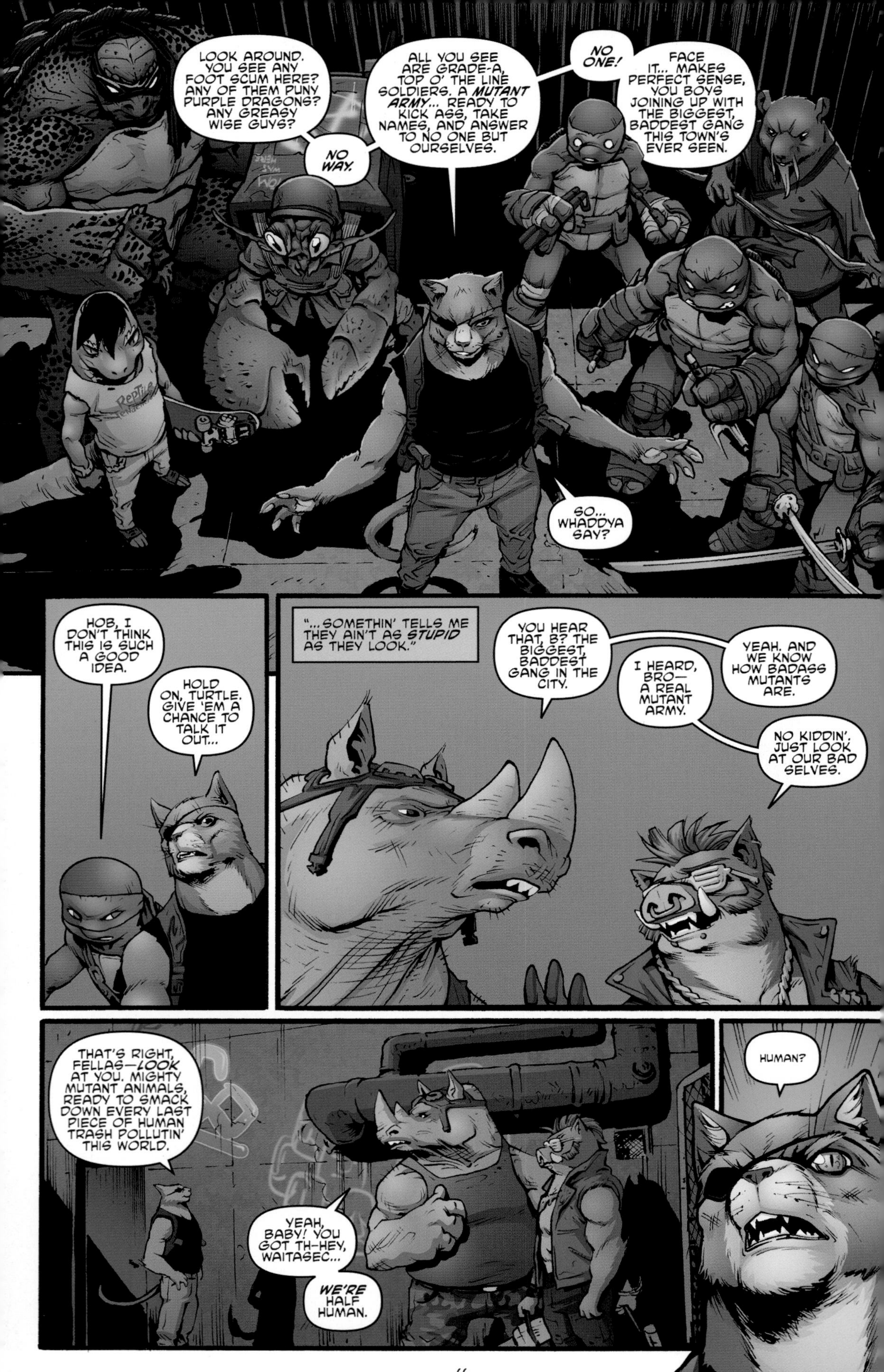
LOOK AROUND. YOU SEE ANY FOOT SCUM HERE? ANY OF THEM PUNY PURPLE DRAGONS? ANY GREASY WISE GUYS?
NO WAY.
ALL YOU SEE ARE GRADE-A, TOP O' THE LINE SOLDIERS. A MUTANT ARMY... READY TO KICK ASS, TAKE NAMES, AND ANSWER TO NO ONE BUT OURSELVES.
NO ONE!
FACE IT... MAKES PERFECT SENSE, YOU BOYS JOINING UP WITH THE BIGGEST, BADDEST GANG THIS TOWN'S EVER SEEN.
SO... WHADDYA SAY?
HOB, I DON'T THINK THIS IS SUCH A GOOD IDEA.
HOLD ON, TURTLE. GIVE 'EM A CHANCE TO TALK IT OUT...
"...SOMETHIN' TELLS ME THEY AIN'T AS STUPID AS THEY LOOK."
YOU HEAR THAT, B? THE BIGGEST, BADDEST GANG IN THE CITY.
I HEARD, BRO— A REAL MUTANT ARMY.
YEAH. AND WE KNOW HOW BADASS MUTANTS ARE.
NO KIDDIN'. JUST LOOK AT OUR BAD SELVES.
THAT'S RIGHT, FELLAS—LOOK AT YOU. MIGHTY MUTANT ANIMALS, READY TO SMACK DOWN EVERY LAST PIECE OF HUMAN TRASH POLLUTIN' THIS WORLD.
YEAH, BABY! YOU GOT TH-HEY, WAITASEC...
WE'RE HALF HUMAN.
HUMAN?

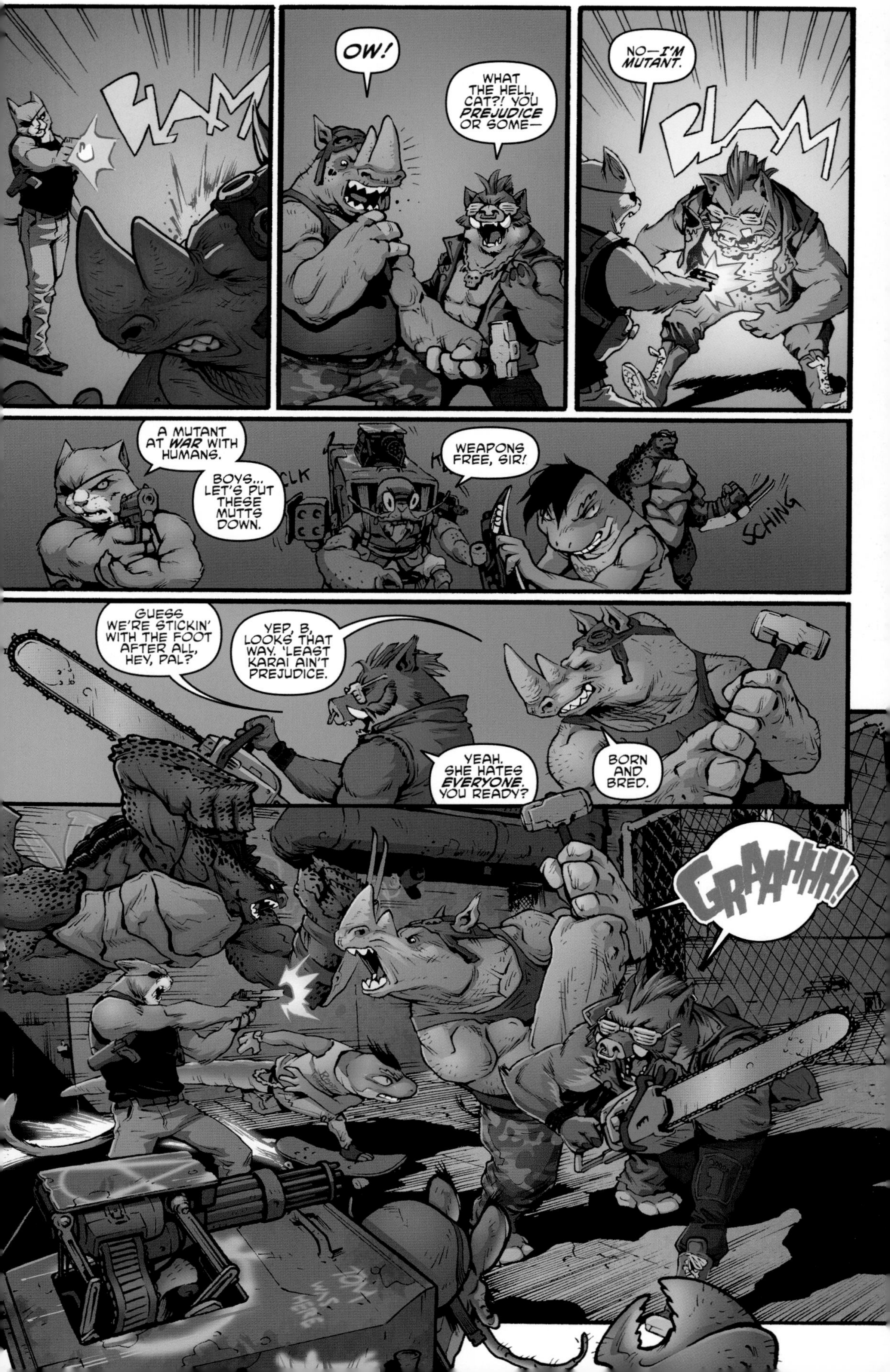
WAM
OW!
WHAT THE HELL, CAT?! YOU PREJUDICE OR SOME—
NO—I'M MUTANT.
BLAM
A MUTANT AT WAR WITH HUMANS.
BOYS... LET'S PUT THESE MUTTS DOWN.
CLK
WEAPONS FREE, SIR!
SCHING
GUESS WE'RE STICKIN' WITH THE FOOT AFTER ALL, HEY, PAL?
YEP, B, LOOKS THAT WAY. 'LEAST KARAI AIN'T PREJUDICE.
YEAH. SHE HATES EVERYONE. YOU READY?
BORN AND BRED.
GRAAHHH!

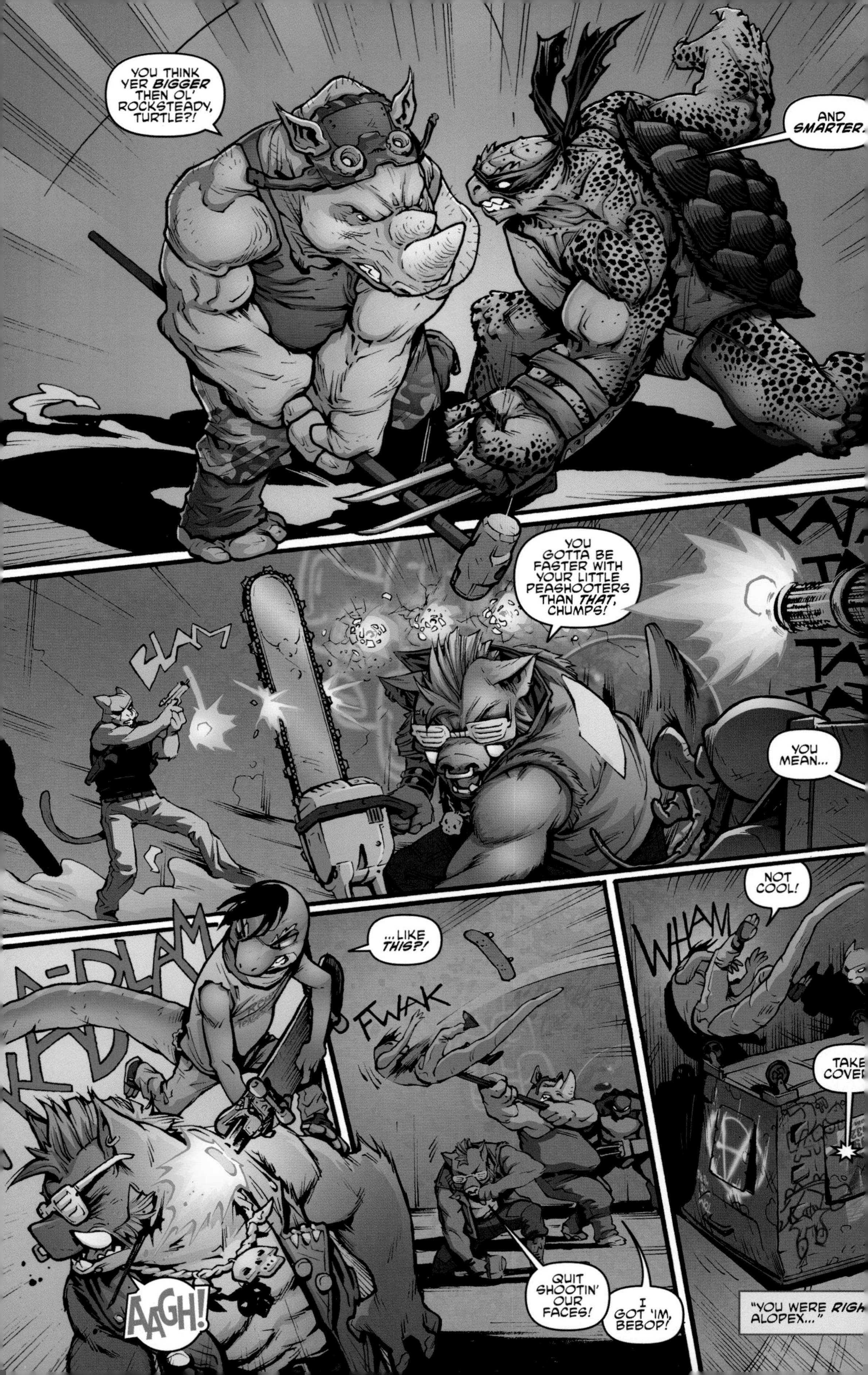

YOU THINK YER BIGGER THEN OL' ROCKSTEADY, TURTLE?!
AND SMARTER.
YOU GOTTA BE FASTER WITH YOUR LITTLE PEASHOOTERS THAN THAT, CHUMPS!
BLAM
YOU MEAN...
...LIKE THIS?!
FWAK
AAGH!
QUIT SHOOTIN' OUR FACES!
I GOT 'IM, BEBOP!
NOT COOL!
WHAM
TAKE COVE
"YOU WERE RIGH ALOPEX..."

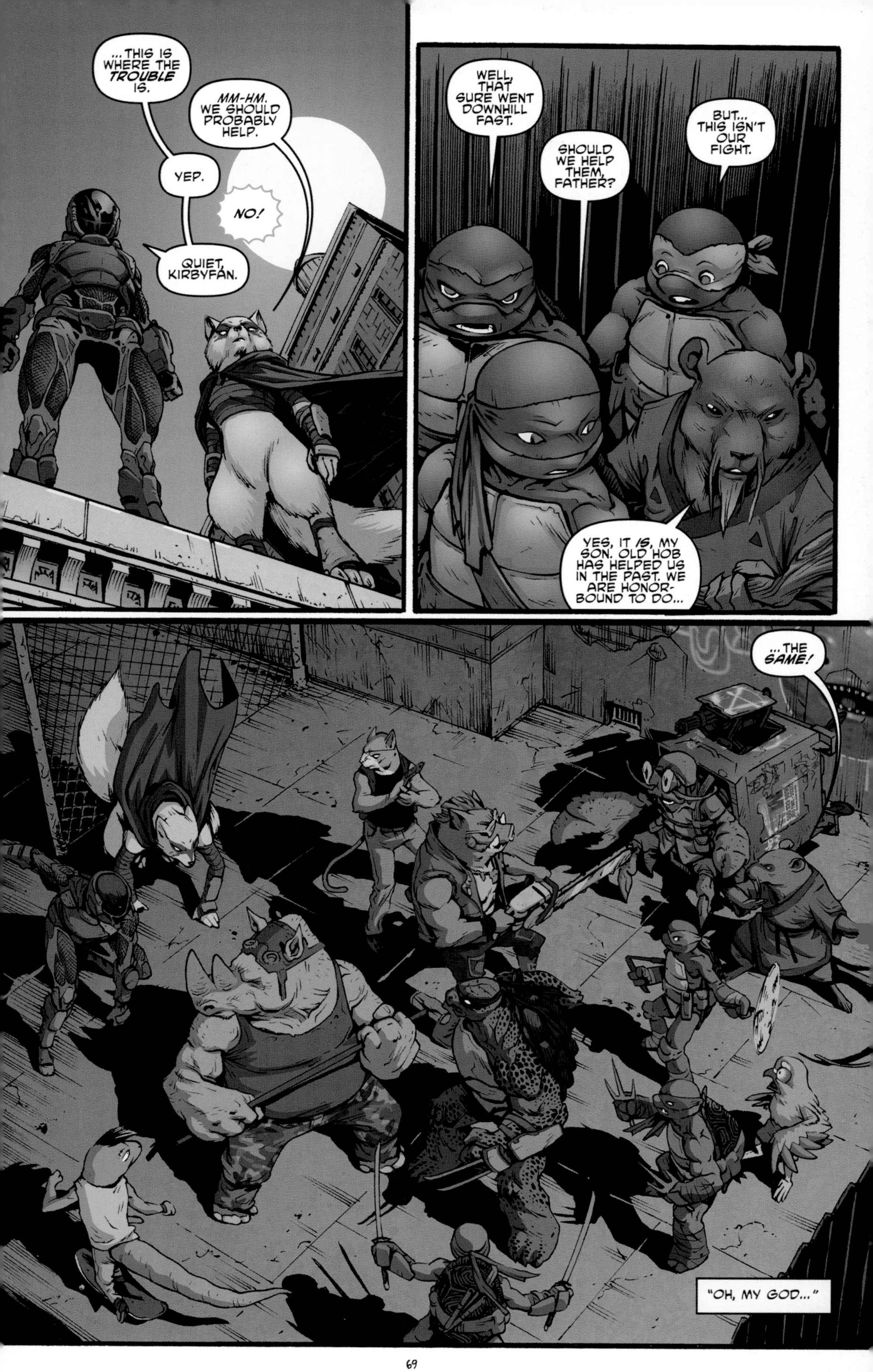
...THIS IS WHERE THE *TROUBLE* IS.
MM-HM. WE SHOULD PROBABLY HELP.
YEP.
NO!
QUIET, KIRBYFAN.
WELL, THAT SURE WENT DOWNHILL FAST.
SHOULD WE HELP THEM, FATHER?
BUT... THIS ISN'T OUR FIGHT.
YES, IT *IS*, MY SON. OLD HOB HAS HELPED US IN THE PAST. WE ARE HONOR-BOUND TO DO...
...THE *SAME!*
"OH, MY GOD..."

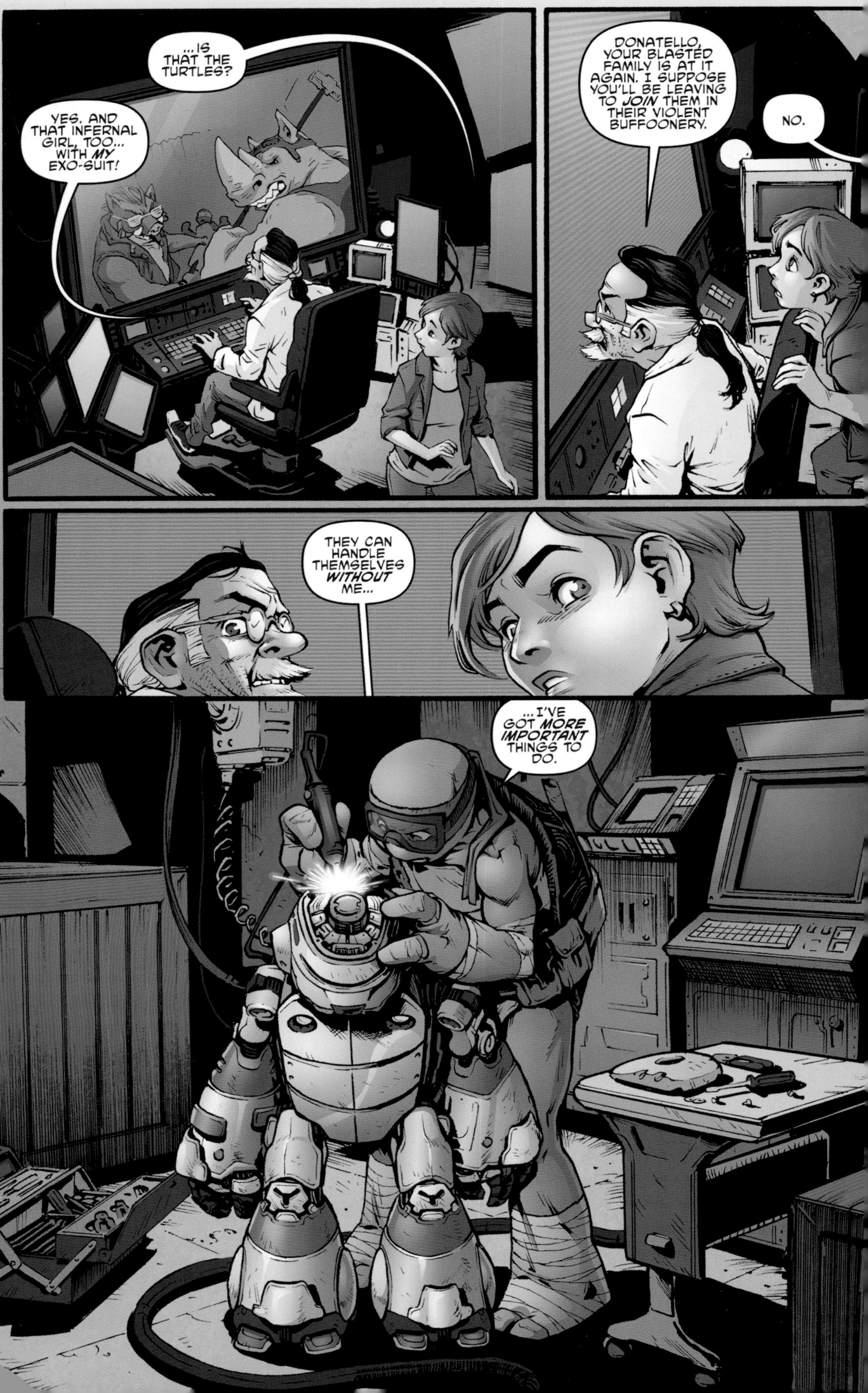
...IS THAT THE TURTLES?
YES. AND THAT INFERNAL GIRL, TOO... WITH *MY* EXO-SUIT!
DONATELLO, YOUR BLASTED FAMILY IS AT IT AGAIN. I SUPPOSE YOU'LL BE LEAVING TO *JOIN* THEM IN THEIR VIOLENT BUFFOONERY.
NO.
THEY CAN HANDLE THEMSELVES *WITHOUT* ME...
...I'VE GOT *MORE IMPORTANT* THINGS TO DO.

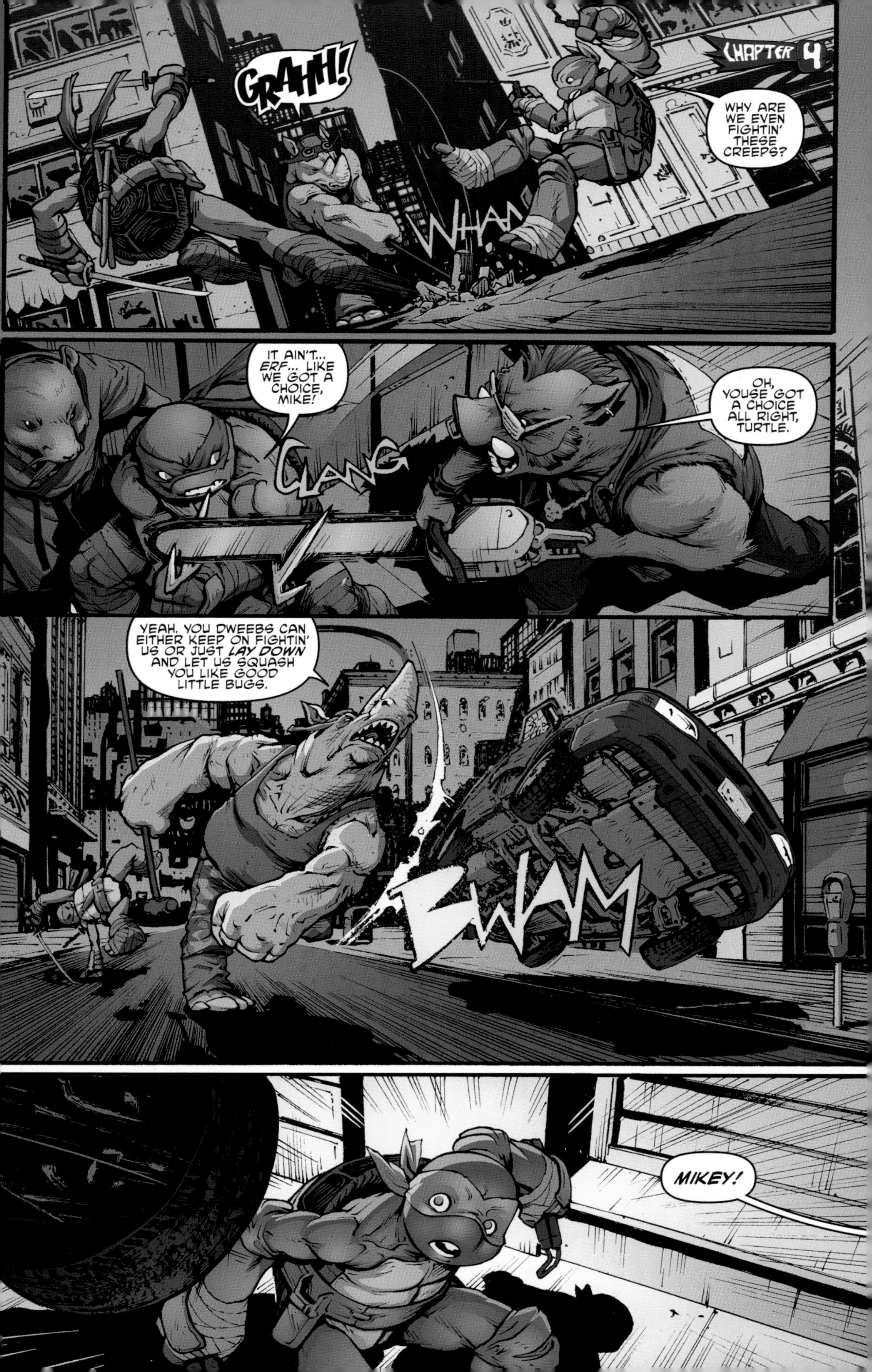
CHAPTER 4
GRAHH!
WHY ARE WE EVEN FIGHTIN' THESE CREEPS?
WHAM
IT AIN'T... ERF... LIKE WE GOT A CHOICE, MIKE!
CLANG
OH, YOUSE GOT A CHOICE ALL RIGHT, TURTLE.
YEAH. YOU DWEEBS CAN EITHER KEEP ON FIGHTIN' US OR JUST LAY DOWN AND LET US SQUASH YOU LIKE GOOD LITTLE BUGS.
WAM
MIKEY!

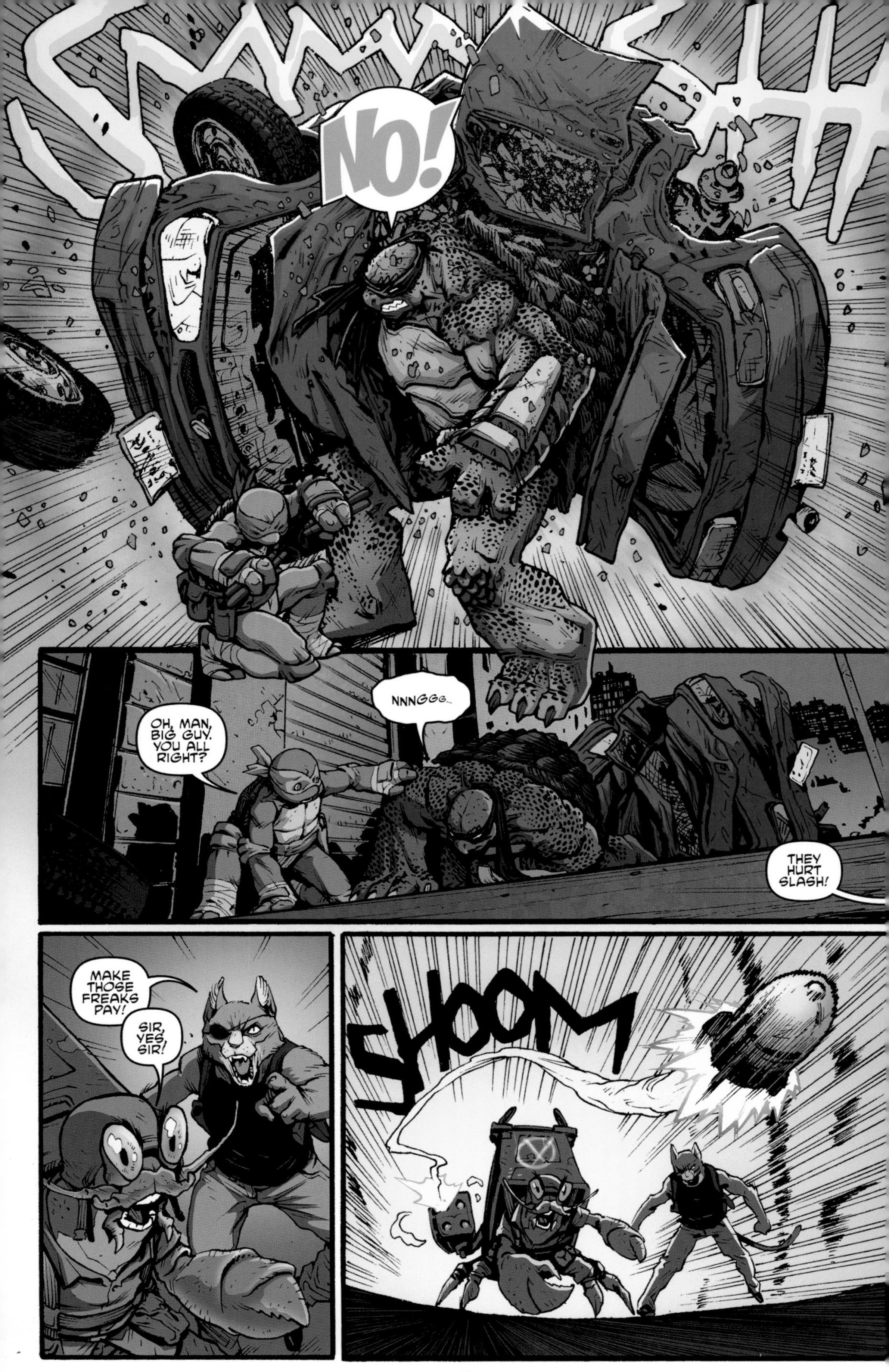

SMASH
NO!
OH, MAN, BIG GUY. YOU ALL RIGHT?
NNNGGG...
THEY HURT SLASH!
MAKE THOSE FREAKS PAY!
SIR, YES, SIR!
SHOOM

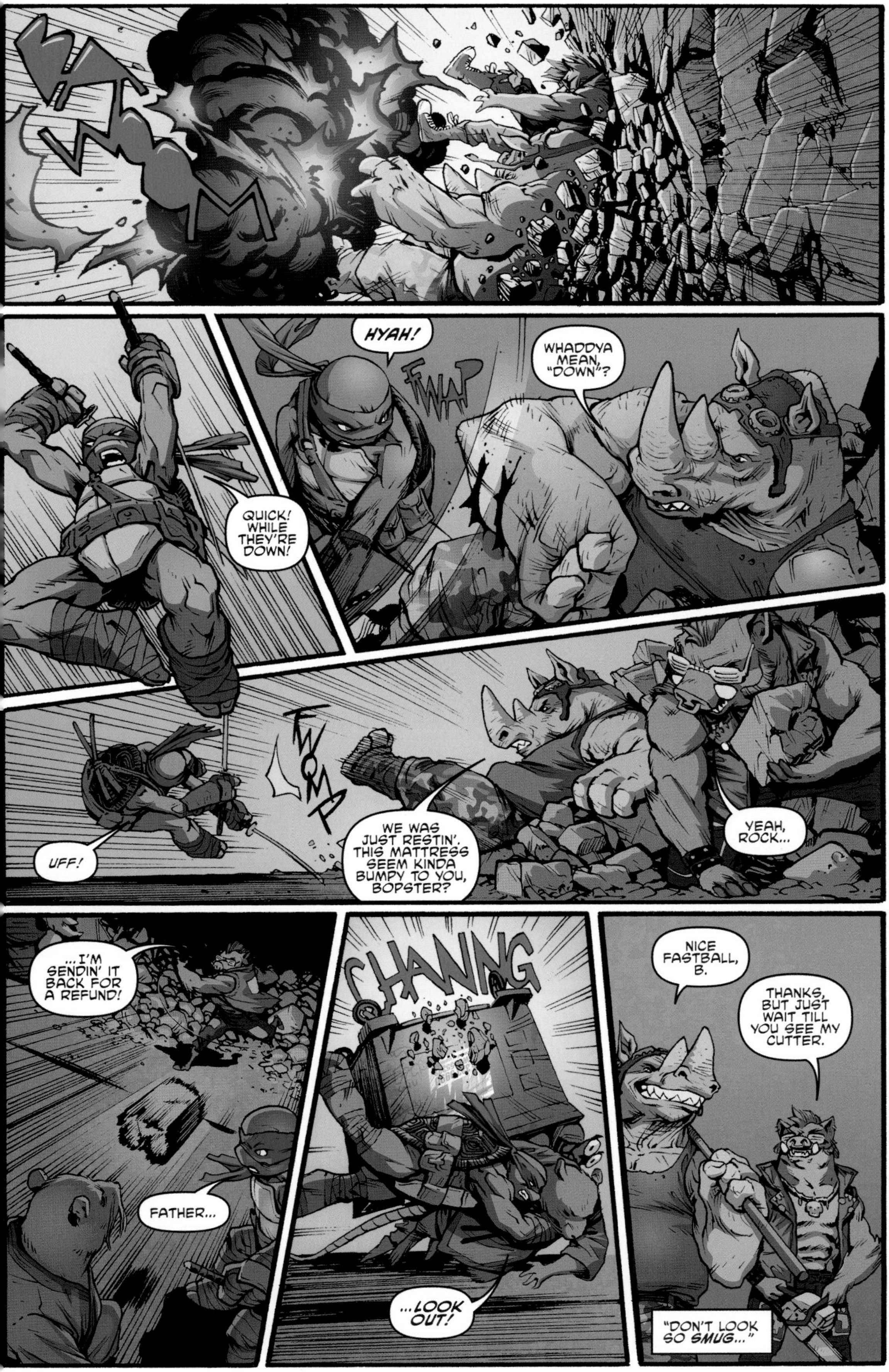

WHAMM
QUICK! WHILE THEY'RE DOWN!
HYAH!
FWAP
WHADDYA MEAN, "DOWN"?
FWOMP
UFF!
WE WAS JUST RESTIN'. THIS MATTRESS SEEM KINDA BUMPY TO YOU, BOPSTER?
YEAH, ROCK...
...I'M SENDIN' IT BACK FOR A REFUND!
FATHER...
CHANNG
...LOOK OUT!
NICE FASTBALL, B.
THANKS, BUT JUST WAIT TILL YOU SEE MY CUTTER.
"DON'T LOOK SO SMUG..."

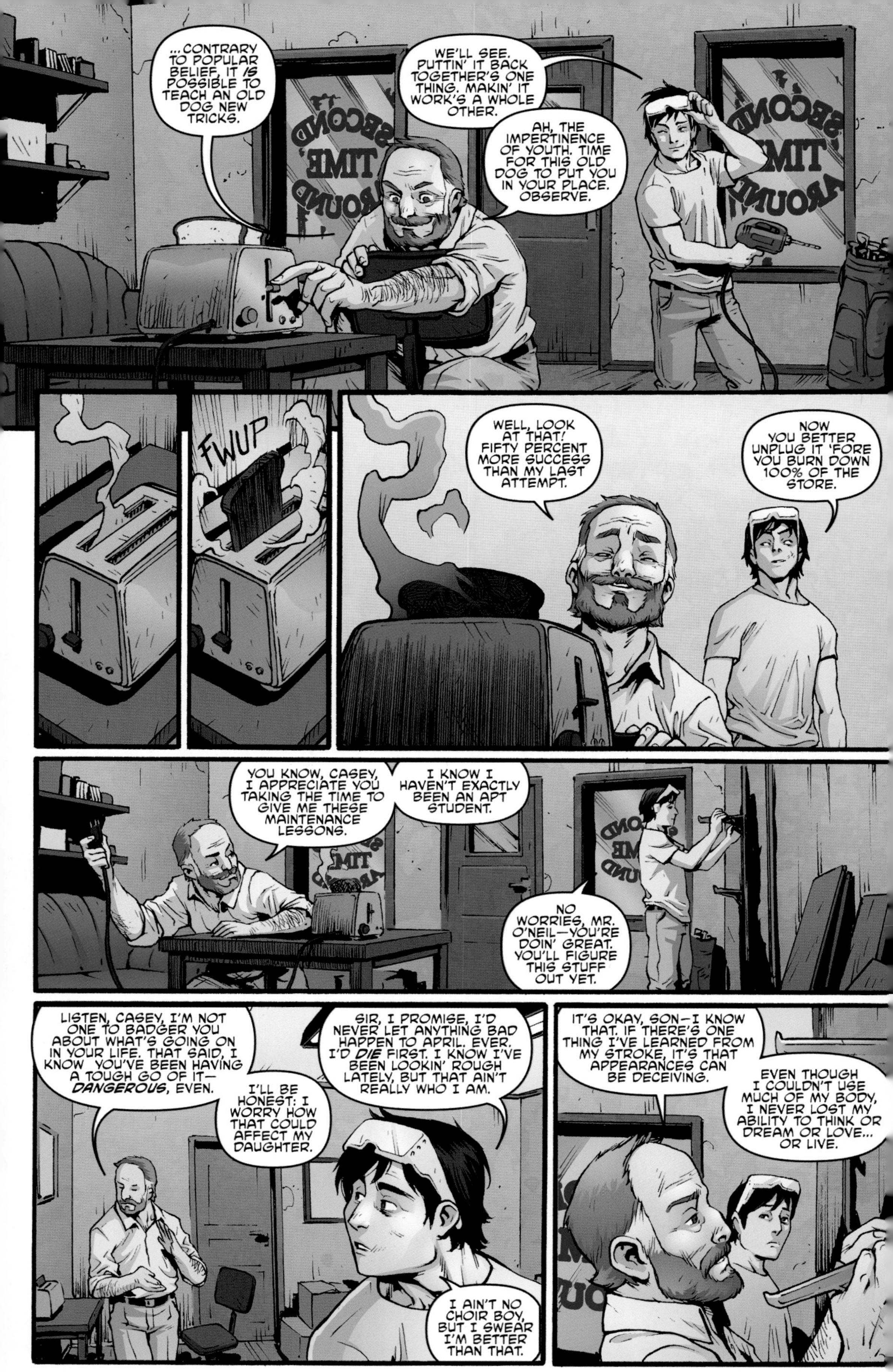
...CONTRARY TO POPULAR BELIEF, IT IS POSSIBLE TO TEACH AN OLD DOG NEW TRICKS.
WE'LL SEE. PUTTIN' IT BACK TOGETHER'S ONE THING. MAKIN' IT WORK'S A WHOLE OTHER.
AH, THE IMPERTINENCE OF YOUTH. TIME FOR THIS OLD DOG TO PUT YOU IN YOUR PLACE. OBSERVE.
SECOND TIME AROUND
FWUP
WELL, LOOK AT THAT! FIFTY PERCENT MORE SUCCESS THAN MY LAST ATTEMPT.
NOW YOU BETTER UNPLUG IT 'FORE YOU BURN DOWN 100% OF THE STORE.
YOU KNOW, CASEY, I APPRECIATE YOU TAKING THE TIME TO GIVE ME THESE MAINTENANCE LESSONS.
I KNOW I HAVEN'T EXACTLY BEEN AN APT STUDENT.
NO WORRIES, MR. O'NEIL—YOU'RE DOIN' GREAT. YOU'LL FIGURE THIS STUFF OUT YET.
LISTEN, CASEY, I'M NOT ONE TO BADGER YOU ABOUT WHAT'S GOING ON IN YOUR LIFE. THAT SAID, I KNOW YOU'VE BEEN HAVING A TOUGH GO OF IT—DANGEROUS, EVEN.
I'LL BE HONEST: I WORRY HOW THAT COULD AFFECT MY DAUGHTER.
SIR, I PROMISE, I'D NEVER LET ANYTHING BAD HAPPEN TO APRIL. EVER. I'D DIE FIRST. I KNOW I'VE BEEN LOOKIN' ROUGH LATELY, BUT THAT AIN'T REALLY WHO I AM.
I AIN'T NO CHOIR BOY, BUT I SWEAR I'M BETTER THAN THAT.
IT'S OKAY, SON—I KNOW THAT. IF THERE'S ONE THING I'VE LEARNED FROM MY STROKE, IT'S THAT APPEARANCES CAN BE DECEIVING.
EVEN THOUGH I COULDN'T USE MUCH OF MY BODY, I NEVER LOST MY ABILITY TO THINK OR DREAM OR LOVE... OR LIVE.

SO DESPITE THE OBVIOUS SETBACKS, I KNEW I STILL HAD SOMETHING TO OFFER THIS WORLD AND I NEVER ONCE THOUGHT ABOUT GIVING UP...

...NEVER ONCE STOPPED MOVING FORWARD.

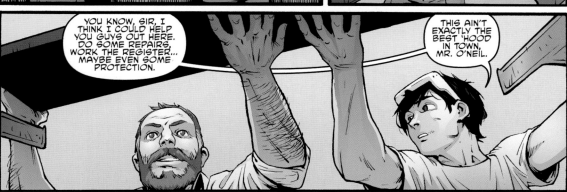

YOU KNOW, SIR, I THINK I COULD HELP YOU GUYS OUT HERE. DO SOME REPAIRS, WORK THE REGISTER... MAYBE EVEN SOME PROTECTION.

THIS AIN'T EXACTLY THE BEST 'HOOD IN TOWN, MR. O'NEIL.

WELL, WE CAN'T PAY YOU YET, BUT WE CAN GIVE YOU ROOM AND BOARD... AND A REAL WAGE WHEN WE START MAKING MONEY.

HELP US GET THE STORE UP AND RUNNING THE RIGHT WAY.

WE'LL HANDLE THE ADMINISTRATIVE STUFF AND LEAVE THE PRACTICAL MATTERS TO YOU.

AND THOUGH I LOATHE VIOLENCE, I'D ALSO BE *LYING* IF I DENIED HAVING A CAPABLE FIGHTER ON-SITE WOULD HELP THIS OLD SCIENTIST SLEEP EASIER AT NIGHT.

SO WHAT DO YOU SAY, SON... YOU READY TO OFFICIALLY JOIN THE SECOND TIME AROUND TEAM?

YOU DON'T EVEN GOTTA ASK, MR. O'NEIL...

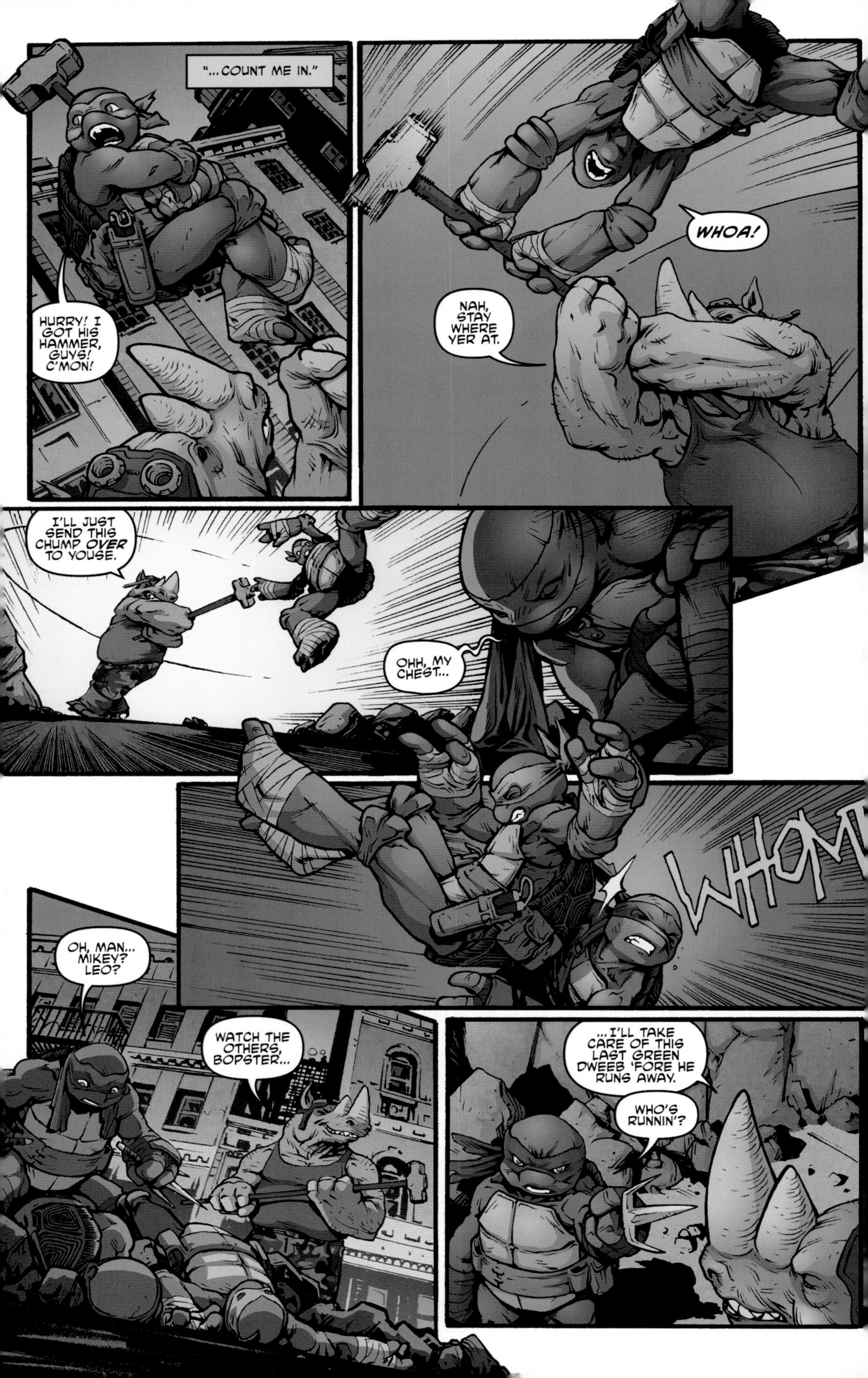
"...COUNT ME IN."
HURRY! I GOT HIS HAMMER, GUYS! C'MON!
WHOA!
NAH, STAY WHERE YER AT.
I'LL JUST SEND THIS CHUMP OVER TO YOUSE.
OHH, MY CHEST...
WHOM
OH, MAN... MIKEY? LEO?
WATCH THE OTHERS, BOPSTER...
...I'LL TAKE CARE OF THIS LAST GREEN DWEEB 'FORE HE RUNS AWAY.
WHO'S RUNNIN'?

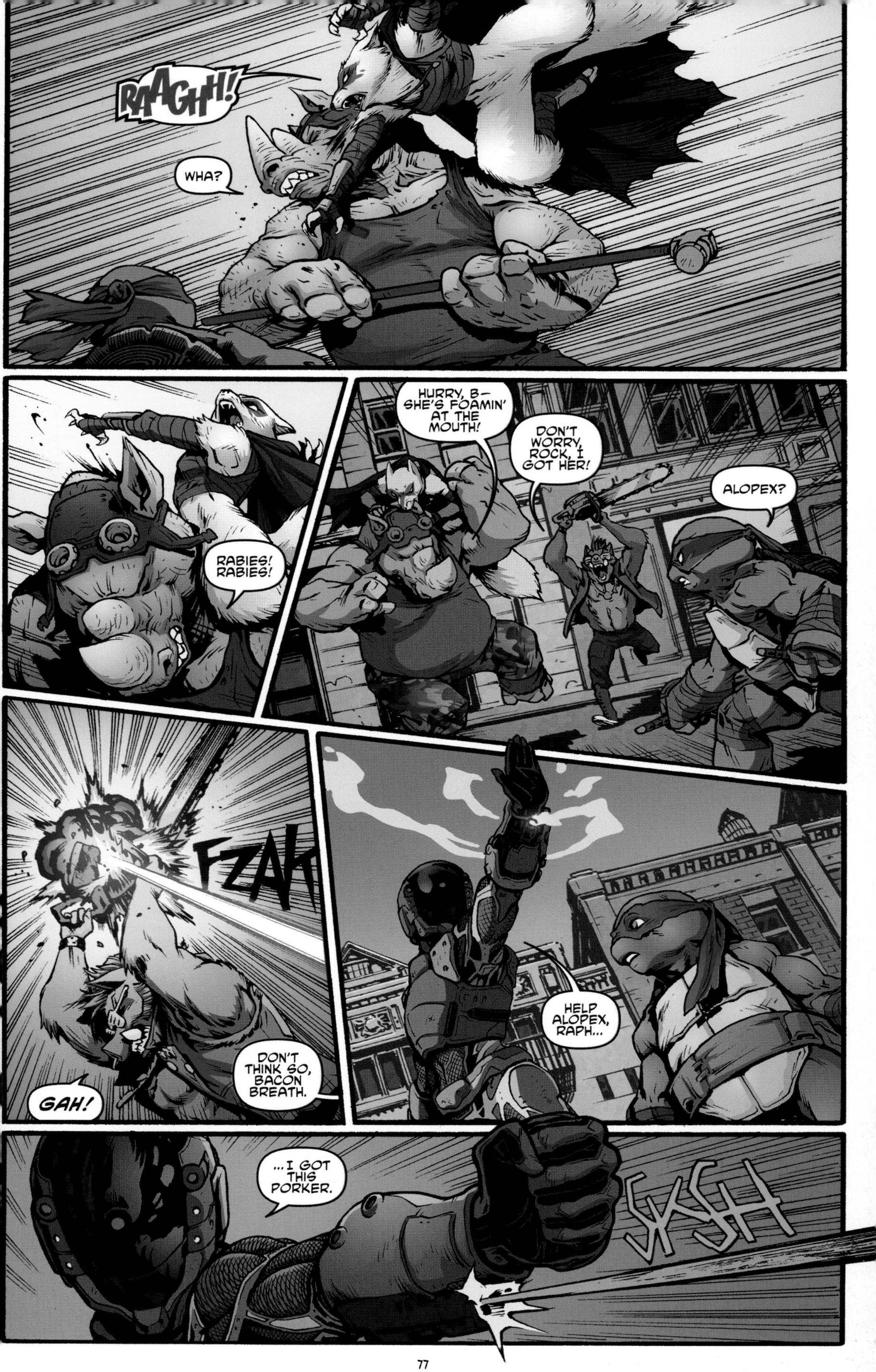
RAAGHH!
WHA?
RABIES! RABIES!
HURRY, B– SHE'S FOAMIN' AT THE MOUTH!
DON'T WORRY, ROCK, I GOT HER!
ALOPEX?
FZAK
DON'T THINK SO, BACON BREATH.
GAH!
HELP ALOPEX, RAPH...
...I GOT THIS PORKER.
SKSH

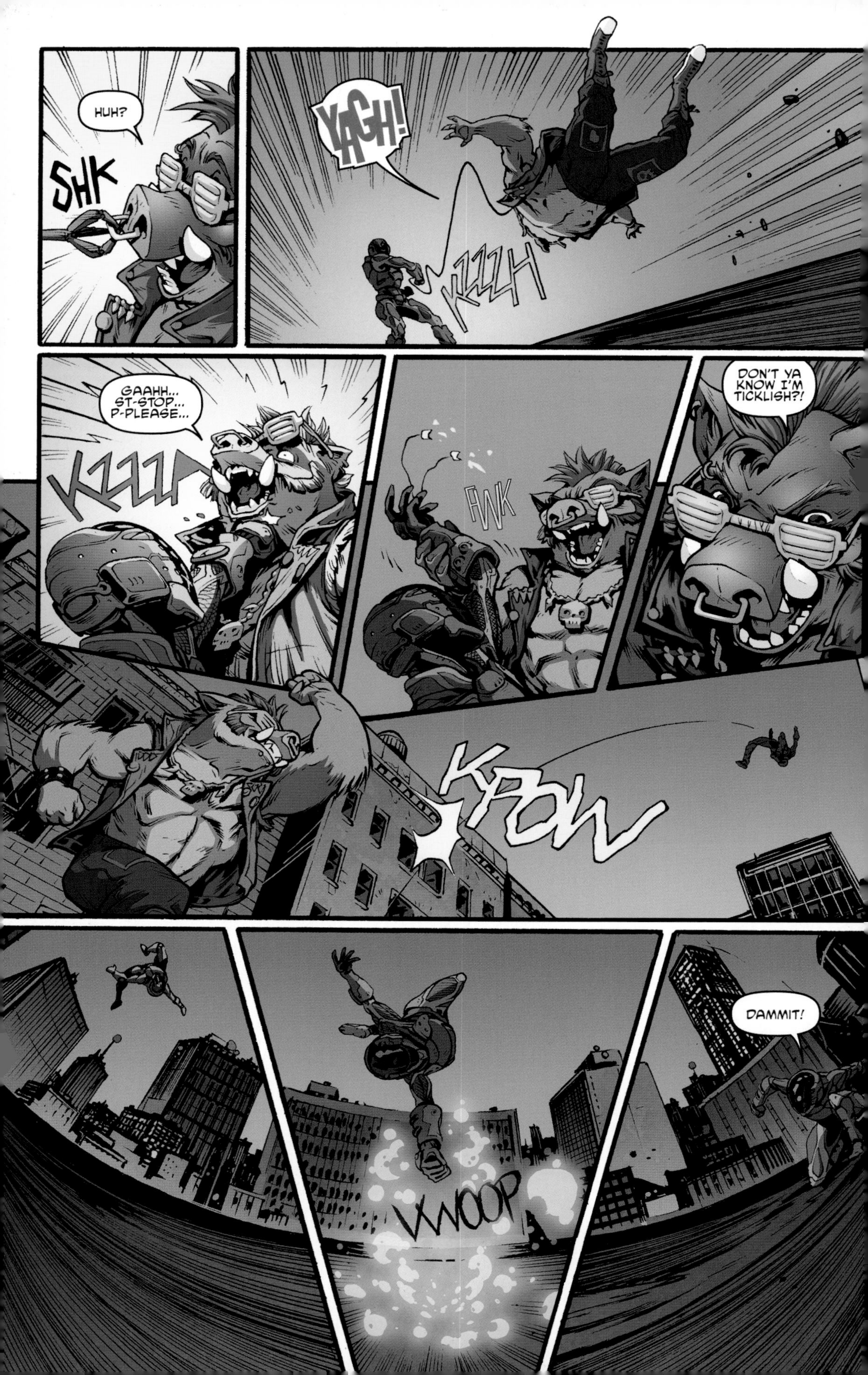
HUH?
SHK
YAGH!
KZZZH
GAAHH... ST-STOP... P-PLEASE...
KZZZT
FWK
DON'T YA KNOW I'M TICKLISH?!
KPOW
VWOOP
DAMMIT!

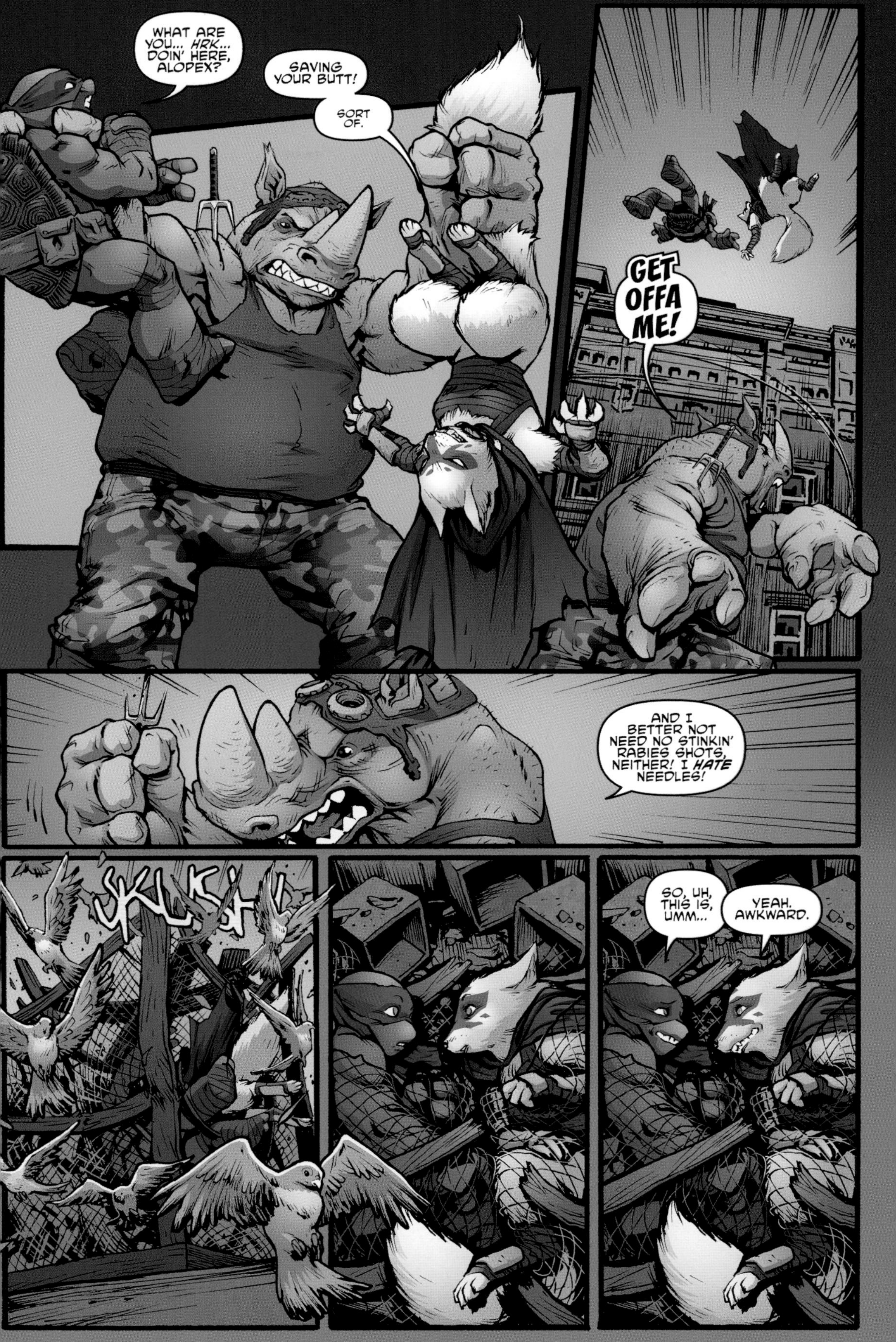
WHAT ARE YOU... HRK... DOIN' HERE, ALOPEX?
SAVING YOUR BUTT!
SORT OF.
GET OFFA ME!
AND I BETTER NOT NEED NO STINKIN' RABIES SHOTS, NEITHER! I HATE NEEDLES!
SO, UH, THIS IS, UMM...
YEAH. AWKWARD.

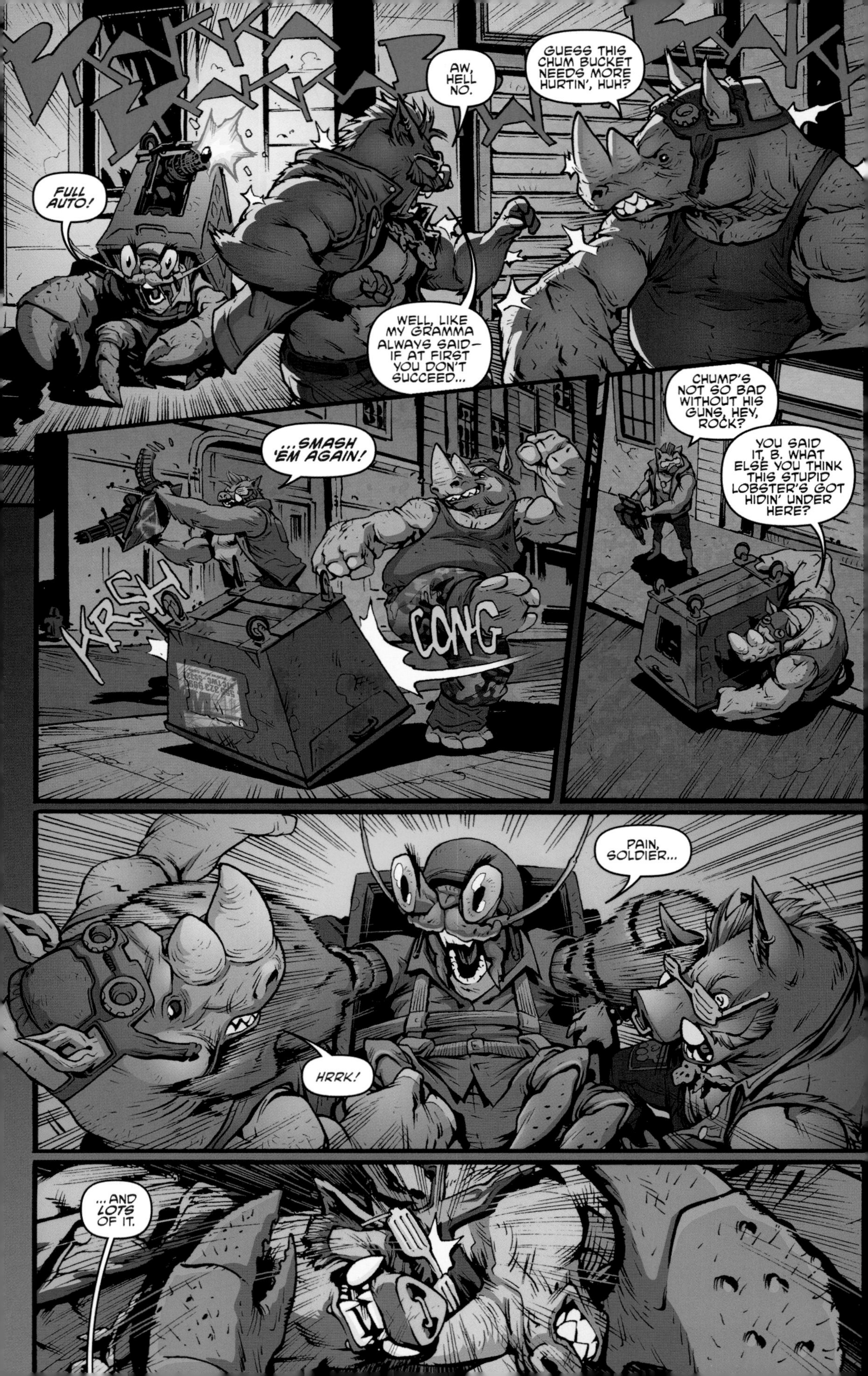
AW, HELL NO.
GUESS THIS CHUM BUCKET NEEDS MORE HURTIN', HUH?
FULL AUTO!
WELL, LIKE MY GRAMMA ALWAYS SAID–IF AT FIRST YOU DON'T SUCCEED...
...SMASH 'EM AGAIN!
KRSH
CONG
CHUMP'S NOT SO BAD WITHOUT HIS GUNS, HEY, ROCK?
YOU SAID IT, B. WHAT ELSE YOU THINK THIS STUPID LOBSTER'S GOT HIDIN' UNDER HERE?
PAIN, SOLDIER...
HRRK!
...AND LOTS OF IT.

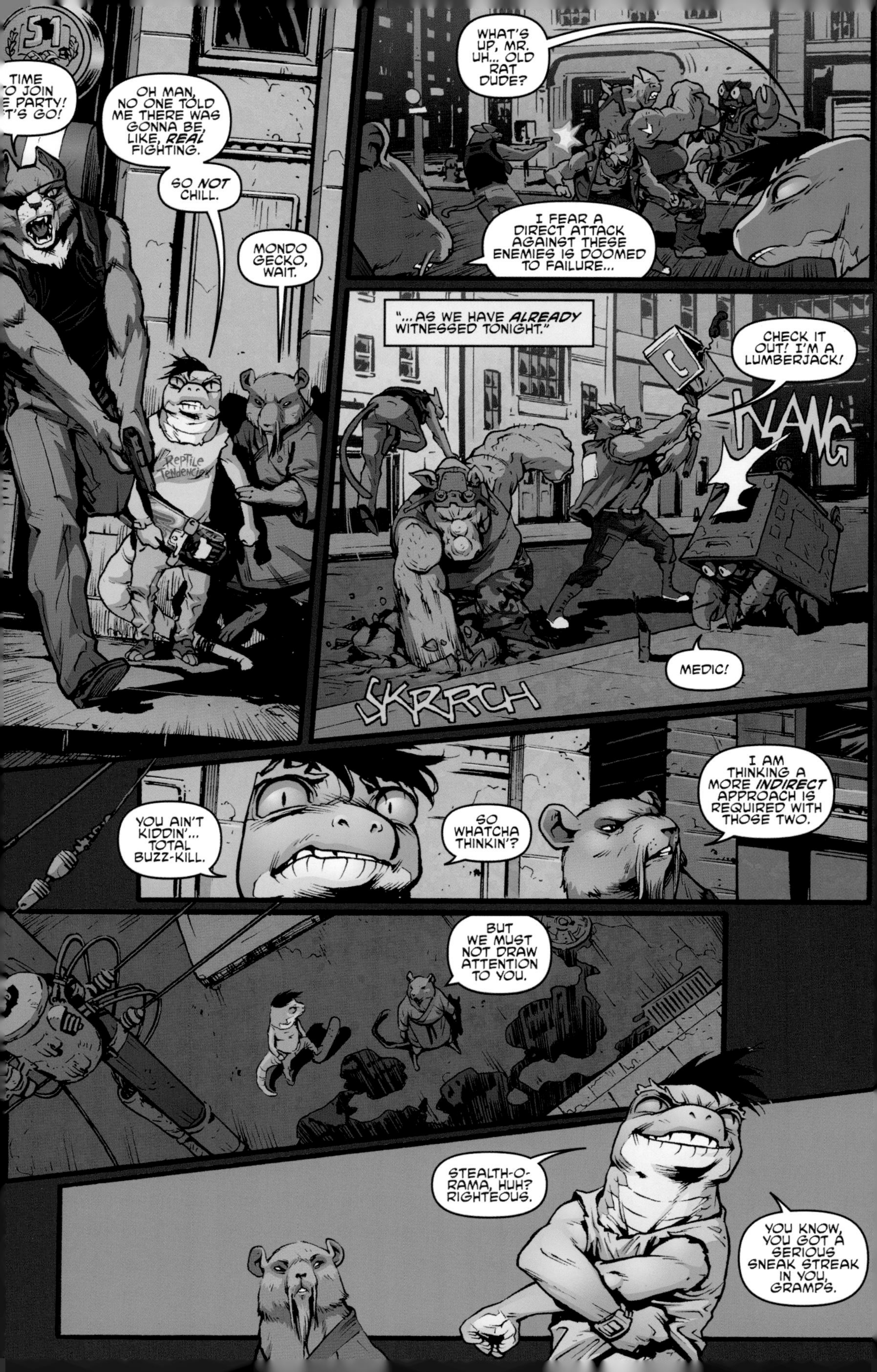
TIME
O JOIN
E PARTY!
T'S GO!
OH MAN, NO ONE TOLD ME THERE WAS GONNA BE, LIKE, REAL FIGHTING.
SO NOT CHILL.
MONDO GECKO, WAIT.
REPTILE TENDENCIES
WHAT'S UP, MR. UH... OLD RAT DUDE?
I FEAR A DIRECT ATTACK AGAINST THESE ENEMIES IS DOOMED TO FAILURE...
"...AS WE HAVE ALREADY WITNESSED TONIGHT."
CHECK IT OUT! I'M A LUMBERJACK!
KLANG
MEDIC!
SKRRCH
YOU AIN'T KIDDIN'... TOTAL BUZZ-KILL.
SO WHATCHA THINKIN'?
I AM THINKING A MORE INDIRECT APPROACH IS REQUIRED WITH THOSE TWO.
BUT WE MUST NOT DRAW ATTENTION TO YOU.
STEALTH-O-RAMA, HUH? RIGHTEOUS.
YOU KNOW, YOU GOT A SERIOUS SNEAK STREAK IN YOU, GRAMPS.

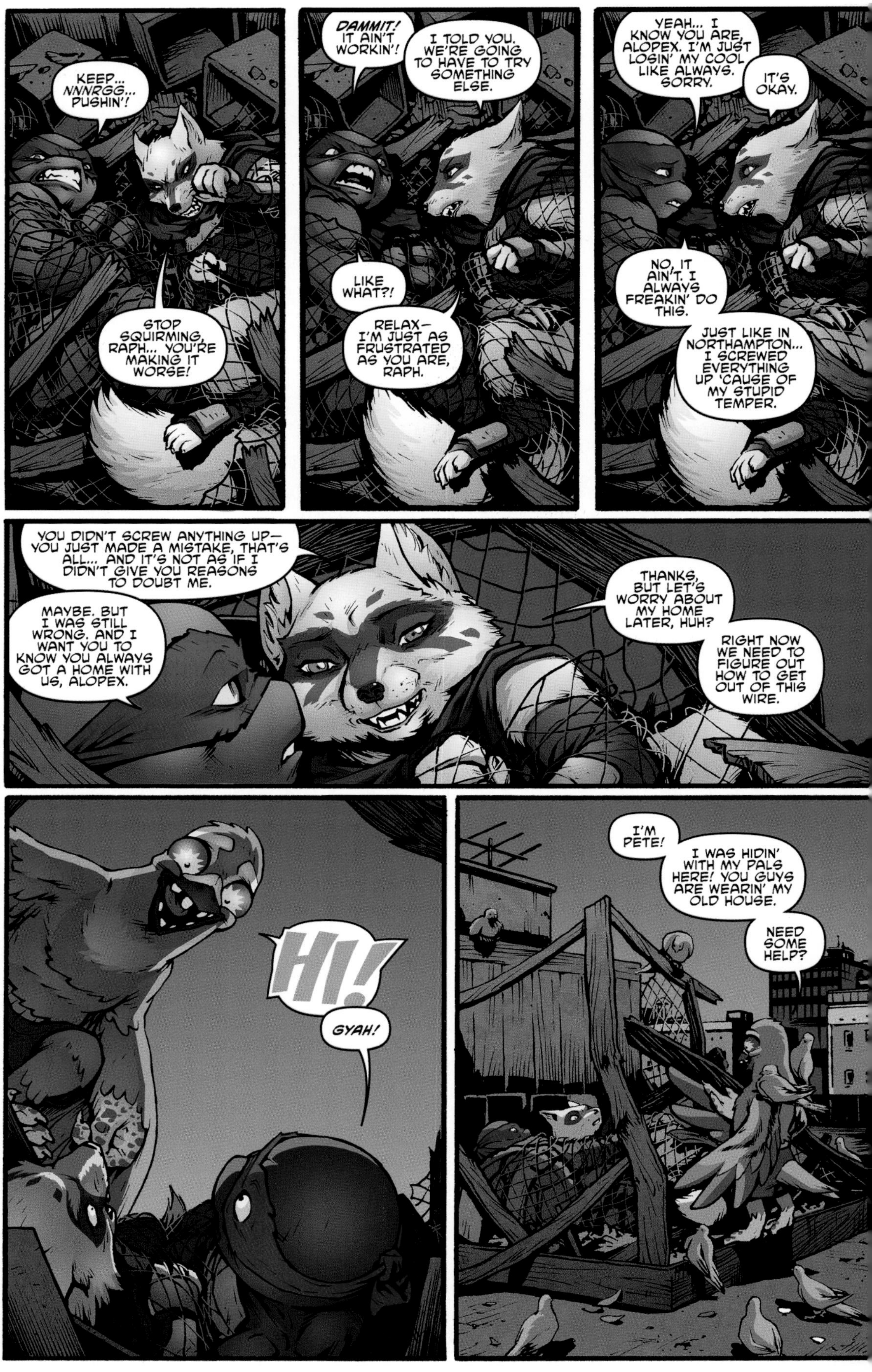
KEEP... NNNRGG... PUSHIN'!
STOP SQUIRMING, RAPH... YOU'RE MAKING IT WORSE!
DAMMIT! IT AIN'T WORKIN'!
I TOLD YOU. WE'RE GOING TO HAVE TO TRY SOMETHING ELSE.
LIKE WHAT?!
RELAX— I'M JUST AS FRUSTRATED AS YOU ARE, RAPH.
YEAH... I KNOW YOU ARE, ALOPEX. I'M JUST LOSIN' MY COOL LIKE ALWAYS. SORRY.
IT'S OKAY.
NO, IT AIN'T. I ALWAYS FREAKIN' DO THIS.
JUST LIKE IN NORTHAMPTON... I SCREWED EVERYTHING UP 'CAUSE OF MY STUPID TEMPER.
YOU DIDN'T SCREW ANYTHING UP— YOU JUST MADE A MISTAKE, THAT'S ALL... AND IT'S NOT AS IF I DIDN'T GIVE YOU REASONS TO DOUBT ME.
MAYBE. BUT I WAS STILL WRONG. AND I WANT YOU TO KNOW YOU ALWAYS GOT A HOME WITH US, ALOPEX.
THANKS, BUT LET'S WORRY ABOUT MY HOME LATER, HUH?
RIGHT NOW WE NEED TO FIGURE OUT HOW TO GET OUT OF THIS WIRE.
HI!
GYAH!
I'M PETE!
I WAS HIDIN' WITH MY PALS HERE! YOU GUYS ARE WEARIN' MY OLD HOUSE.
NEED SOME HELP?

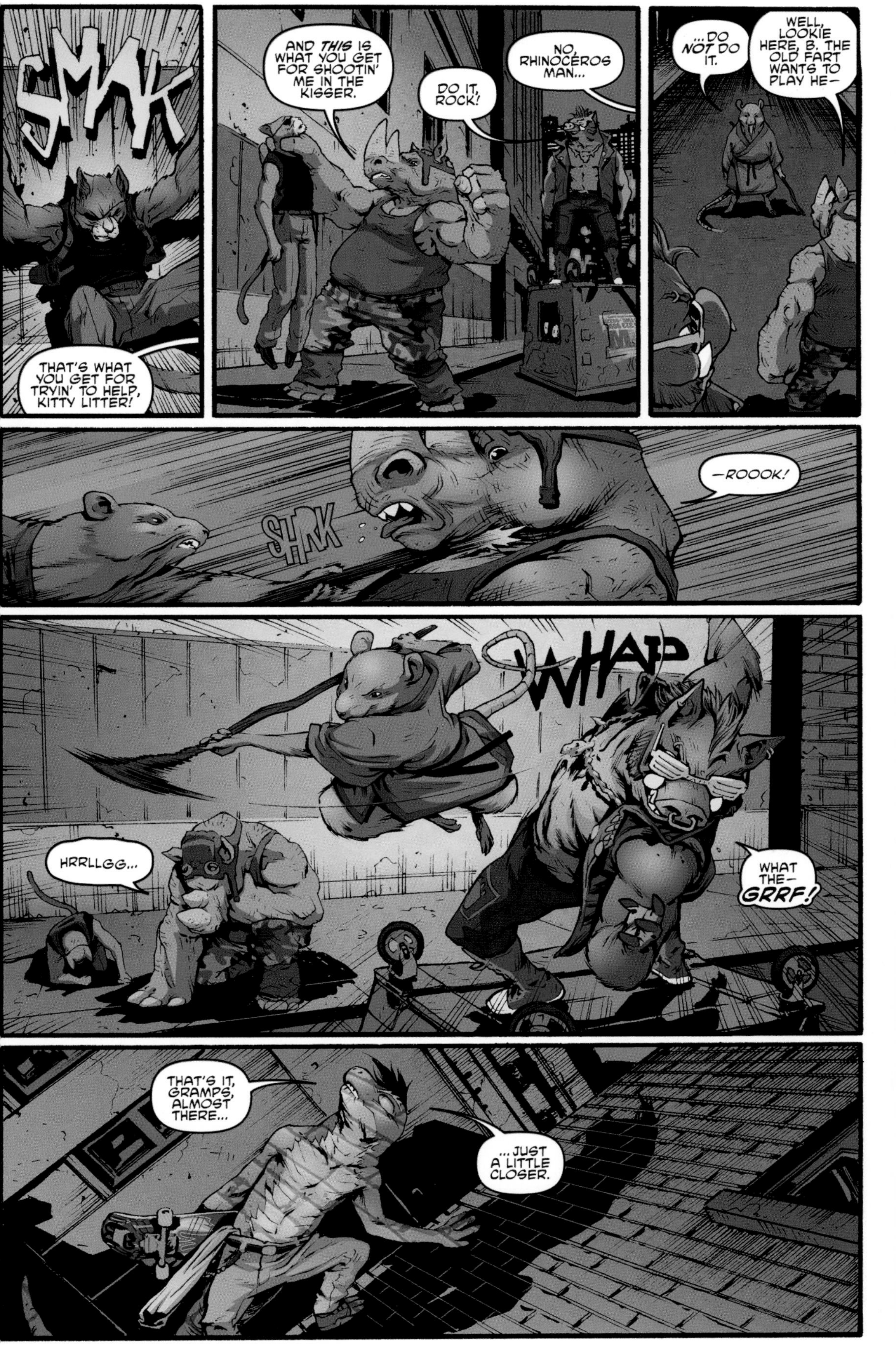
SMAK
THAT'S WHAT YOU GET FOR TRYIN' TO HELP, KITTY LITTER!
AND THIS IS WHAT YOU GET FOR SHOOTIN' ME IN THE KISSER.
DO IT, ROCK!
NO, RHINOCÉROS MAN...
...DO NOT DO IT.
WELL, LOOKIE HERE, B. THE OLD FART WANTS TO PLAY HE—
SHRK
—ROOOK!
WHAP
HRRLLGG...
WHAT THE—GRRF!
THAT'S IT, GRAMPS, ALMOST THERE...
...JUST A LITTLE CLOSER.

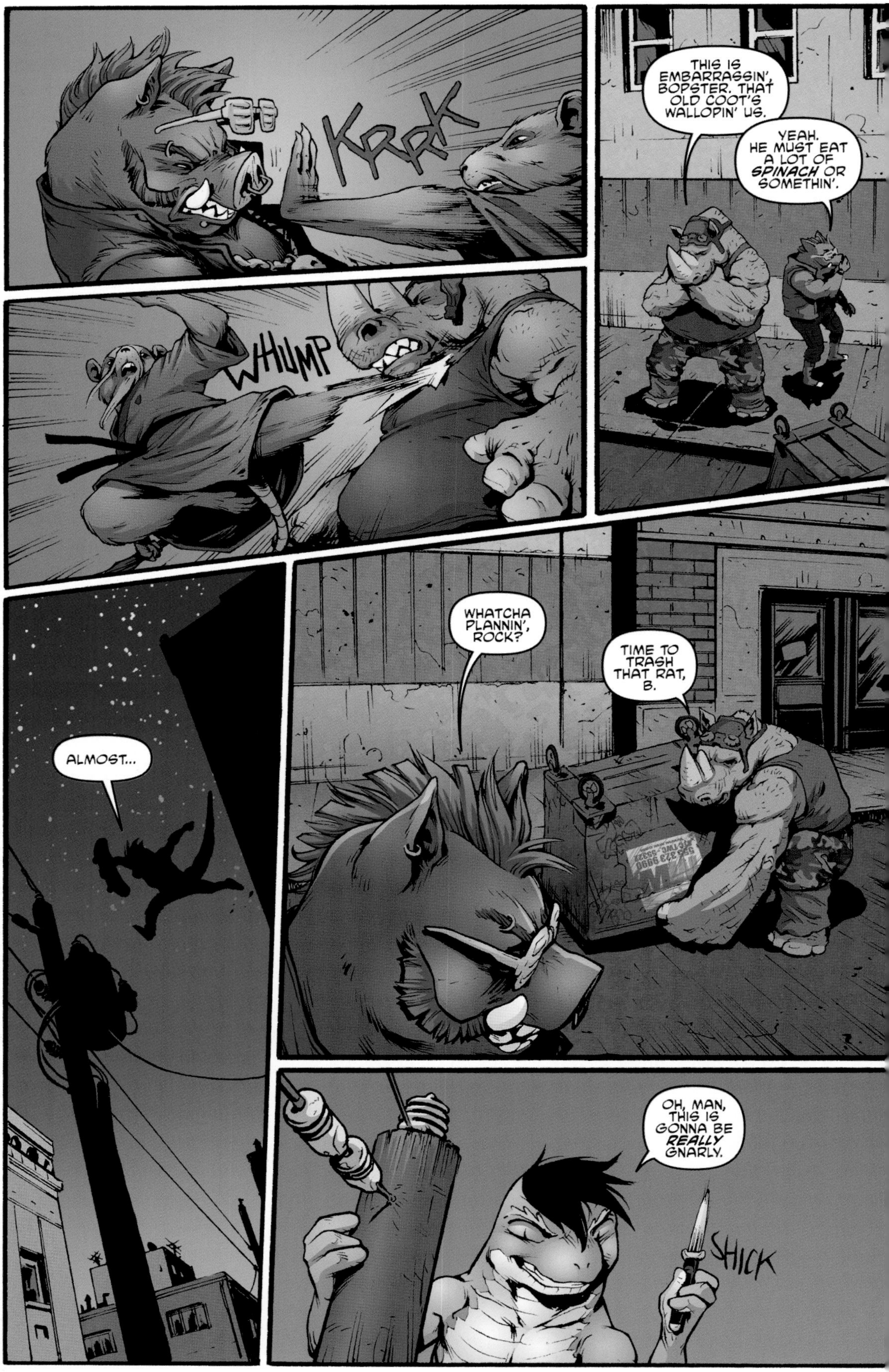
KRRK
THIS IS EMBARRASSIN', BOPSTER. THAT OLD COOT'S WALLOPIN' US.
YEAH. HE MUST EAT A LOT OF SPINACH OR SOMETHIN'.
WHUMP
ALMOST...
WHATCHA PLANNIN', ROCK?
TIME TO TRASH THAT RAT, B.
OH, MAN, THIS IS GONNA BE REALLY GNARLY.
SHICK

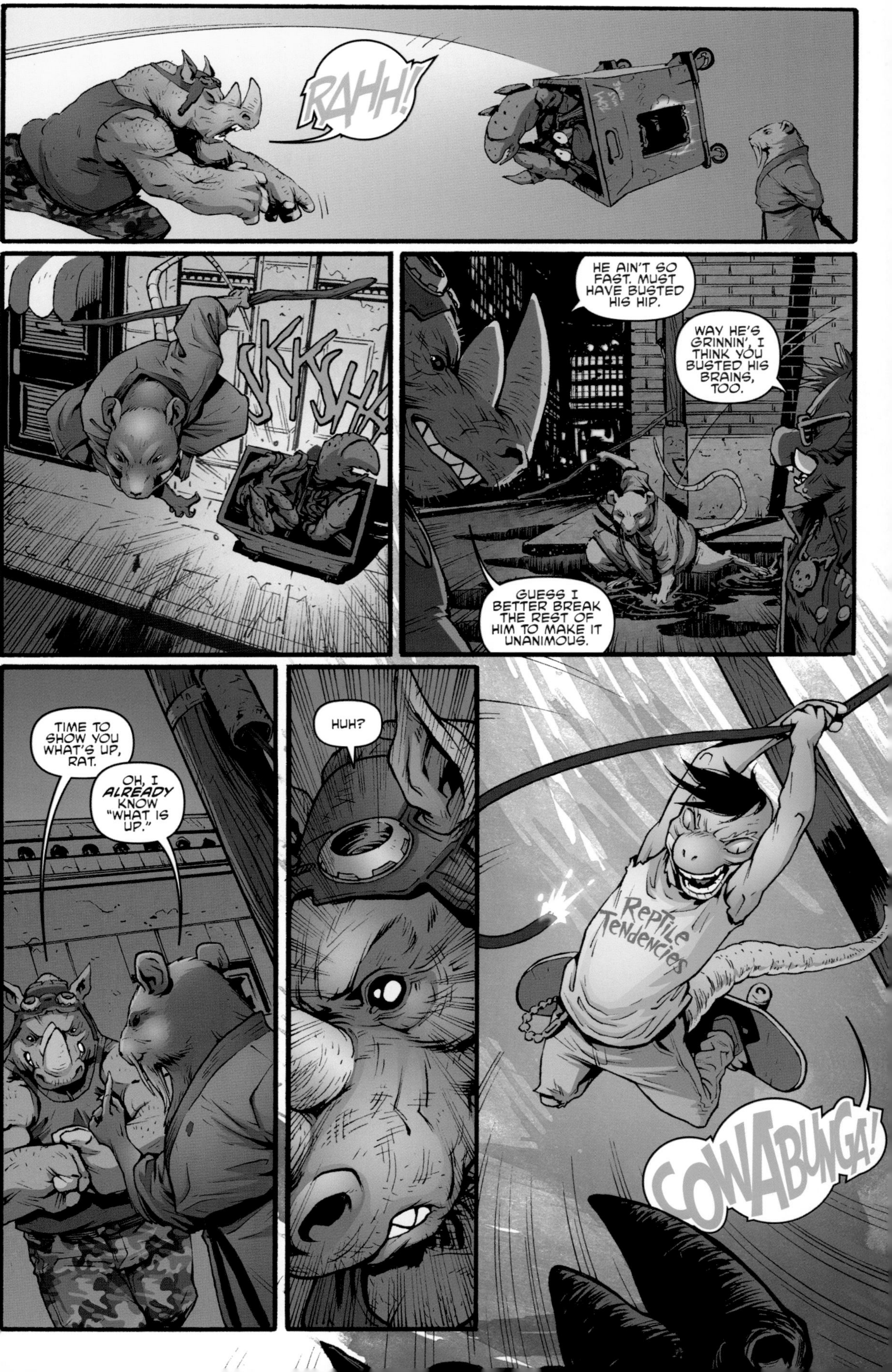
RAHH!
SKKSHH
HE AIN'T SO FAST. MUST HAVE BUSTED HIS HIP.
WAY HE'S GRINNIN', I THINK YOU BUSTED HIS BRAINS, TOO.
GUESS I BETTER BREAK THE REST OF HIM TO MAKE IT UNANIMOUS.
TIME TO SHOW YOU WHAT'S UP, RAT.
OH, I ALREADY KNOW "WHAT IS UP."
HUH?
Reptile Tendencies
COWABUNGA!

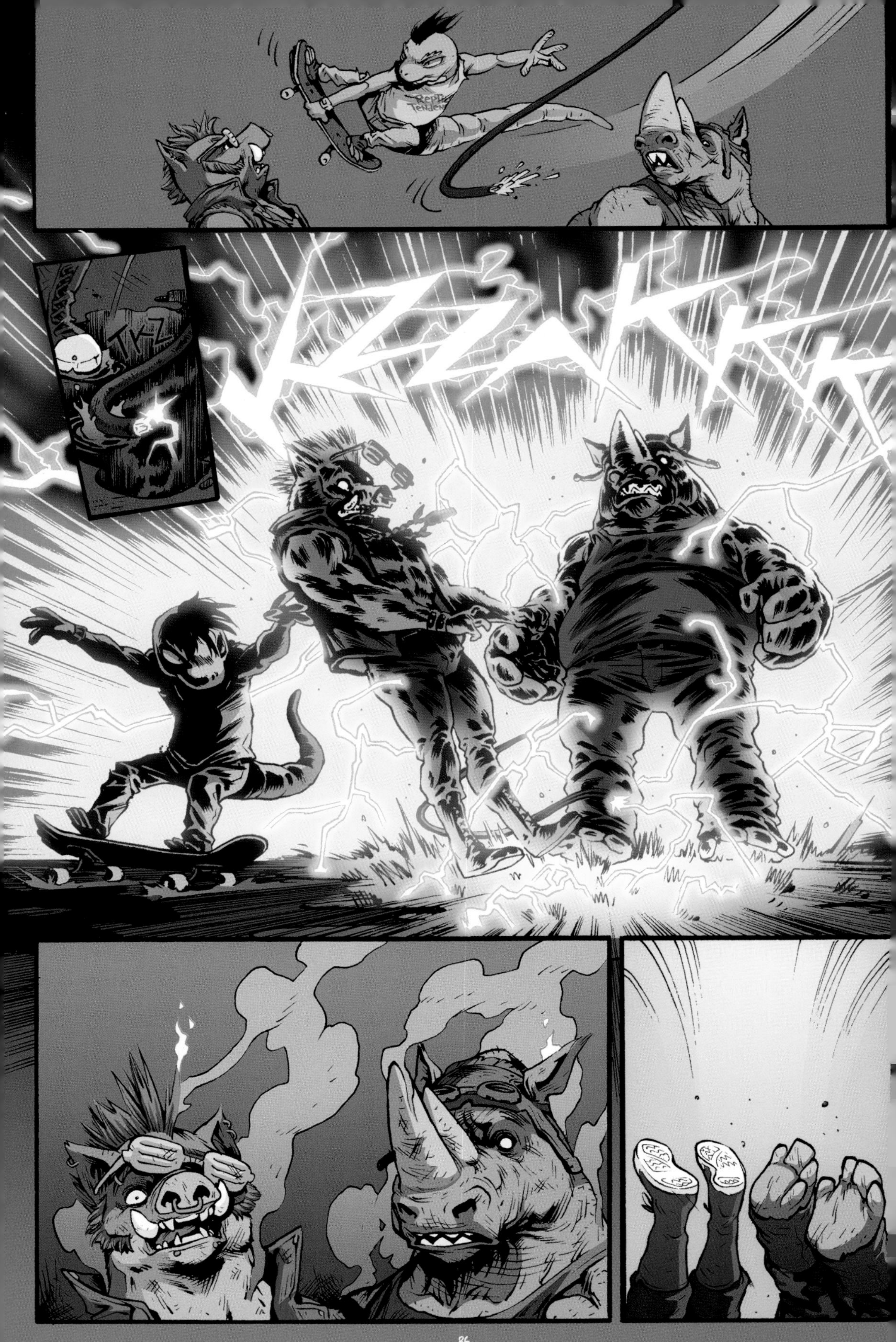
TK-Z
KZZAKKK

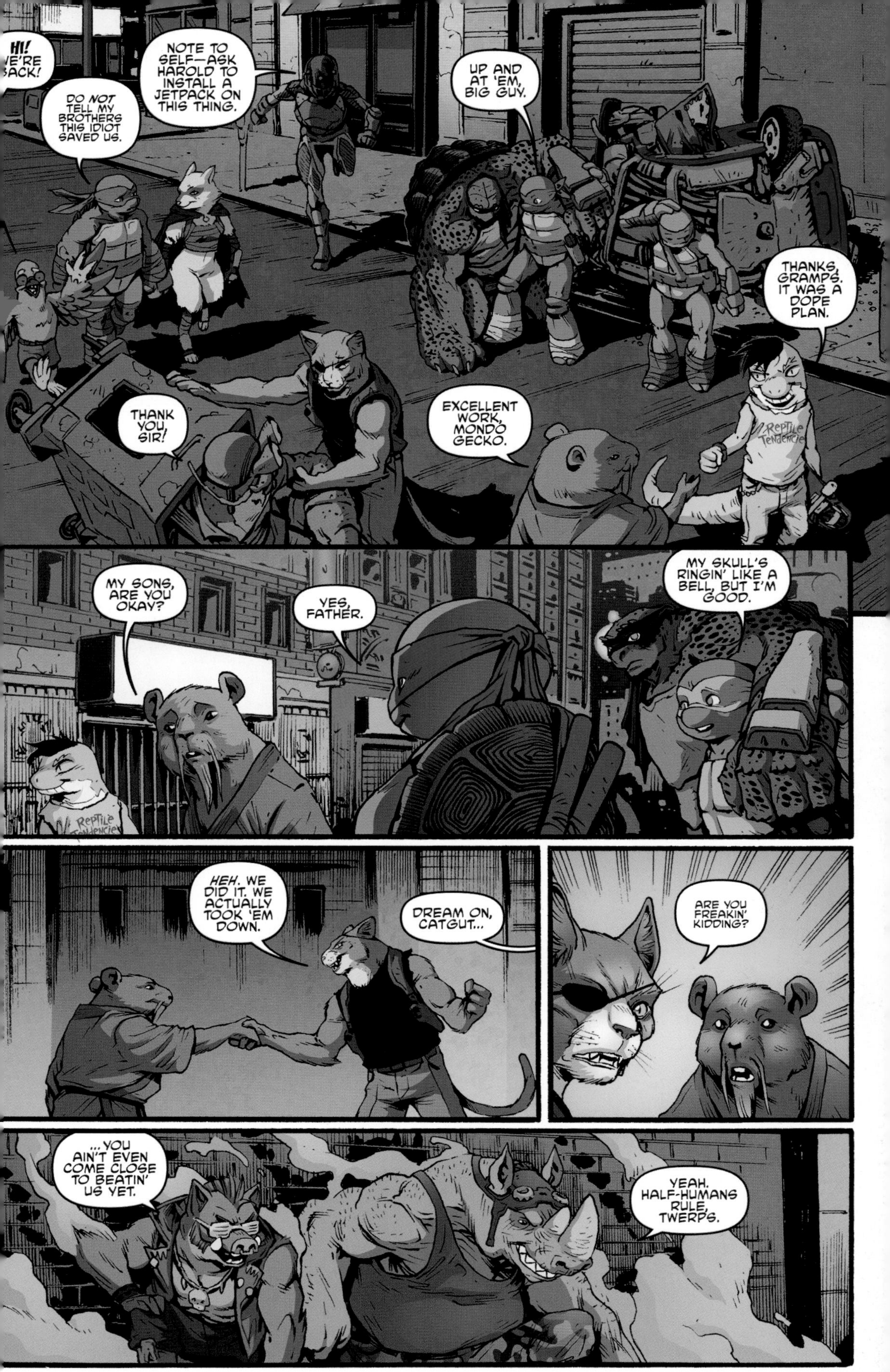
HI! WE'RE BACK!
DO NOT TELL MY BROTHERS THIS IDIOT SAVED US.
NOTE TO SELF—ASK HAROLD TO INSTALL A JETPACK ON THIS THING.
UP AND AT 'EM, BIG GUY.
THANKS, GRAMPS. IT WAS A DOPE PLAN.
THANK YOU, SIR!
EXCELLENT WORK, MONDO GECKO.
REPTILE TENDENCIES
MY SONS, ARE YOU OKAY?
YES, FATHER.
MY SKULL'S RINGIN' LIKE A BELL, BUT I'M GOOD.
REPTILE TENDENCIES
HEH. WE DID IT. WE ACTUALLY TOOK 'EM DOWN.
DREAM ON, CATGUT...
ARE YOU FREAKIN' KIDDING?
...YOU AIN'T EVEN COME CLOSE TO BEATIN' US YET.
YEAH. HALF-HUMANS RULE, TWERPS.

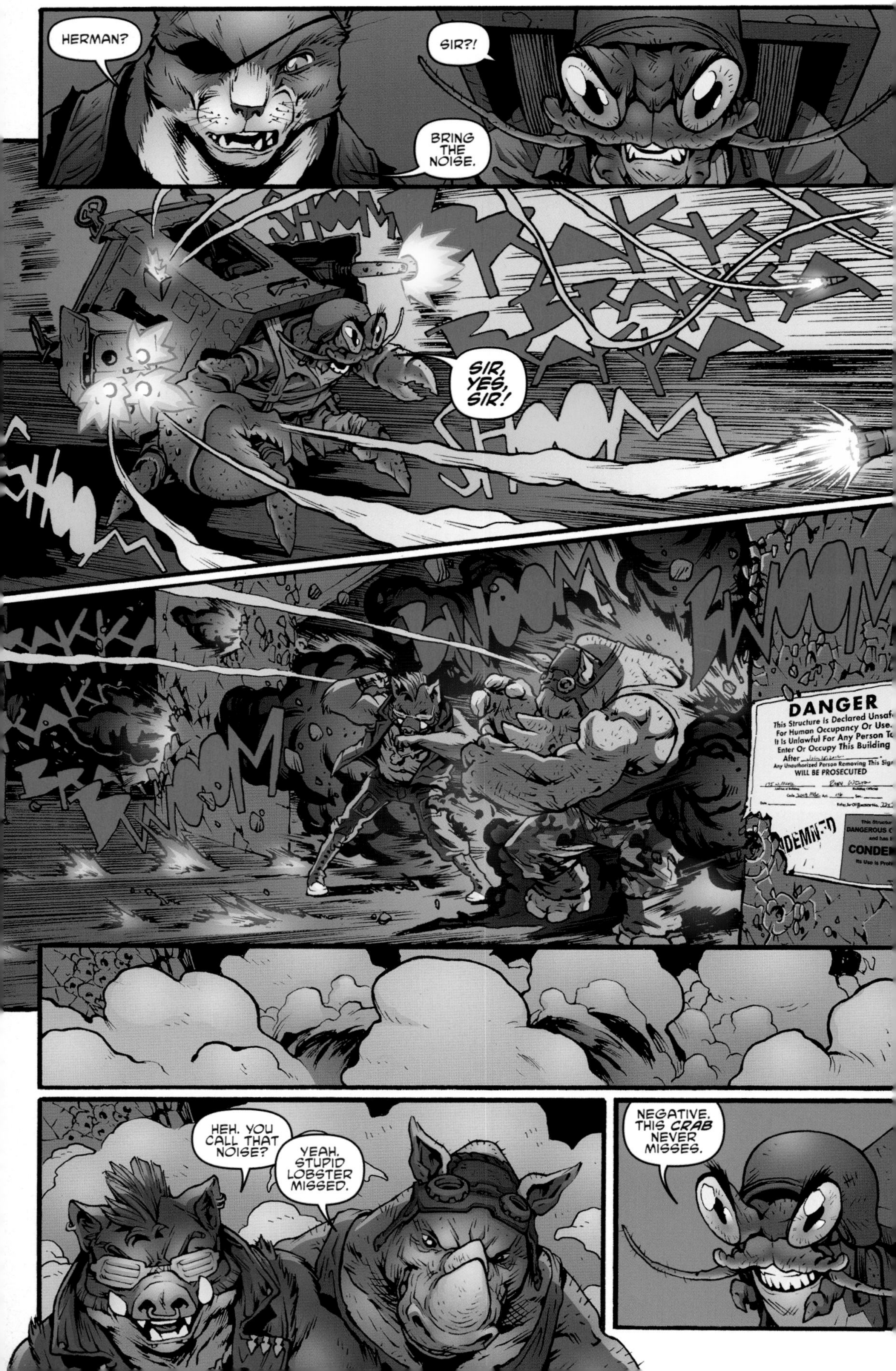
HERMAN?
SIR?!
BRING THE NOISE.
SIR, YES, SIR!
DANGER
This Structure Is Declared Unsaf
For Human Occupancy Or Use.
It Is Unlawful For Any Person To
Enter Or Occupy This Building
After
Any Unauthorized Person Removing This Sign
WILL BE PROSECUTED
HEH. YOU CALL THAT NOISE?
YEAH. STUPID LOBSTER MISSED.
NEGATIVE. THIS CRAB NEVER MISSES.

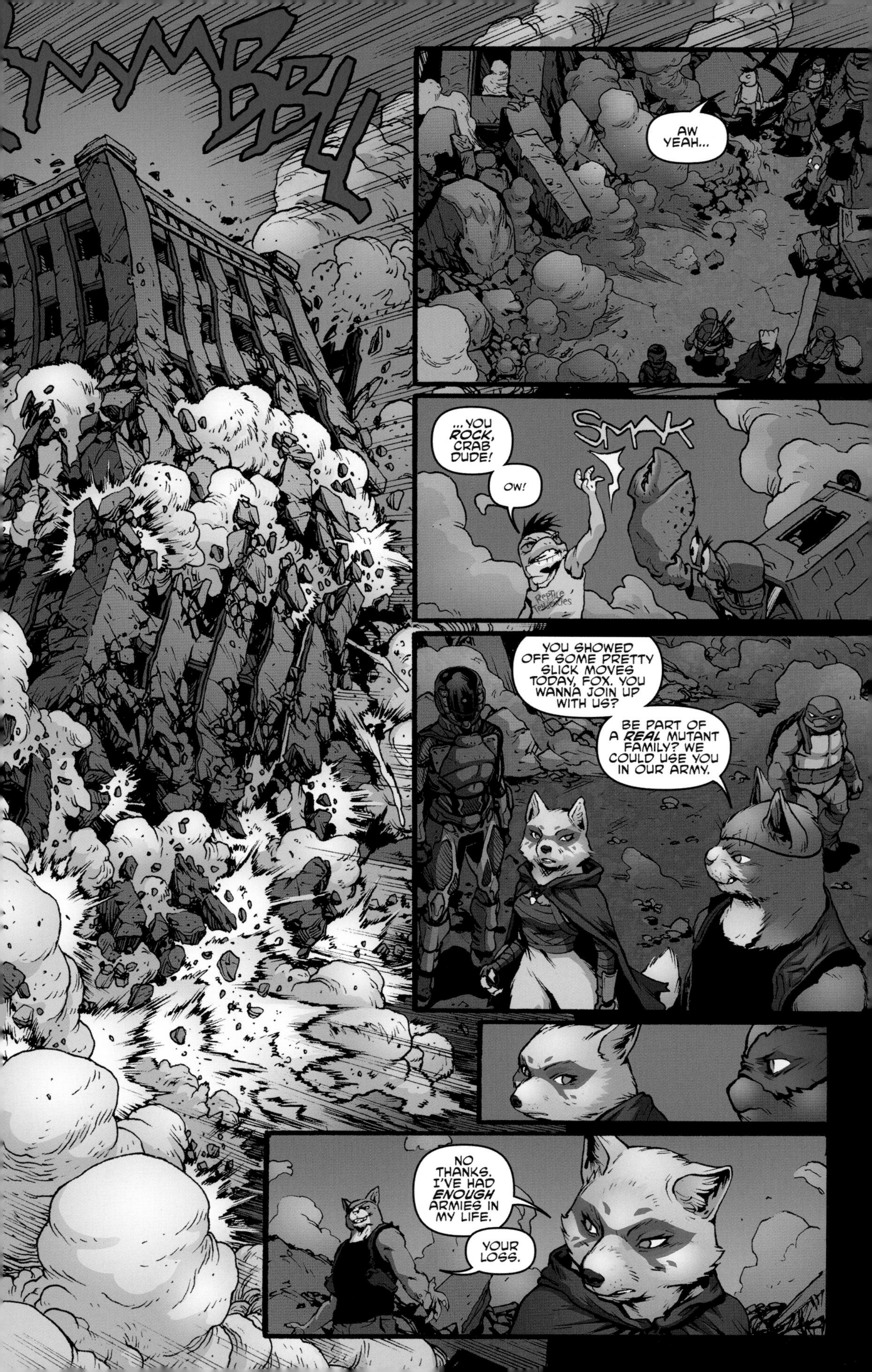

AW YEAH...
...YOU ROCK, CRAB DUDE!
SMAK
OW!
YOU SHOWED OFF SOME PRETTY SLICK MOVES TODAY, FOX. YOU WANNA JOIN UP WITH US?
BE PART OF A REAL MUTANT FAMILY? WE COULD USE YOU IN OUR ARMY.
NO THANKS. I'VE HAD ENOUGH ARMIES IN MY LIFE.
YOUR LOSS.

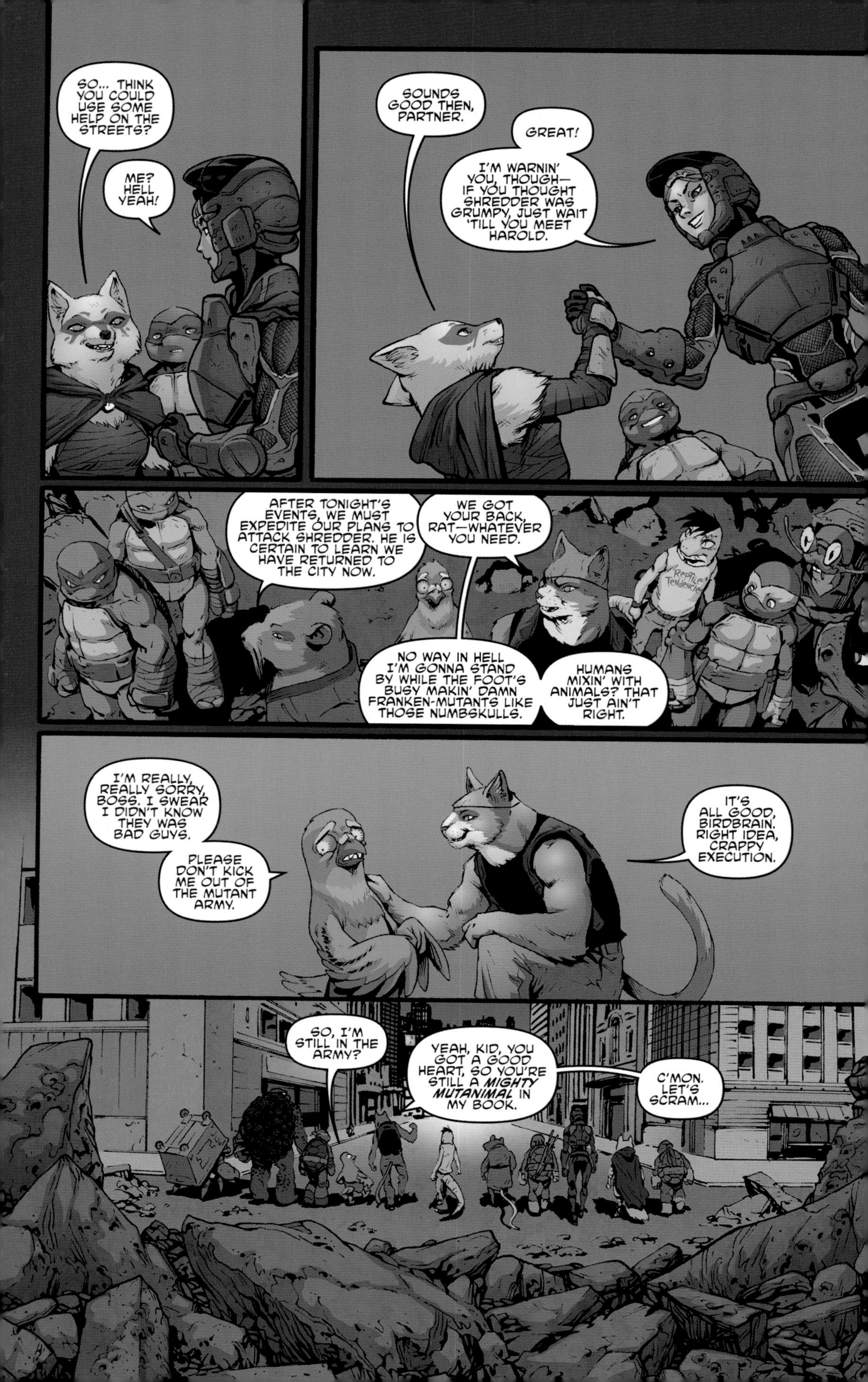
SO... THINK YOU COULD USE SOME HELP ON THE STREETS?
ME? HELL YEAH!
SOUNDS GOOD THEN, PARTNER.
GREAT!
I'M WARNIN' YOU, THOUGH— IF YOU THOUGHT SHREDDER WAS GRUMPY, JUST WAIT 'TILL YOU MEET HAROLD.
AFTER TONIGHT'S EVENTS, WE MUST EXPEDITE OUR PLANS TO ATTACK SHREDDER. HE IS CERTAIN TO LEARN WE HAVE RETURNED TO THE CITY NOW.
WE GOT YOUR BACK, RAT—WHATEVER YOU NEED.
NO WAY IN HELL I'M GONNA STAND BY WHILE THE FOOT'S BUSY MAKIN' DAMN FRANKEN-MUTANTS LIKE THOSE NUMBSKULLS.
HUMANS MIXIN' WITH ANIMALS? THAT JUST AIN'T RIGHT.
REPTILE TENDENCIES
I'M REALLY, REALLY SORRY, BOSS. I SWEAR I DIDN'T KNOW THEY WAS BAD GUYS.
PLEASE DON'T KICK ME OUT OF THE MUTANT ARMY.
IT'S ALL GOOD, BIRDBRAIN. RIGHT IDEA, CRAPPY EXECUTION.
SO, I'M STILL IN THE ARMY?
YEAH, KID, YOU GOT A GOOD HEART, SO YOU'RE STILL A *MIGHTY MUTANIMAL* IN MY BOOK.
C'MON. LET'S SCRAM...

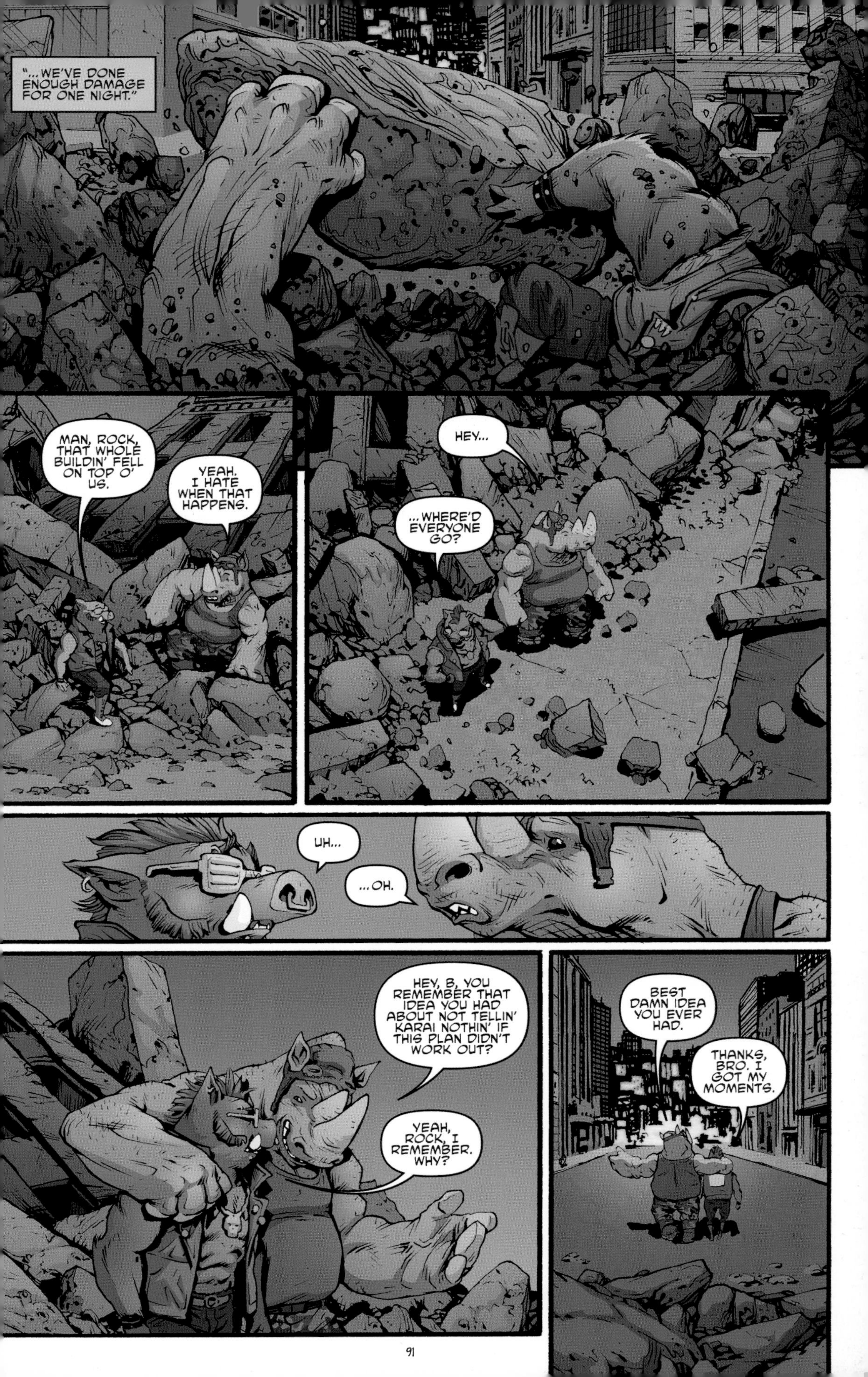
"...WE'VE DONE ENOUGH DAMAGE FOR ONE NIGHT."
MAN, ROCK, THAT WHOLE BUILDIN' FELL ON TOP O' US.
YEAH. I HATE WHEN THAT HAPPENS.
HEY...
...WHERE'D EVERYONE GO?
UH...
...OH.
HEY, B, YOU REMEMBER THAT IDEA YOU HAD ABOUT NOT TELLIN' KARAI NOTHIN' IF THIS PLAN DIDN'T WORK OUT?
YEAH, ROCK, I REMEMBER. WHY?
BEST DAMN IDEA YOU EVER HAD.
THANKS, BRO. I GOT MY MOMENTS.

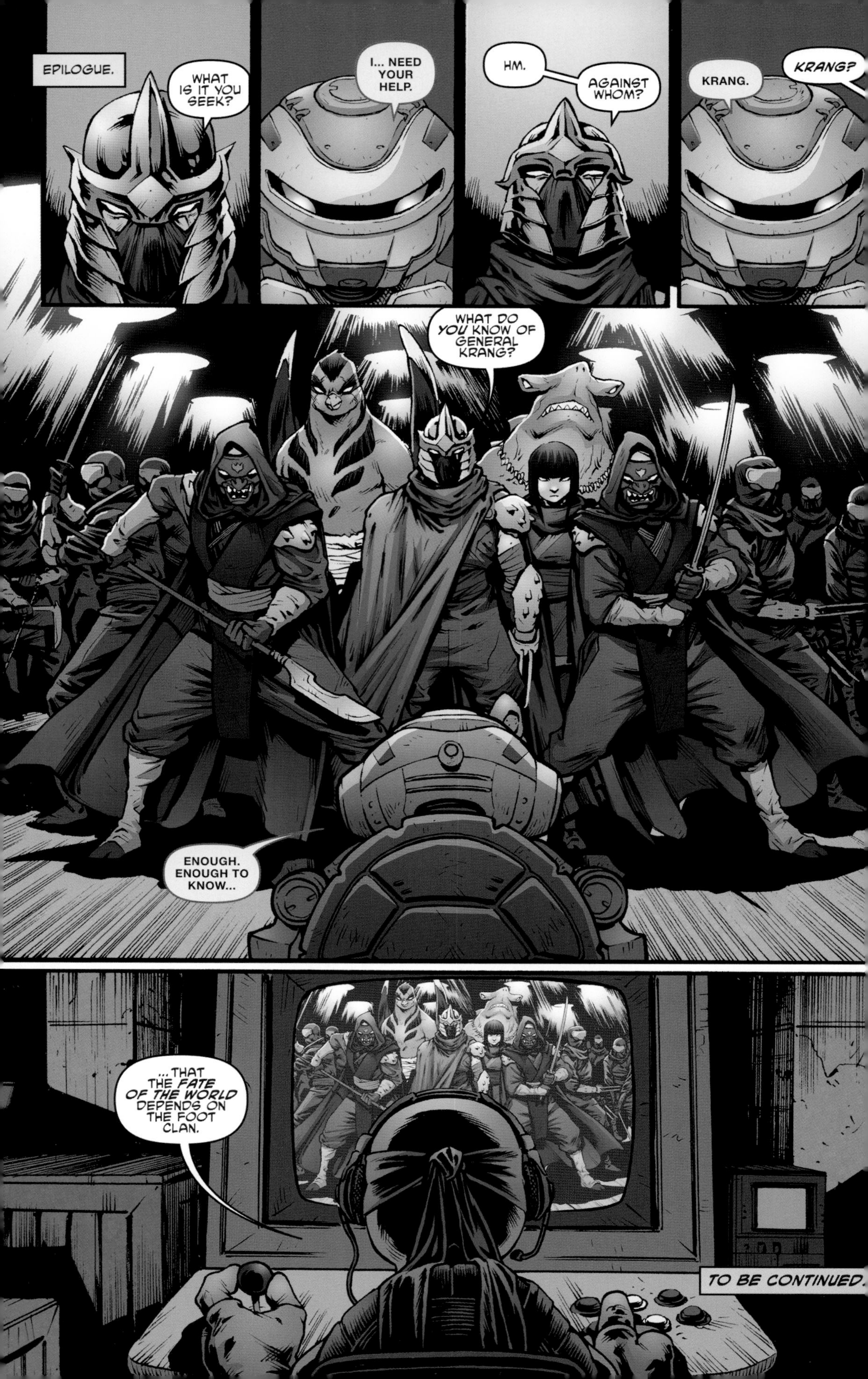
EPILOGUE.
WHAT IS IT YOU SEEK?
I... NEED YOUR HELP.
HM.
AGAINST WHOM?
KRANG.
KRANG?
WHAT DO YOU KNOW OF GENERAL KRANG?
ENOUGH. ENOUGH TO KNOW...
...THAT THE FATE OF THE WORLD DEPENDS ON THE FOOT CLAN.
TO BE CONTINUED.

ART GALLERY

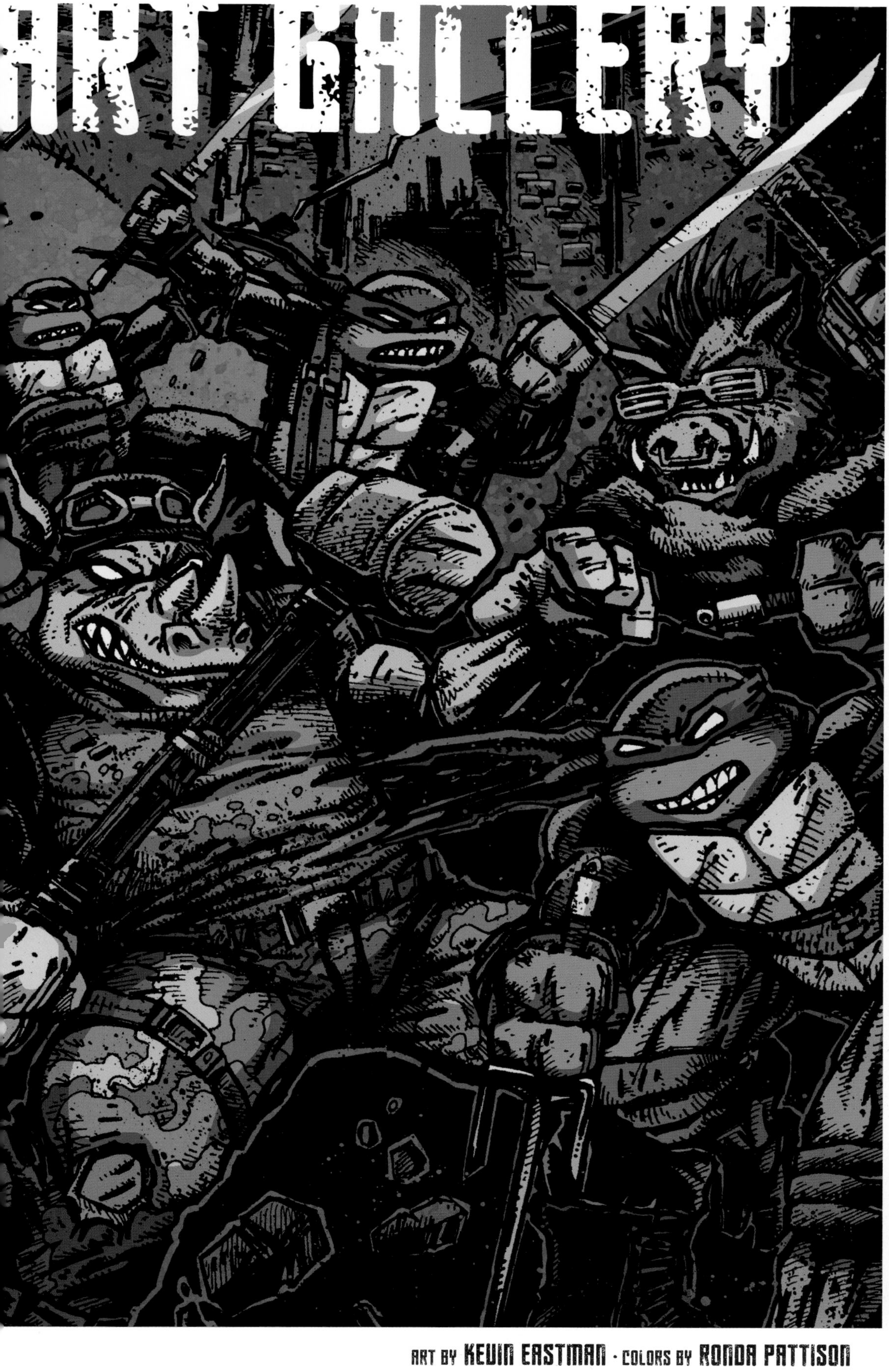

ART BY KEVIN EASTMAN · COLORS BY RONDA PATTISON

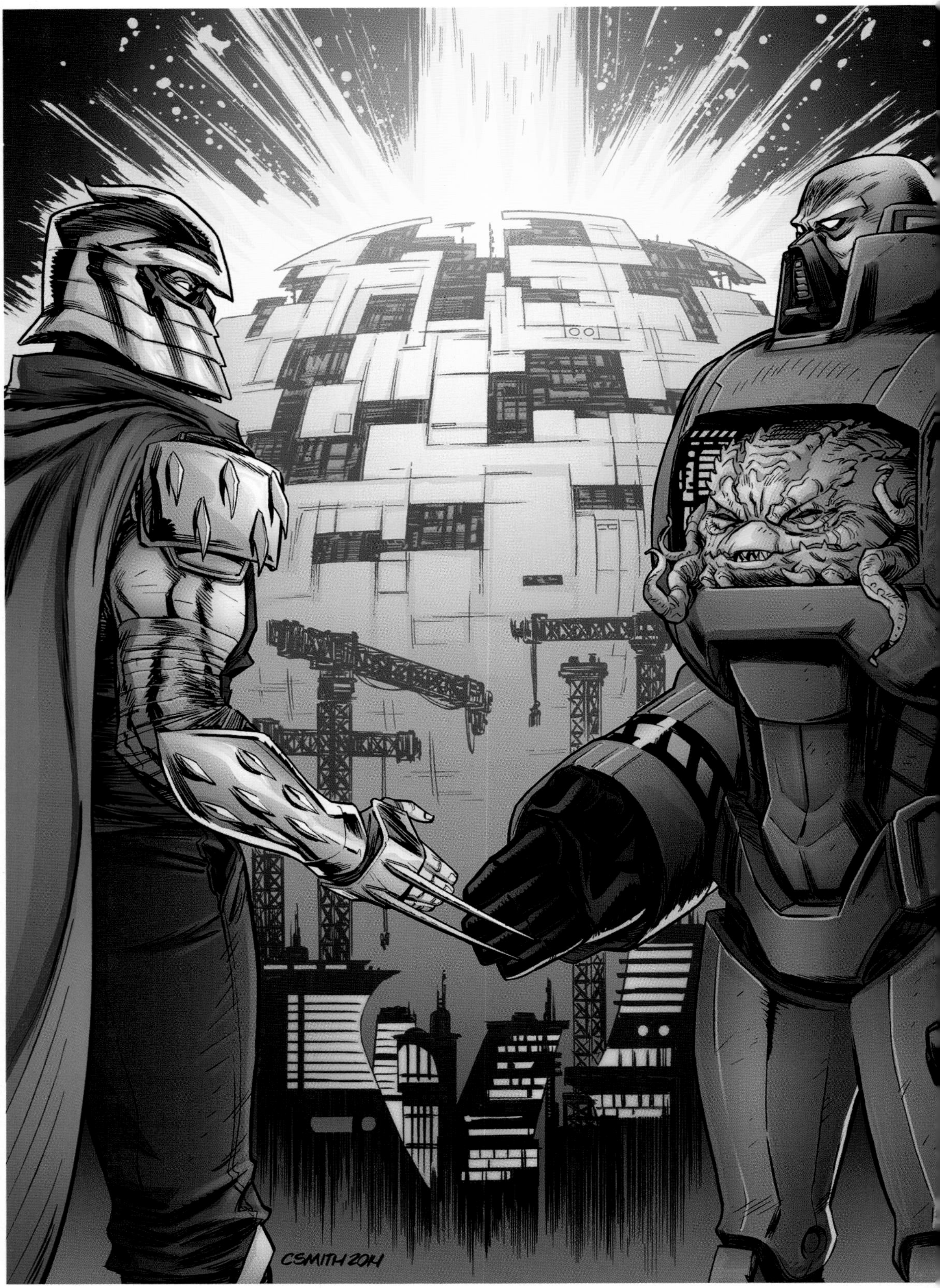
CSMITH 2014

ART BY CORY SMITH

OPPOSITE PAGE: ART BY KEVIN EASTMAN · COLORS BY RONDA PATTISON

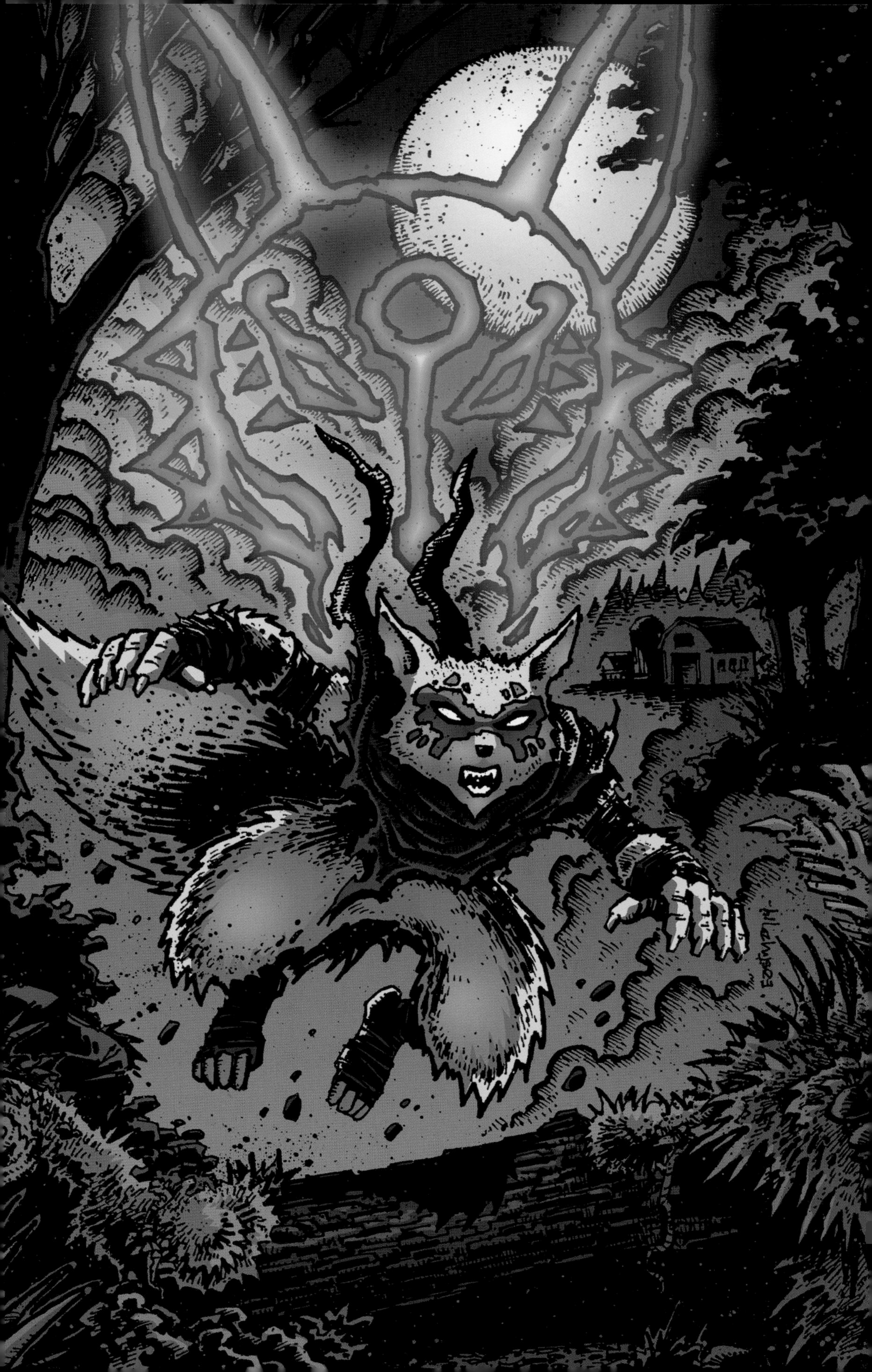

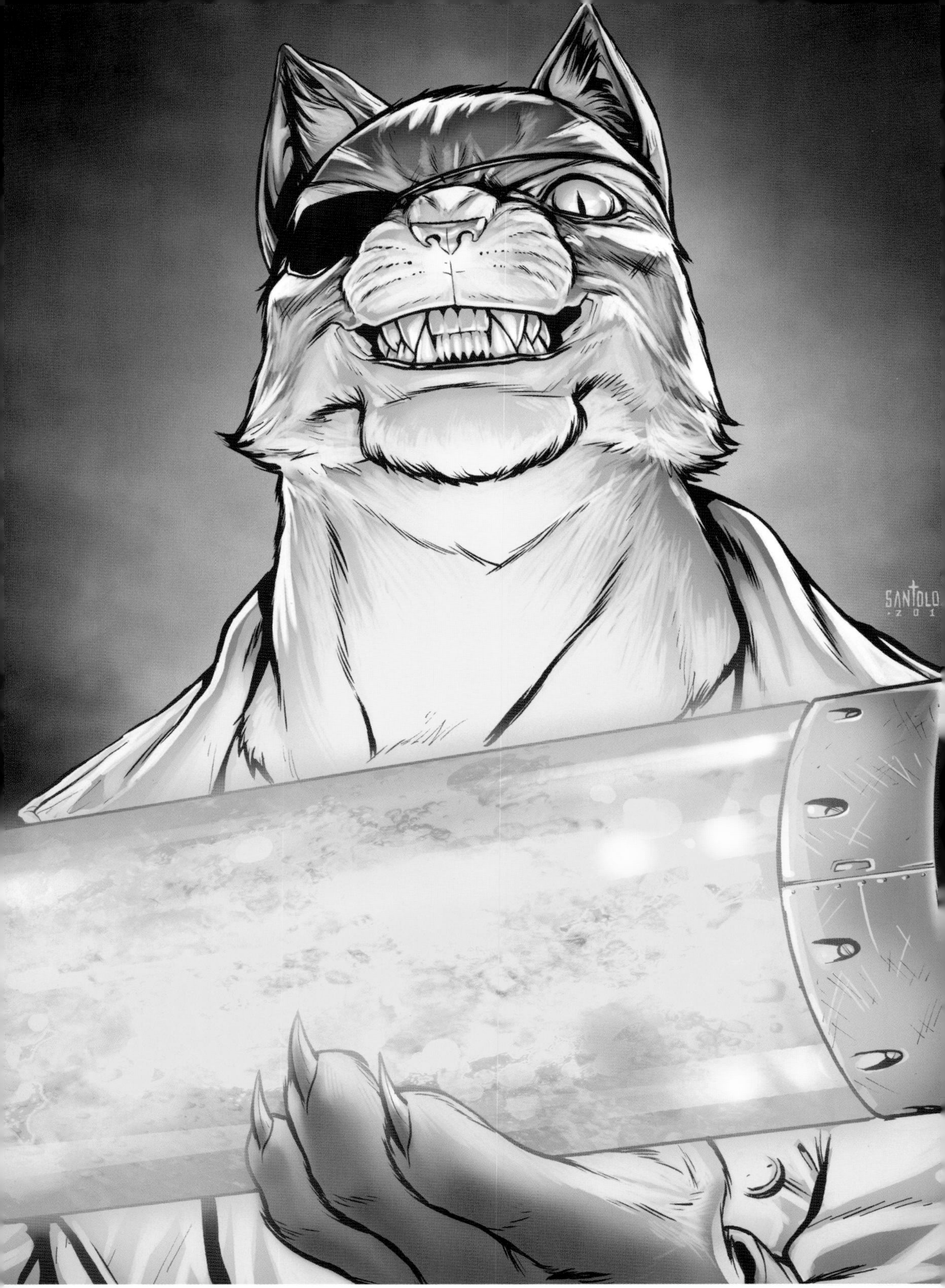
SANTOLO
·201

ART BY MATEUS SANTOLOUCO

OPPOSITE PAGE: ART BY KEVIN EASTMAN · COLORS BY RONDA PATTISON

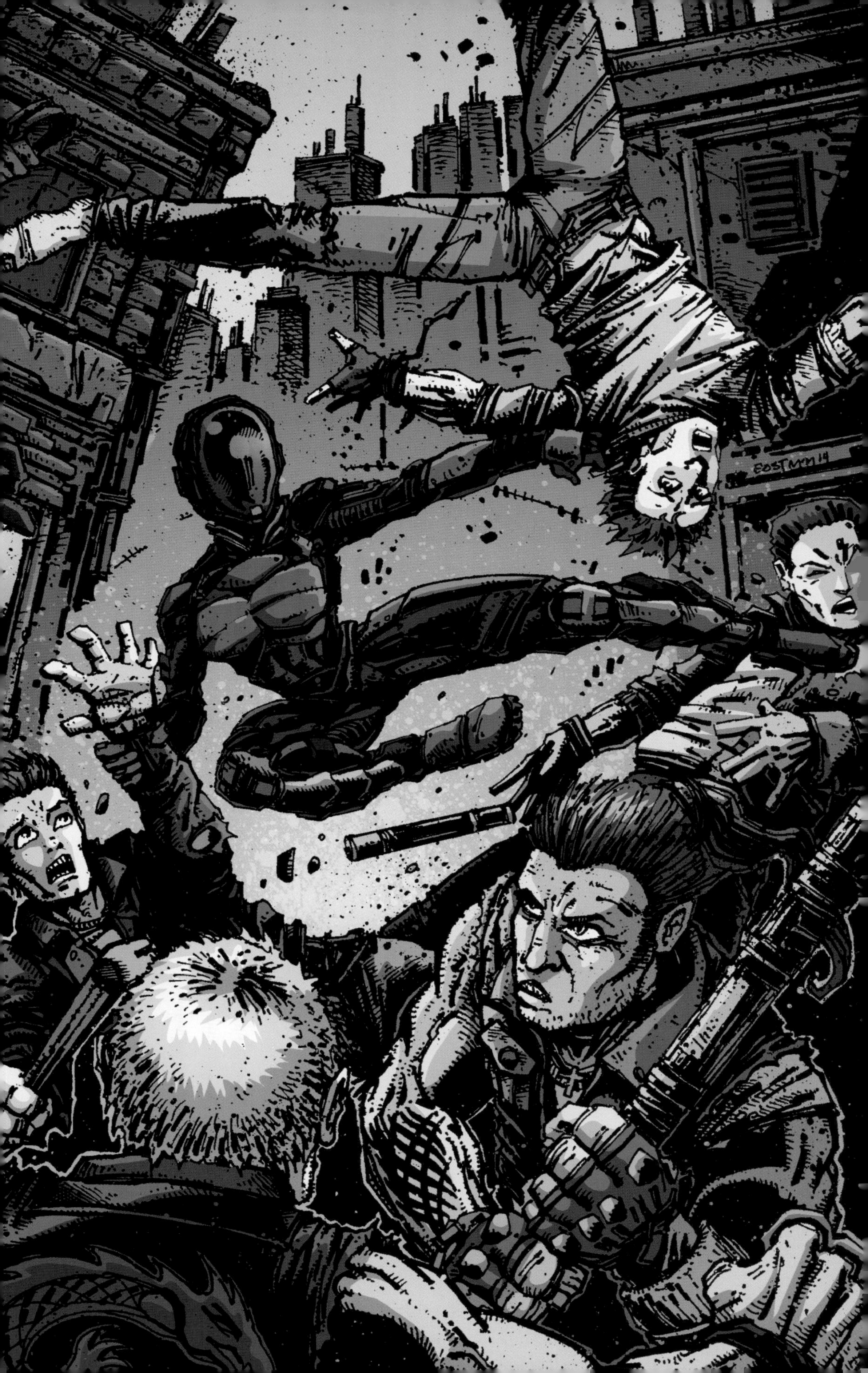

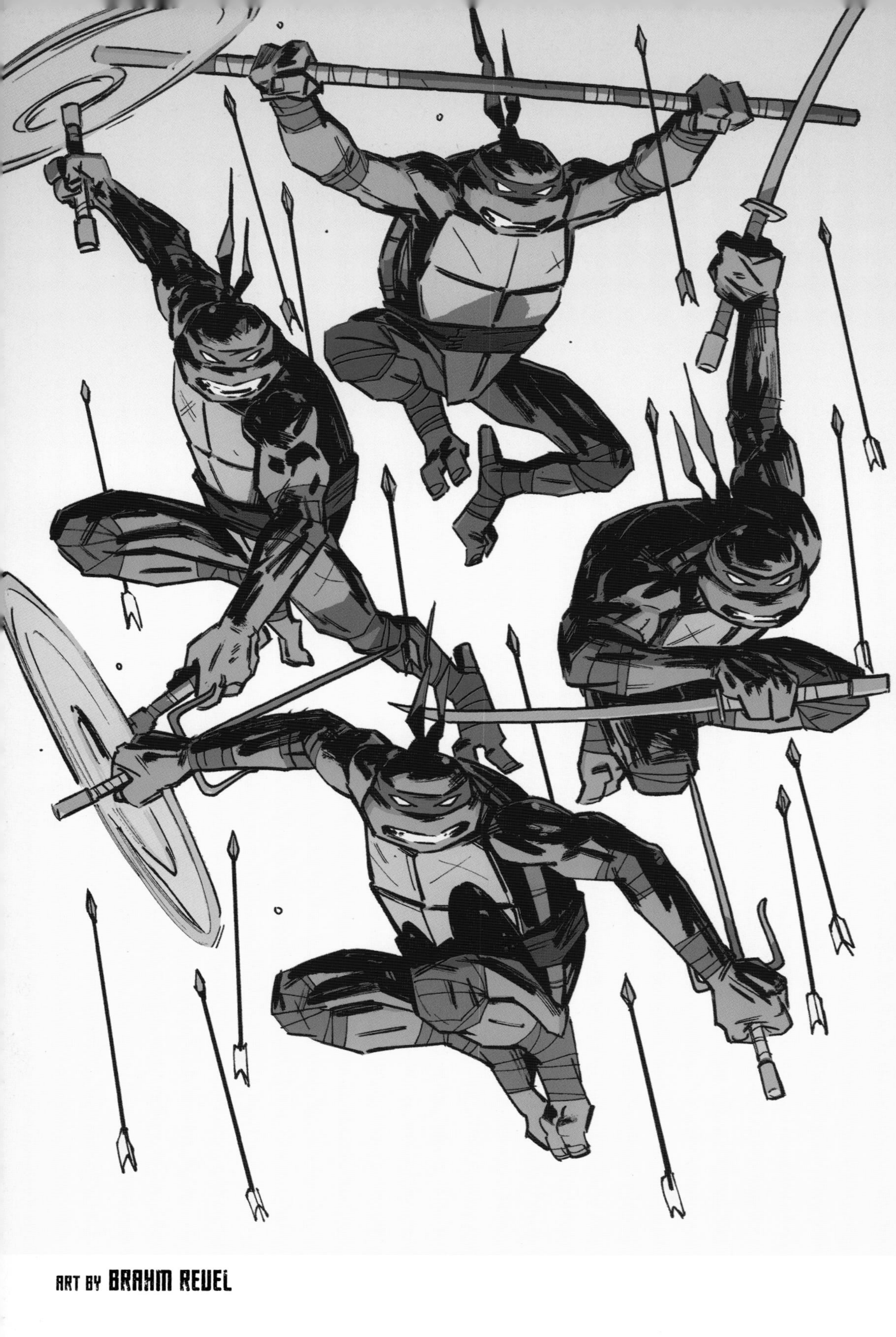

ART BY BRAHM REVEL

OPPOSITE PAGE: ART BY MATEUS SANTOLOUCO

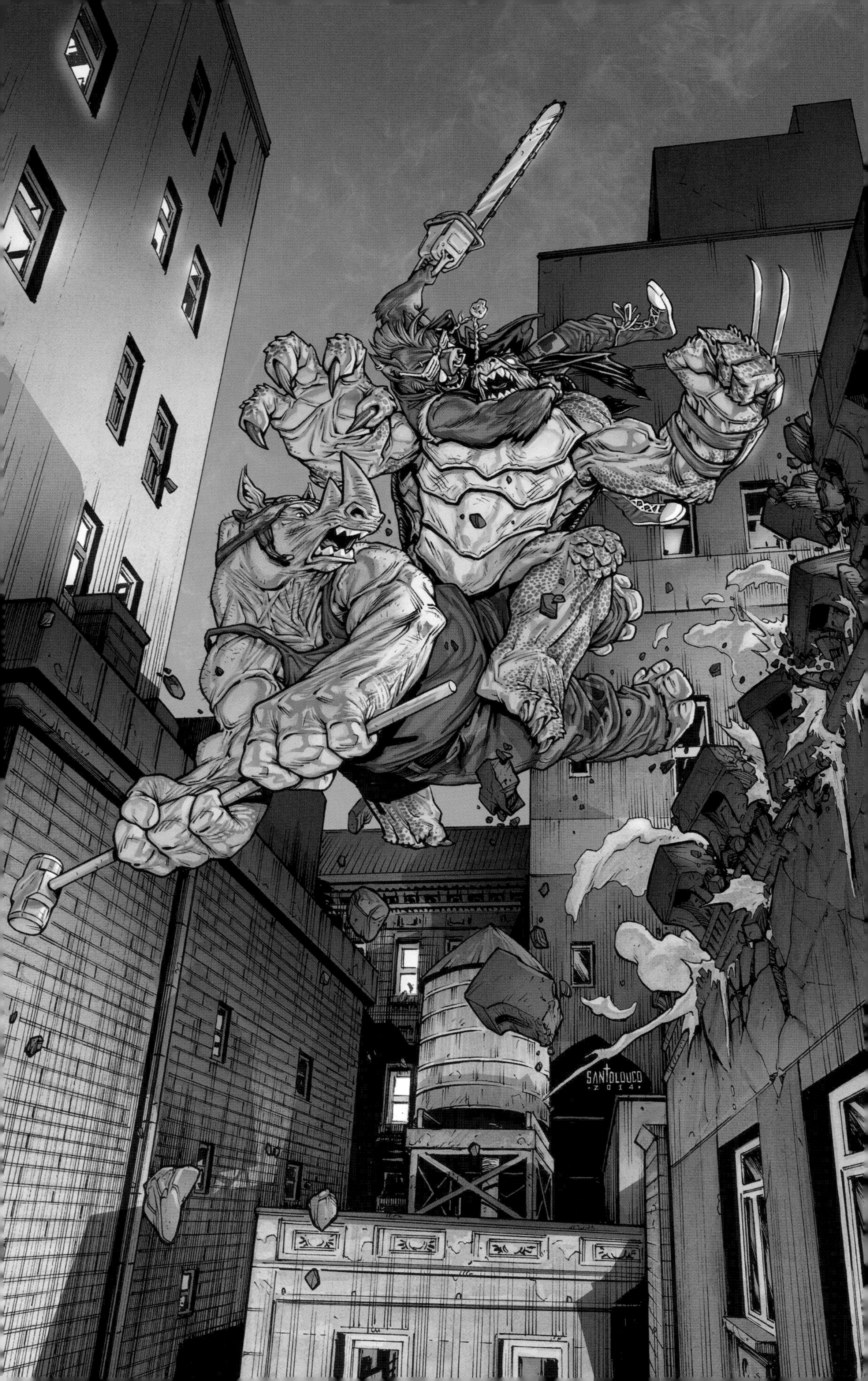
SANTOLOUCO
2014

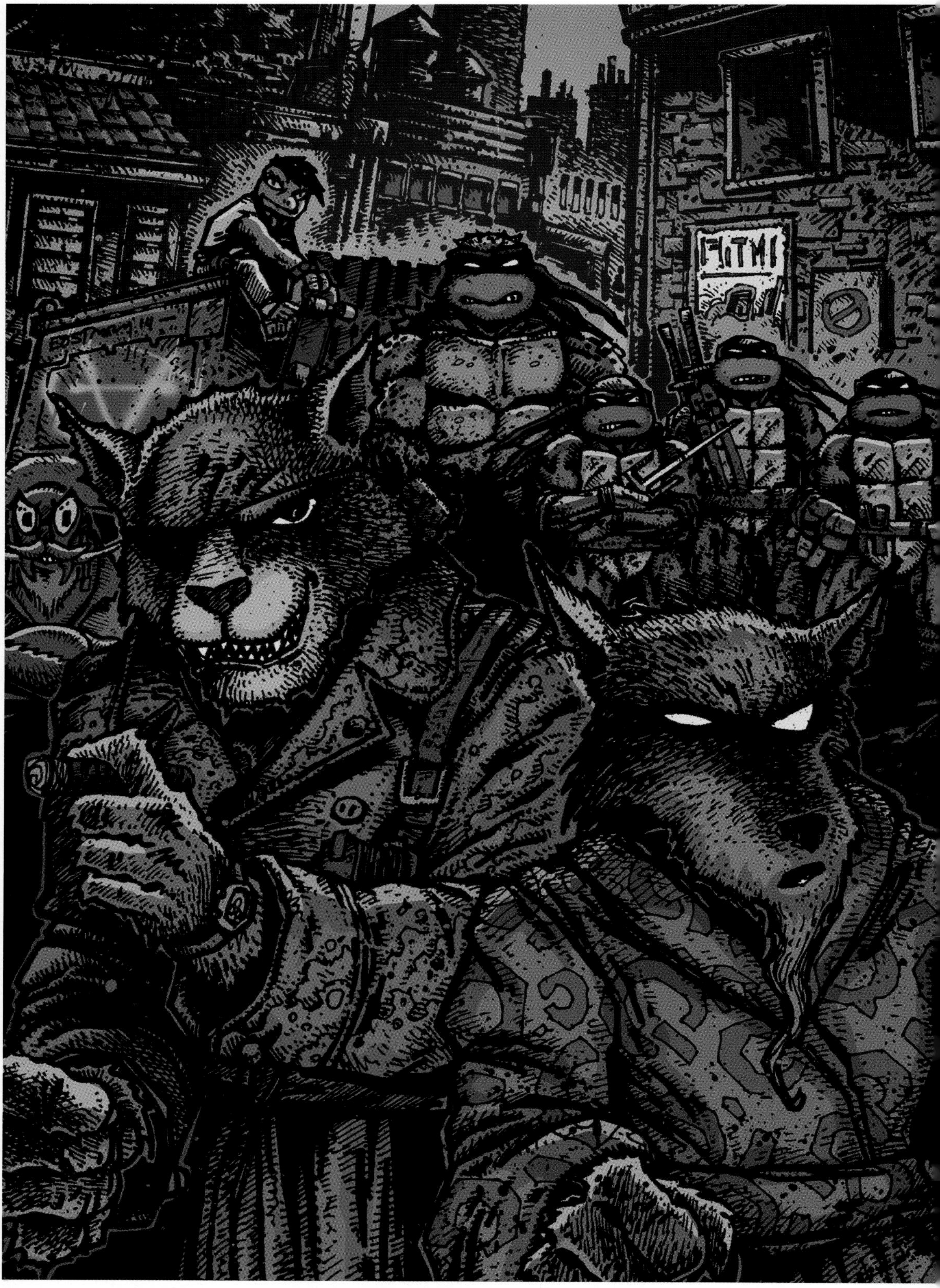

ART BY KEVIN EASTMAN · COLORS BY RONDA PATTISON

OPPOSITE PAGE: ART BY ULISES FARINAS

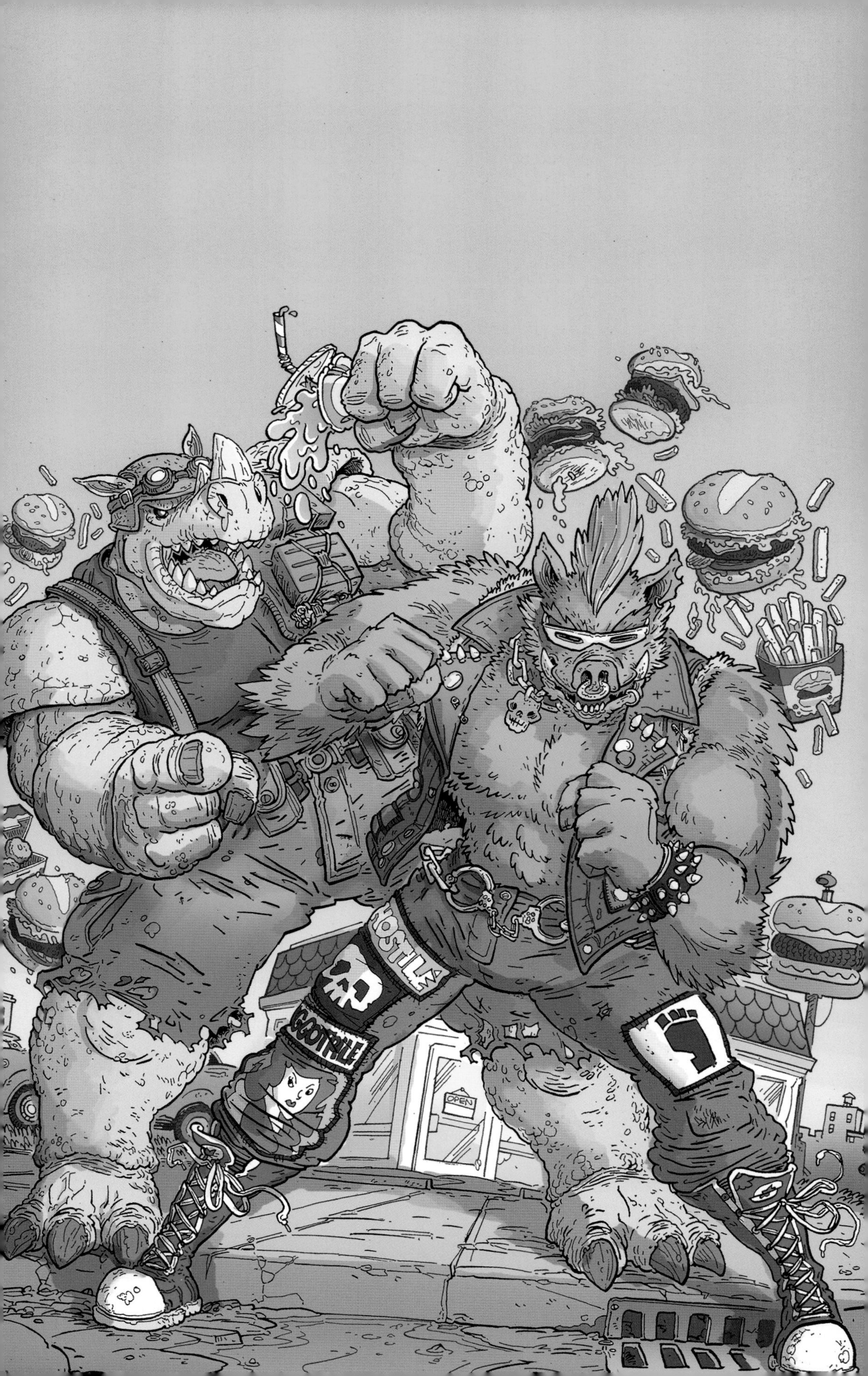
OPEN

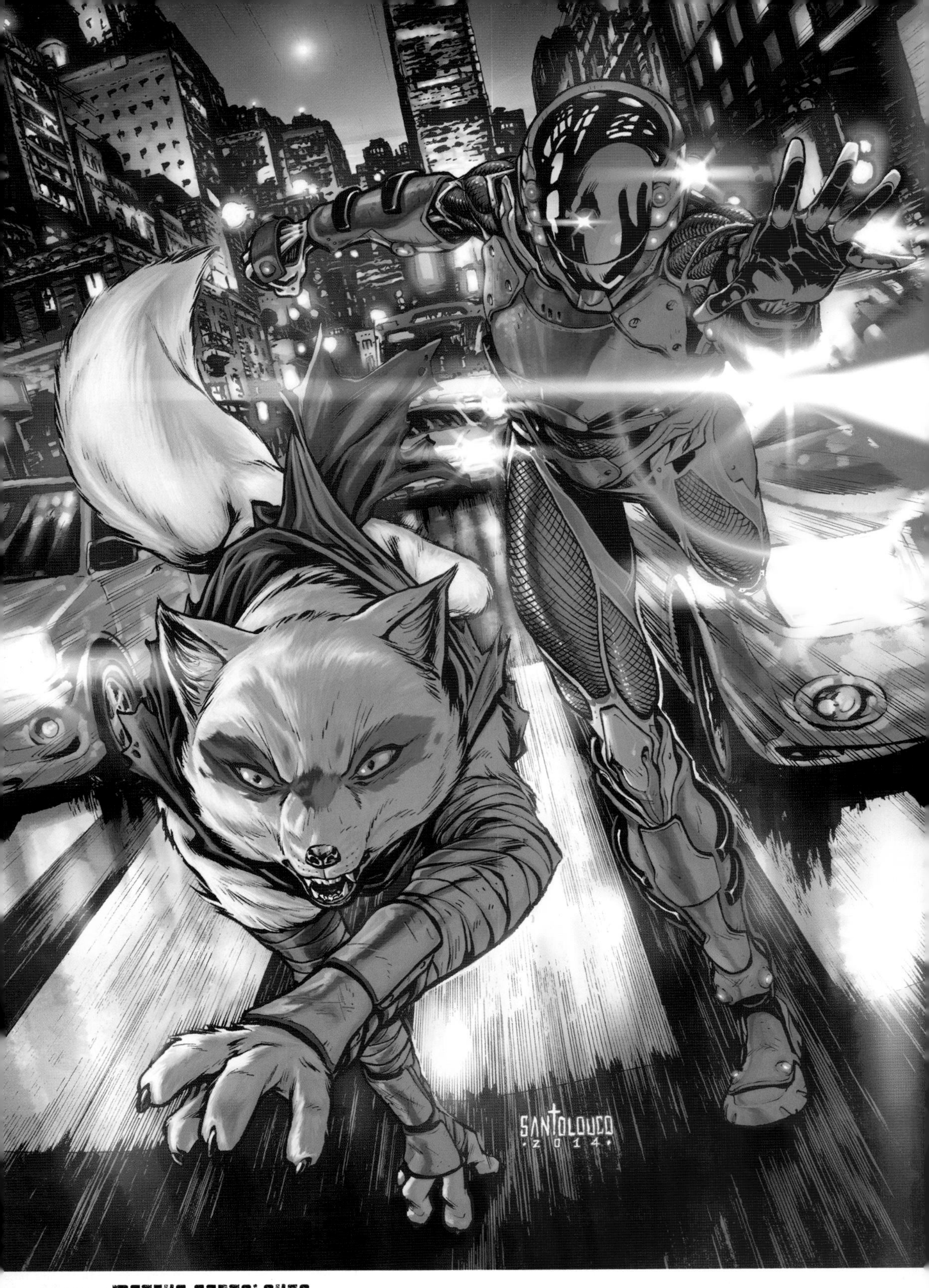
SANTOLOUCO
2014

ART BY MATEUS SANTOLOUCO

OPPOSITE PAGE: ART BY BUSTER MOODY

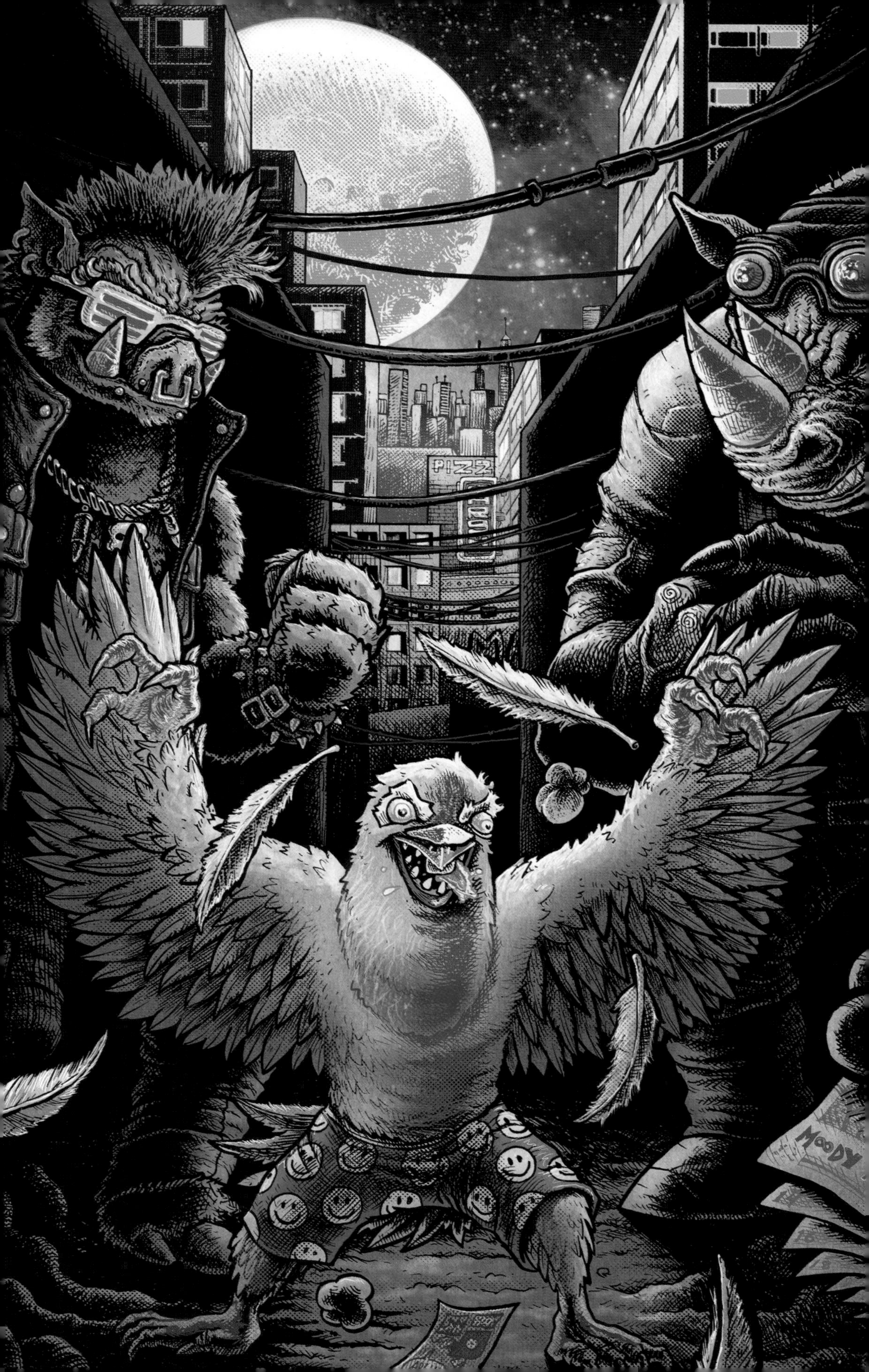
PIZZ
MOODY

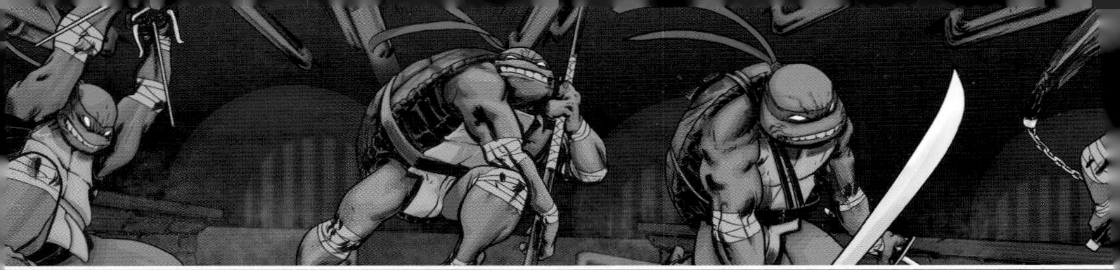

TEENAGE MUTANT NINJA TURTLES

MORE TURTLE ACTION

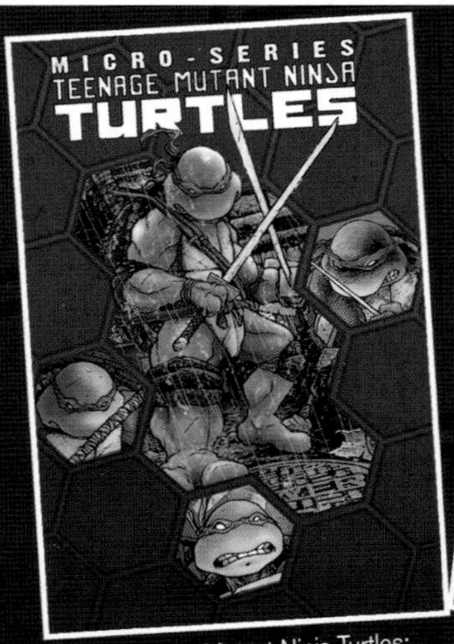
MICRO-SERIES
TEENAGE MUTANT NINJA
TURTLES

Teenage Mutant Ninja Turtles:
Micro-Series, Vol. 1
ISBN: 978-1-61377-232-4

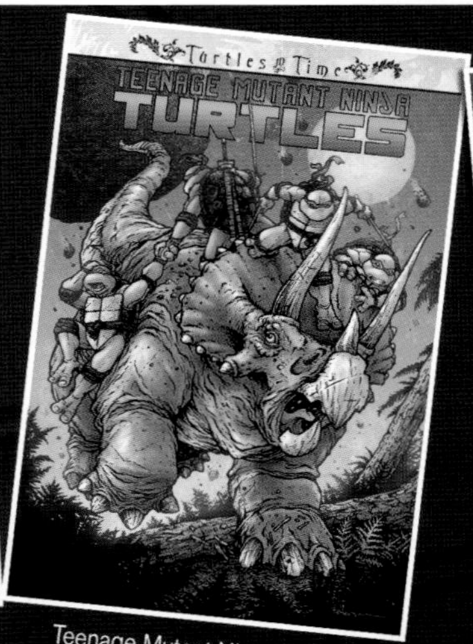
Turtles in Time
TEENAGE MUTANT NINJA
TURTLES

Teenage Mutant Ninja Turtles:
Turtles in Time
ISBN: 978-1-63140-181-7

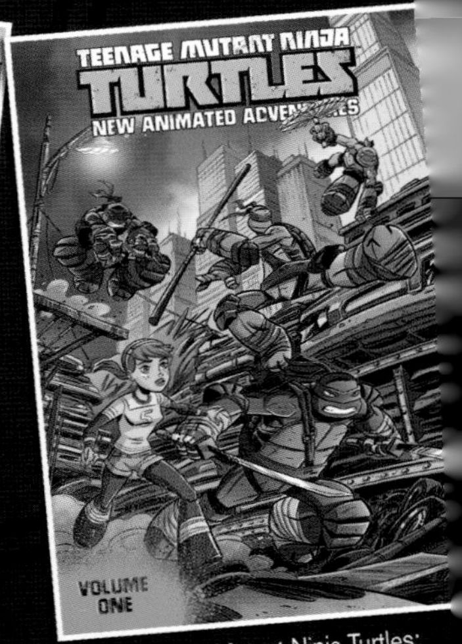
TEENAGE MUTANT NINJA
TURTLES
VOLUME
ONE

Teenage Mutant Ninja Turtles:
New Animated Adventures, Vol. 1
ISBN: 978-1-61377-856-2

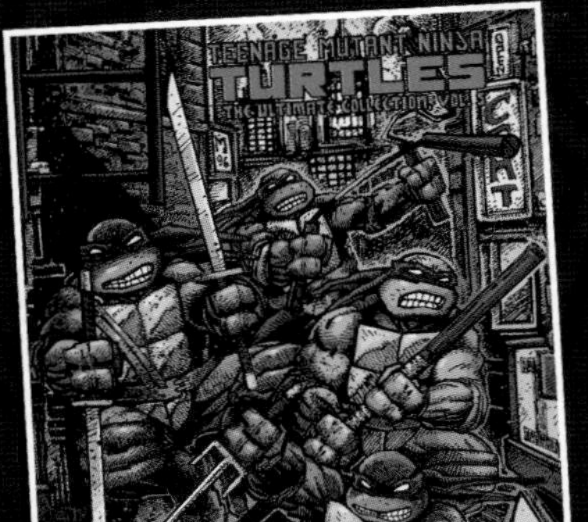
TEENAGE MUTANT NINJA
TURTLES

Teenage Mutant Ninja Turtles:
The Ultimate Collection, Vol. 5
ISBN: 978-1-61377-553-0

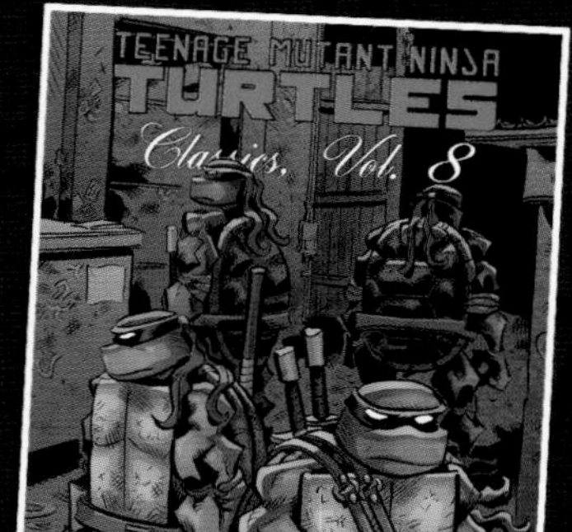
TEENAGE MUTANT NINJA
TURTLES
Classics, Vol. 8

Teenage Mutant Ninja Turtles
Classics, Vol. 8
ISBN: 978-1-61377-961-3

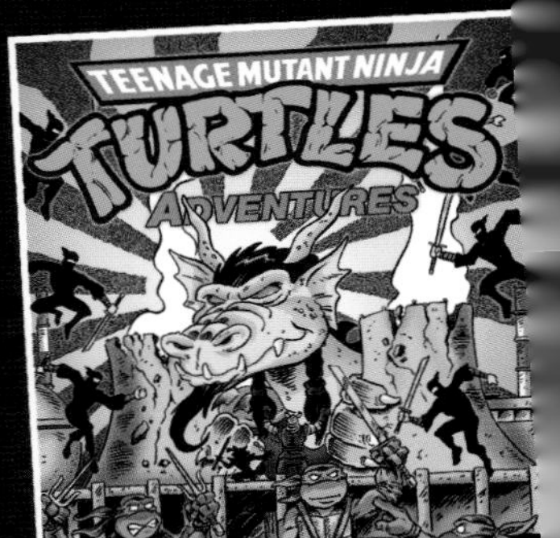
TEENAGE MUTANT NINJA
TURTLES
ADVENTURES

Teenage Mutant Ninja Turtles
Adventures, Vol. 8
ISBN: 978-1-63140-082-7

ON SALE NOW

www.idwpublishing.com

IDW

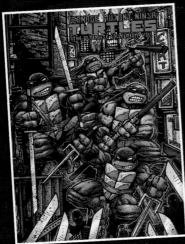

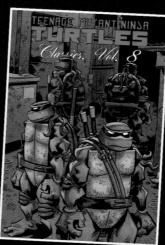

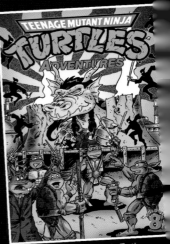